WORKHORSE NUMBERS

Tables for a World, a State,
Ball Games,
and the Doom of
a Republic

Norman Richardson

Inquiries should be made to:
Seaview Press
PO Box 234
Henley Beach, South Australia 5022
Telephone 08 8235 1535; fax 08 8235 9144
E-mail: seaview@seaviewpress.com.au
Web site: http://www.seaviewpress.com.au

Printed by:
Copy Master
234 Currie Street
Adelaide, South Australia 5000

Cartoons by John Martin.

National Library of Australia Cataloguing-in-Publication entry

Richardson, Norman, 1929- .
Workhorse numbers : tables for a world, a state, ball games and the doom of a republic.

ISBN 1 74008 091 2.

1. Correlation (Statistics). 2. Coincidence. 3.
Mathematics - Philosophy. 4. Symbolism of numbers. I.
Title.

519.537

CONTENTS

FOREWORD

I MEANT to call this book "An Idiot's Guide to Workhorse Numbers" till I realised this would risk offence to my potential readership and other authors. Those authorities who brandish titles like the said "Idiot's Guide to ...", where the "idiot" is the clueless buyer, must surely resent a newcomer holding *himself* out as an idiot and, at the same time, a purveyor of knowledge — one of themselves. That is, muddying the waters. Moreover, the reader, in this topsy-turvy world, might well be miffed to find the intended *idiot* was the looked-for *guide*. For, with regard to the just demands of my theme, I own to feeling less than adequate.

* * *

Having spent a double handful of my adult years on audit and tax work as a low–middle rank civil servant in post WW2 Britain, I found myself one day passing through the portals of the Vocational Guidance Association in London to seek advice on a replacement career. The advice given me, following tests and interviews, included to avoid anything to do with figures. Nevertheless, as circumstances conduced, there came more years in or between tax jobs with accounting firms of the metropolis.

When the utility of all this had run its course, exposing the futility underlying it, I took advantage of the cheap fare offered by a new entrant in the travel market and joined their inaugural flight to Singapore, with onward passage by ship to Fremantle, Western Australia.

It was not immediately that my intellectual interests, such as they are, showed development. My first big essay — on the topic of human vigilance — was predictably struck down by the "anonymous reviewers" of a prestigious journal. Just enough indirect encouragement from one kind scientist relieved my disappointment.

Then acceptance of a stripped-down version of the same paper by another journal, oriented more to publication than rejection of work "of scientific merit", renewed my confidence. The years that followed were accompanied by further papers.

Meanwhile, a remark by a senior partner — a Scotsman — at one of the London firms which once employed me has sometimes rankled, "It's difficult to get guid information out of that chap."

This book is an oblique attempt to compensate for past failings by offering a novel version of old ideas regarding the relation between — yes — numbers and reality. More specifically, the idea of a numeric factor, which somehow complements "real factors" in diverse areas. My book is dedicated, with due diffidence indeed, to all seekers of "guid information", that is, good numerical information.

It is also dedicated to those "anonymous reviewers" of my papers, who have shown me favour, and, going back again in time, to those to whom I owe my upbringing and formal education.

At the same time is acknowledged the handiwork of that mysterious force which allows hopes to be placed on one individual but places the means to fulfil any of them in the path of another. Also are acknowledged assistance and tolerance by the staff of various libraries.

My thanks for the expert help and services required to bring my book into the light of day go especially to Bill, Susan, and Miranda of Seaview Press.

PREFACE

THE SHORT pieces and longer papers or articles collected here were written at different times and have not been published before. With topics ranging from planet Earth to cricket and baseball, they have a common objective. This is to challenge the reader to join in the non-trivial pursuit of reality as *number*.

For the best of reasons — the author is not a mathematician — no mathematical skills are assumed, except the most basic ones of addition, subtraction, multiplication, and division. A pre-existing awareness of powers and roots would also be useful, but its lack or desuetude should be no obstacle to a reader touched by the fascination of the "numeric factor". A glossary of special terms (which I hope I have used correctly) is included.

Most important, tables are appended, which include many of the numbers more likely to turn up in "empirical" data from almost any source. To anticipate Chapter 1, "The Numbers Show", our Showman, never one to mince words, wraps it up as follows: "Sounds a lot of numbers. What you find, though, is, the same numbers keep repeating — a bit like spring onions and radishes".

To encourage readers to acquaint themselves with the least transparent of the tables in terms of construction, that is, our *e*-based ratios (*e*–BR) table (see Appendix B), each of Chapters 1–12 of this book is followed by one of the Showman's "Green Quiz" questions. These concern the number of hectares of parks and gardens ("P'n'G") in cities around the world, which the Showman swears are related to numbers in our *e*-BR table.

One chapter differs somewhat from the others, as it contains much material not directly related to numbers. This is Chapter 11, "The Last Elections of Weimar". Early in the 1930s the fate of Europe and the world, as well as of the Weimar Republic and Germany, were balanced on a knife edge. The coming of the Nazi dictatorship is history to the majority but the causes of the collapse of democracy in Germany are of perennial interest not only to those for whom the Nazi period stirs unquiet memories.

The political scene in Germany, as the Republic neared its end, was one of turbulence, amid which the four general elections of the "year of elections", 1932, formed eddies. It is an extraordinary, as well as previously unrecognised fact that into the turmoil intruded the "numeric factor" to contribute — of all things — *harmony* — if only of the numeric kind. To the extent, however, that the *German* Nazi share of votes in the Reichstag election of November interlocks in an exact manner with that Nemesis of Nazidom, F. D. Roosevelt's *United States* Democratic vote *two days* later. Whether this was by coincidence, magic, resonance, or what else, is too important to decide without first reading this book.

CHAPTER ONE
THE NUMBERS SHOW

ROLL UP! Roll up! for the greatest show on earth! Bringing to you, for the first time ever, the most amazing, astounding, an' remarkable revelations in the entire history of the game you love the most — C-R-I-C-K-E-T, CRICKET. That's test cricket to you, sir.

Ladeez an' gentlemen, they say love makes the world go round. Love an' money. What about numbers? Listen, it's been said the whole caboodle is MADE of mathematics. When you really get down to it, what's out there IS numbers.[1] I don't go that far. I'd rather leave a bit of room for other things. Particularly ... cricket ...

Have you heard that a cricket match is won — or lost — in the mind? Well, friends, I will show you, fair an' square, cards on the table, it's numbers, N-U-M-B-E-R-S, NUMBERS that settle the

---

[1] Cf. Paul Davies (1993) reports, "A colleague of mine once remarked that in his opinion the world was *nothing but* bits and pieces of mathematics" (p. 93).

issue. Yes sir, what you say comes into it, but it's numbers settle the issue.

Now, speaking of tables, if you take a good look at this particular table you will notice the letter e –

Test Match Wins[2] Shape up on $1/e$ = .368 and $1 - (1/e)$ = .632

England		W. Indies		Australia
.348	(Av) .366	.385	(Av) .398	.411
	$(1/e =)$ .368		$(.632^2 =)$ .400	

S. Africa		Pakistan
.220	(Av) .231	.243
	$(.368 \times .632 =)$ .233	

N. Zealand		India
.137		.161
$(.368^2 =)$ .135		$(.632^4 =)$ .160

Sri Lanka

.054

$([.368 \times .632]^2 =)$ .054

What does it mean e? It's a constant, of course. Like the government. Or a tune you can't get out of your head. It's mathematics for 2.718. You'd think the person who invented it couldn't think of a half-way decent number. Like 12 — I'll tell you about that as well in a minute. If you want the real thing though, numerically speaking, as like as not, e is it. Yes sir, every country is there, that ever played a test match, that is, up to 1992. No, sir, there's not half a chance it's just coincidence. There's not a chance in a hundred it's just chance.

You can't make head or tail of it, madam? Look at the top line, where it says England, W. Indies an' Orstraila. These countries have the best percentages, or call them ratios of wins. As you can see, West Indies an' Orstraila average .398 wins. Against all comers. Yes, madam, .632 is the difference between $1 \div 2.718$ (that's the reciprocal of e) and 1, an' if you multiply .632 by itself, you get .400. That's right, whichever country you look at its ratio fits the pattern. But remember, it's all based on e. [3]

---

[2] Including all tests up to August 9, 1992, as given by *Wisden Cricketers' Almanack* 1993.

[3] A table of win-ratios updated to August 31, 1998 is included in the chapter headed "Quantisation Effects in Test Cricket" (see Chapter 6, p. 37). This again shows a relation to our e-BR table. (See Appendix B, p. 190.)

What about 12? I was coming to that. Now, you can have 12, you can have 1 divided by 12, which is a twelfth — the reciprocal of 12 to you, sir. You can have a twenty-fourth, a thirty-sixth, a forty-eighth, an' needn't stop there. Then you have your roots. Yes, sonny, the square root of a number multiplied by itself gives you the number. Your square, fourth an' eighth roots. Your cube, sixth an' twelfth roots. You can go on. Sounds a lot of numbers. What you find, though, is, the same numbers keep repeating — a bit like spring onions an' radishes.

Now, I must correct myself here, friends, because when I said the rad — er *ratio* of matches a country won has to do with *e*, if you go back to that table there you see under England the number .348. That's near enough the cube root of a twenty-fourth, which is .347, if you round it up. So the top countries' line-up you can say is anchored in the 12-based division of numbers.

The Numbers Show (Suite)

Mesdames an' Messieurs, pardon my French, but here's a question I've got for you — who won the World Cup — the cricket World Cup, of course. You, sir! The Ozzies? — Orstraila! Orstraila won it. Where was it played? Right, in Paris, France. An' who did Orstraila beat? — In the final … The Springboks! South Africa, to you, madam.

Eh bien, *mes amis*, comprenday vous? … The question is, how many did Orstraila make in the final, an' how many did they make in the semis, when they came through against Pakistan on run rate? — 213 against Pakistan an' 133 in the finals. Right. Now there's something about 213 an' something about 133 I want to show you.

Start with 213. Put a decimal point in front of it an' what do you get? — Point 213, of course. Then take point 213 away from 1 an' to save you the trouble I'll tell you what you get: point 787. Now divide decimal point 213 by .787 an' you get .271, rounded up, that is. We're not finished yet.

Now we start all over again. We take .271 away from 1 an' divide it by — ? That's right, my young friend — .729. — An' we get … ? …point 371. By the way, 1/.371 is 2.695 an' that number ought to ring a bell with some of you whiz kids, 'cos, of course, it's just a whisker away from that stupid-clever number *e*, 2.718, that is.

No, I'm not forgetting the 133; we're coming to that. We just put the decimal point in front, take the square root — of .133 — an' we've got ... point 365, rounded up again.

Then we do a magic average of .371 and .365 an' — surprise, surprise — we get .368 — that's $1/e$ to three decimal places exactly.[4]

I'll tell you something else, though — If we do it all over again without any rounding up, what we get isn't .368, it's .36789, an' — believe it or not, my friends — .36789 is the same as $1/e$ to *five* decimal places, except for 1/100,000 — that's all the difference there is.

You were ahead of me, were you, *jeune ami*? 'Cos you swiped my copy of that table?[5] So .213 is like F11 in the table an' .133 is like E1. — Is that so? And do you know something else, *p'tit*? ... The probability of Orstraila's figures matching those numbers just by chance is as high as an ant's knee?

Reference for Chapter 1

DAVIES, P., *The mind of God: science and the search for ultimate meaning.* (Harmondsworth, Middx.: Penguin, 1993).

---

[4] Stop, there! To recap:
Semi-final: Australia 213; .213/(1-.213 = .787) = .271. And .271/(1-.271 = .729) = .371.
Final: Australia 133; $\sqrt{.133}$ = .365
Mean of .371 and .365 = .368 = $1/e$ to three decimal places.

[5] Table of e-based ratios (e-BR) — see Appendix B.

The Green Quiz

Ladeez an' gentlemen, boys an' girls. You've heard of parks 'n' gardens. Every city has them, an' some have more than others. Now, this city in Orstraila wanted to prove it had what it takes on the green side. So they have a survey done — see? — of cities round the world, to find how many *hectares* they've got of P'n'G, OK? They knew how many *they* had, this Big Smoke in Orstraila, that is.

So what do they come up with? They were pretty pleased, I'll tell you, 'cos none of those places in America, Europe, an' the rest, came in ahead of this Orstrailin one.

Now, this is going to be a quiz, an' this is how it works: to make it easy for you, I *give* you the name of the city, an' all *you* have to do is get the number of hectares of P'n'G they've got in that particular city. On top of that, I give you a clue.

By a stroke of luck — an' I don't mean chance — it's like our win ratios all over again, remember? — that started off with *e*?

Quite right, sir, our *e*-based ratios are decimals, decimal fractions, if you prefer, an' our P'n'Gs are whole numbers — integers to you — but the fact is, they pair off with each other like lads an' lasses in the spring, if you take no notice of the decimal point. The most they have is three digits, though, not four, like the table.

That reminds me, the way you find the number — 'cos I don't want you to guess — is *from the table*[6]. So it's cut the cackle an' get down to the 'orses.

Green Quiz Question No 1

The name of our first city means "muddy estuary" — I don't know why. That's Kuala Lumpur, if you didn't know; an' its P'n'Gs come in near the *square* of that little *e*, with the 1 an' a slash in front, like this, 1/*e*.

The Green Quiz question is, how many hectares of P'n'G has KL got, give or take one?

What is the letter an' column number of this number in the table?

---

[6] That is, the table of *e*-based ratios (*e*-BR) — Appendix B. Note: the answers to the Green Quiz are on p. 183.

CHAPTER TWO
NO HEAD FOR CRICKET: A FLIGHT OF THE IMAGINATION

JEFF AND I were trying to explain cricket to the alien. As usual, Ee-yip, as we called him, was getting things round the wrong way.

You have to make allowances for galactic time slip, of course, as they get *here* before they started from back *there*.

When we played the Ashes tape, every time Warney[7] bowled his flipper Ee-yip squeaked — just like that — Yipee! backwards, okay?

He surely had a head for figures — it was built that way. The trouble was, he kept putting *numbers* ahead of the *game*. Complete cart-before-horse case.

---

[7] Warney: Shane Warne — Australia's record wicket-taker.

Mind you, Jeff thought he knew what the little weirdo was on about, at first. Seems that, if you play around with *pi*, no, *e* (I should remember because it was — in the jargon — exchanging alternate binary-coded decimals for the expansion of the natural log base — a real mouthful that — that set up first contact with Ee-yip's home planet) you can fit any test-playing country into the same pattern of win ratios.

Jeff wrote it all down but I can only remember the top countries' line-up went something like this:

England		W. Indies		Australia
	Average		Average	
.348	.366	.385	.398	.411

I didn't deny that .366 is nearly .368, which is $1 \div e$. And .398 is only a couple of winks away from .400, which is $(1 - .368 = .632)$ squared.[8]

Et après? — as the French say. It can be that a cricket match is won, or lost, in the mind, but only an alien has a mind that *is* a computer.

The real flaw in Ee-yip's logic circuit showed when he started to connect his *e*-based numbers to actual scores. As if the decimal point in the first lot of numbers *n'existe point!*

I've still got the bit of paper Jeff — he was just as scornful now as I was — wrote Ee-yip's numbers on for the last Ashes series.[9] Funny, when we (I mean Ee-yip) pooled all the innings totals for each game and took half as the average for each side, the Brisbane and Perth games came out the same.

Ee-yip, though, made out the figures (582 and 582.5) were linked to what he called the "*e* quotient" (meaning $.368 \div .632$), which comes to .582, as it happens. Don't forget the decimal point, we warned him.

Then he found the figure for the Adelaide test (the one England won) was 628 — a wee bit short of 632, not to say a light year ahead of *point* 632, $(1 - .368$, remember?) I pointed out.

The Melbourne and Sydney tests, lumped together, came within a touch of 482, Ee-yip's "*e* product" (this time $.368 \times .632$, if you like), or its square root or something.[10] Or rather the digits did.

---

[8] Table references are given in footnotes for most of the numbers mentioned.

Thus we have .368: F1, .632: F2, .400: E2. (See *e*-BR table at Appendix B.)

[9] of 1994/95.

[10] Note: .582: F3, .482: G4 (see Appendix B).

When did the teams decide on what runs total they'd combine to target? — the little freak demanded. Was it before or after the toss was coined? he meant the coin was tossed.

He couldn't see that the whole idea of cricket is to score as many as possible and stop the other side doing that.

By this time Jeff and I were pretty peeved with Ee-yip. But, if possible, there was even worse to come.

Unfortunately, he'd hooked into the match totals for the back series of Australia versus England tests. This time he pooled the scores for each *series* before sharing them out.

We didn't mind this but asked why on earth he took out all the "catch-up" scores — that's where a team is set a target and reaches it. He said, because these scores were "meaningless". At least he knew the word.

Then he averaged two ways, with and without these games, the ones won like I said. And took the average of both. Jeff suggested he was having a bob both ways and I was inclined to agree with him.

Ee-yip had homed in on the period from the 'Thirties Depression to post-WW2. Jeff made a note of Ee-yip's "correlations", for his paper on the mind of the Alien. Here are some specimens:

1932/33 (yes, the "Bodyline" series) 481. *Point* 482 is the square root of that *e* product.

1936/37 ("The Don's" first series as captain) 520. We thought he'd stumped himself there but he got out of it by "factoring" .368, well, finding the pair of divisible "factors" totalling 1, really. The square root of the smaller one came to (*point*) 519.[11] Something like that. It's all so improbable.

1938 (Bradman's pre-war England tour) 632.5. *Point* 632 again. And

1946/47 (the first post-war England team visit) 633. Again *point* 632.

1948 ("the Invincibles" tour) 480. Short of that product again.

Then he made a mix-up of the old bowling records. Why did the Windies' Lance Gibbs retire after 10*e*K balls? — he wanted to know. (In fact, it wasn't that, quite, unless you call Lance's 27,115, 27,183 — that's 10 x 2.7183 x 1,000, alright? 2.7183 is *e*, if I forgot to mention it). Was it in the Laws of Cricket? Jeff, who is a real cricket buff, answered that one.

---

[11] Note: .519 : G5 (see Appendix B).

Ee-yip still couldn't — or wouldn't — see reason. Instead, he "proved" each country's top delivery merchant — old-timers like Benaud, Kapil and Imran — could be fitted into his oddball *e*-based pattern.

The only one I can remember off the top of my head, the only "correlation", that is, is Benaud's figure — after Ee-yip had finished with it — came near *point* 519 (yes, *point* 519). How can you bowl less than one ball? — Jeff wondered.

And that wasn't the half of it. Team records, individual records, partnership records, batting, bowling, catching records. You name them, Ee-yip twisted them round to fit his *e*-BR (*e*-based ratios, you may know). Or twisted his *e*-BR to fit the statistics.

We fibbed to him about Gary Sobers' innings record, that held up from 1957/58 to 1994. You can see why. For an alien (they work by fuzzy logic at the best of times) it's just one small step from 365 to *point 368*.

We couldn't stop him tangling with Bradman's captain's knocks in the last three games of the 1936/37 series, when the Aussies came from two tests down to keep the Ashes. Jeff says the figures were 270, 212 and 169. 1 think the 270 was supposed to be a factor of *point* 368. And 212 a factor of 270, or the other way round. I forget what Ee-yip made of the 169.[12] Jeff doesn't remember either.

We did our best to show him the basics. We told him about keeping your eye on the ball, keeping a straight bat, keeping a stiff upper lip (where the Poms excel). About inswingers, outswingers and wrong'uns. About square leg, fine leg, long hop and slip. About sledging [13]...

Ee-yip is due to lift off for his home planet at 12. That's another number I ought to remember. Jeff and I heard enough about it from Ee-yip. But that's another story. Take it from me, though, you'll never get an alien to understand cricket.

---

[12] Note correlates are: for 270, F5 = .269; for 212, F11 = .212; for 169, F13 = .167 (see Appendix B).

[13] Especially in cricket, verbal abuse to distract an opponent.

Green Quiz Question No 2

It's Barcelona an' London in a close finish, with the Spaniard half a length in front. The clue is, the smaller factor of $1/e$.

The question is, where do you find this factor in the table at Appendix B? Give the letter and column number.

How many hectares of P'n'G have B 'n' L got, give or take a couple?

CHAPTER 3
WHAT-WAS-HIS-NAME WITH THE THINGAMY?

THE FIRST out-of-body experience may have been the realisation of one's existence as a separate member of the proto-group or community. Call it *individuation*. Along with it, or after, must have come the development and manipulation of *ideas* of *things* as a process separable from the selection or manufacture of the things themselves. Call this *ideation*. Ever since then, we may suppose, the ultimate nature of reality has had its protagonists from the side of *materialism* and from that of *idealism* (really, *idea-ism*). Is the world as real as the resistance it offers to one's muscles, or is the existence of anything no more than a conjecture, and if not held in consciousness continuously, may melt into air, into thin air?

One of the earliest great idealists in either sense (idea-ist or idealist), of whom history speaks — what-was-his-name? — Pythagoras, was the first famous thinker who is known to have called himself a "philosopher" (or lover of wisdom). He is best remembered as the mathematician credited with the, um, theorem equating the square on the, ah, hypotenuse with the sum of the squares on the other two sides ... of a right-angled triangle.

The name Pythagoras has survived more properly as the founder of the ethical, religious, and political, as well as mathematical, brotherhood or sect of the Pythagoreans. Of the life and works of Pythagoras himself little is known. Born about 580–570 BC on the Greek (Ionian) island of Samos in the Eastern Mediterranean, he migrated (or was forced to flee) in about 530 to the Greek colony of Croton (now Crotona) in South Italy and there gathered adherents around him.

For a study in contrasts we might set the legendary Pythagoras alongside that mathematical genius of our own time, Paul Erdös, as presented in another Paul, Hoffman's (1999) freewheeling biography. Both were eccentrics of the rarest order. To join in Erdös' private language game, in which children were epsilons and grandchildren, epsilons squared,[14] both were "prime numbers" — inexpressible in terms other than their own.

Among their differences from each other, Erdös was born in Hungary and, instead of establishing a school, became the ultimate peripatetic, his 19 hour days filled with mathematics done on the run at, with, or between colleges or colleagues, visited, it may be, on an impulse; all his possessions hardly filling a suitcase and a plastic bag. Compared to Erdös's well over 1,000 published papers, Pythagoras is believed to have written nothing, or nothing extant. He, Pythagoras, a stickler for secrecy, Erdös willing to "open his brain" to a train conductor — if it was to prove a mathematical theorem.[15]

Their shared *primeness* emphasised difference from the common run of numbers, or men: Pythagoras, whose hair was left to grow and grow, Erdös wearing silk for his troublesome skin, averse to touch.

Both held lofty ideals, but followed separate paths. As the Pythagorean credo included metempsychosis,[16] the master abjured animal food. With only a nod in the same direction, Erdös, on being served meat used to ask, "What was that when it was alive?" With an emphatic nod in the opposite direction, the story goes that Pythagoras celebrated the discovery of his famous theorem with the sacrifice of 100 oxen.

The pursuit of esoteric knowledge or self-immersion in problems of mathematics maintains distance from the market-place we know as the world, just as rational thought stands aside from instinct.

Then a question may present itself to the human mind, which engaged the Greek thinkers of the 6th Century BC: despite diversity and change, is there a single principle at work which orders and unifies all things?

The problem, What is the essence of reality? or What is the *physis*?[17] attracted answers of both our kinds. We wise moderns, expectant of the Theory of Everything (TOE), not timid to perform heroic dissection on the brain of God, may smile at some of the theories put forward by the *materialists*: *water* (Thales), *air* (Anaximenes), *fire* (Heraclitus), or, pluralistically, the four

---

[14] epsilon: the fifth letter of the Greek alphabet (*e*), used by mathematicians to denote a small quantity. Not to be confused with the natural log base, also *e*.

[15] Erdös references from Hoffman, pp. 47, 71.

[16] metempsychosis: the transmigration of souls, including animal.

[17] Perhaps: What is the nature of nature?

elements of water, air, fire and earth (Empedocles), or, laterally, undifferentiated matter (Anaximander).

Let us view with calm detachment the answer of the *idealists*, or *formalists*, as given by Pythagoras: All is number. This at least receives endorsement from its latter day translation: The universe is a computer.[18]

According to the Pythagoreans, not *matter* but *form* or *abstract* structure was the key to understanding nature. Form or structure depended on geometrical shapes and whole numbers or their ratios.

The school's approach to such studies was ethical, rather than pragmatic. Divinity came into the equation, with the circle or sphere the most perfect form and the first 10 natural numbers (the *dekad*) supreme.

The *kosmos* was an ordered harmony (*harmonia*) based on numbers. This conception is thought to have stemmed from the discovery that the most pleasing musical intervals, played on, for example, a lyre, are related to the length of the string in the ratios: (octave) 1 : 2, (fifth) 2 : 3, (fourth) 3 : 4. That is, when the string is shortened to half its length, the pitch is raised by one octave, when to two-thirds of its length, the pitch is raised by the equivalent of five white notes on a piano (as from C to G), and when the string is only shortened to three-quarters, the pitch rises by four white notes (as from C to F).

Similar structures or numerical patterns could occur in widely different contexts. In this perspective, a geometrical shape based on whole numbers is particularly impressive: for example, a right-angle triangle with hypotenuse (the side opposite the right angle) = 2 and each of the other two sides of unit length, that is 1;[19] or a right-angle triangle with sides of 5, 3 and 4. The role of whole numbers, as in these musical and geometrical examples, was large in Pythagorean philosophy, whose numerology assigned to particular numbers particular qualities.

---

[18] See Davies (1993), p. 22, etc.

[19] The finding that $\sqrt{2}$ cannot be expressed as the ratio of whole numbers was a famous scandal to the sect and was suppressed. We might wonder why scandal did not also compromise *pi* (the ratio of the circumference of any circle to its diameter). The answer appears to be that the value of this constant was not even known with any accuracy until much later and its irrationality was not proved until 1768 (Maor, 1994, p. 192). Interestingly, 1768 is also the year the *Encyclopaedia Britannica* was founded.

Harmonia did not extend to the human sphere, at least at the ethical level. This is evident from the Pythagorean belief in the need for (as Christians would say) personal redemption and the moral improvement of society. Few moderns would probably take issue with this. Less clear is how the Pythagoreans, or their descendants — for Pythagoreanism is alleged to be alive and well in some mathematical circles and individuals of the present day — would respond to a modern criticism of the motto, "All is number". This is that fixed numbers or ratios are inapplicable to everyday existence, with all its movements and changes. In fact, it is easy to show by examples that this view does not do justice to the facts, subject, as they say, to certain conditions.

A counter-example, which sprang readily to hand, concerns readership figures for the latest 12 months, claimed for an Australian metropolitan newspaper, *The Advertiser* of Adelaide and its Sunday affiliate, the *Sunday Mail*. These were as follows:[20]

Advertiser	weekdays	587,000
	Saturday	761,000
Mail		818,000

Suppose each set of three digits (disregarding the zeroes) represents one side of a triangle which is to be tested for *rectangularity*. Then $587^2 + 761^2 = 923690$, and $818^2 = 669124$. The result, not unexpectedly, is negative. However, if we compare these numbers — just the digit sequences — with our table of 12-based ratios (12-BR — Appendix A), it turns out that the first (say 9237) approximates to the 32nd root of $1/12^{th}$ (or $12^{-1/32}$) = .9253, and the second (6691) to the 8th root of $1/24^{th}$ or $24^{-1/8}$) = .6722. We have here, then, a scaling effect based on 12.[21]

In this same example, if we average the two smaller numbers, 587 and 761, the mean, 674, is near the first three digits of the square of 818, that is 669. To support this link, the ratio of the *Mail*'s readership to potential readership (number of South Australians aged 14 and over) is, digitally, almost the same, that is, .670, being independent, of course, of the actual readership figures.

As we leave this example, we might as well take a Parthian shot at the ratio between the square of the *Mail*'s figure and the

---

[20] Data from *The Advertiser* dated November 20, 1999.

[21] See later chapters re "trans-decimal" correlations.

sum of the squares of the *Advertiser*'s. This ratio would have been 1 if our notional triangle had been rectangular, but is, in fact, (6691/9237 =) .7244, close to $48^{-1/12}$ = .7243. Notice this figure as it recurs in the next example.

While it seems improbable these effects are due solely to chance, the present purpose is simply to indicate a possible route from Pythagorean philosophy to a far broader "interface" between the world in all its aspects and a range of table numbers.

Any group of numbers may conceal a square : square root relation, or one of higher power, if the numbers have a minimum span. A sample which meets this requirement and includes, this time, two sets of three numbers, relates to the recent test cricket series between Australia and Pakistan. The scores were:[22]

1st Test, Brisbane

Pakistan	1st innings	367	Australia	1st innings	575
	2nd innings	281		2nd innings	74
	Total	648		Total	649

2nd Test, Hobart

Pakistan	1st innings	222	Australia	1st innings	246
	2nd innings	392		2nd innings	369
	Total	614		Total	615

3rd Test, Perth

Pakistan	1st innings	155	Australia	1st innings	451
	2nd innings	276		2nd innings	-
	Total	431		Total	451

This nondescript looking array of numbers has some remarkable features, though these again do not include rectangularity. On the other hand, the squares, sums of squares, and their ratios fit our tables well. The ratio of the square of the Australian total at Brisbane to the sum of the squares of the same team's totals at Hobart and Perth repeats — or, as we shall say, resonates with — the figure in the previous example, as follows: $649^2/(615^2 + 451^2)$ = .7242. Recall that the earlier figure was .7244, so the mean, .7243, is the same as $48^{-1/12}$ to four decimal places. This "coincidence", needless to say, was entirely unexpected.

Both countries' match totals, averaged across the first and second tests, come to practically the same figure, as follows: Pakistan 631, Australia 631.5, corresponding to the *e*-based

---

[22] Source: *The Advertiser*.

number (e-BR — see table at Appendix B) F2 = .6321. Also, Pakistan's 367 (1st Test, 1st Innings) and Australia's 369 (2nd Test, 2nd Innings) straddle F1 = .368 to three decimal places, being the *complement* of F2 (.632 + .368 = 1.0).

While Games 1 and 2 show this relationship to e-BR, Game 3 shows a systematic relation of both teams' figures to 12-BR, as 155 is near the *mean* of $48^{-1/2}$ and $36^{-1/2}$ (mean = .1555), 276 is near $48^{-1/3}$ = .275, and 451 is near $24^{-1/4}$ = .452. ($p < .05$)

In view of this preliminary evidence and the abundant support it receives from the following chapters, it is possible to think that the Pythagorean conception of numbers as the framework of reality — but now including the mutable realities of everyday life — was not altogether mistaken; provided the narrow focus on whole numbers and their relations is developed to "legitimate" a far larger "reservoir" of correlates.

References for Chapter 3

The *Encyclopedia Americana International Edition* (Danbury, Connecticut, 1994).

The New Encyclopaedia Britannica (15th ed., Chicago, 1994).

Grand Dictionnaire Encyclopédique Larousse (Paris, 1982).

HOFFMAN, P., *The man who loved only numbers* (London: Fourth Estate, 1999).

Green Quiz Question No. 3

This city is in Canada. Its name is Toronto, an' it has a total of hectares of P'n'G like — listen — the square *of the square* of the *complement* of the *reciprocal* of that little *e*.

What is the location of this number in the table? Give the letter and column number.

How many hectares of P'n'G has Toronto got?

Extra clue: round up.

CHAPTER 4
THE GREAT GLOBE ITSELF

TO US millennium-enders the Earth is both the literal ground of our existence and a colour image in a view from space. Though lacking photography and launch vehicles, the first Pythagoreans were also round-Earthers and held that the universe itself (*kosmos*) was a perfect example of that most perfect three-dimensional form, the sphere.

Today our planet is described as an oblate spheroid, circular round the equator and elliptical in polar circumference. Its area is given as approximately 197m sq. miles or 510m sq. km.[23]

With land and ocean jostling for room, a basic question to consider in a Pythagorean perspective is, do these elements show harmony or due proportion in their shares of the globe, given that on the blue planet ocean appears to have the muscle.

Geologists distinguish between "land" and "continent" and between "water" and "ocean". The natural "physiographic" division between continent and ocean is not the shore-line but the off-shore continental slope. This is where a continent ends and ocean begins. So two different estimates are possible for each element. Nor are these numbers "set in concrete".

Both continents and oceans have as their bases or foundations "lithospheric plates" of crust and mantle, which, contrary to "common sense", are not fixed, but move in relation to one another. At a creeping pace, during millions of years, the continents are brought together to form a single land mass or *Pangaea*, then drift apart again.

---

[23] Our tables (see Appendixes B and C) show 197 is similar to the *e*-based ratio (*e*-BR) F7, which rounds up to .197, and 510 is similar to the square of the fraction 5/7ths, which rounds up to .510. These are examples of "trans-decimal" correlations. Note that when the metre was established as a measure in about 1790 during the French Revolution it was defined as 1/10,000,000th of the distance from the equator to the north pole. By the way, 197 is near the atomic weight of gold = 196.967.

The *Pangaea* of about 160 million years ago comprised the southern super-continent of Gondwana (Gondwanaland), a jigsaw join-up of Australia, South America, Africa, and India, complemented by the northern super-continent of Laurasia. The break-up of these conglomerates featured, for example, the amazing northward slide of India, whose collision with the Eurasian plate caused the upthrust (orogenesis) of the Himalayas.

This alternating process is accompanied by changes in the world-ocean floor, with the average ocean depth at its maximum just before the return movement of the continental cycle, that is the re-amalgamation phase. As it has been stated that the continents are now approaching their maximum separation, the average ocean depth should be near *its* maximum, and the ocean's share of the globe near its minimum.

What, then, is the present state of the elements, numerically speaking? In view of such complications as (to mention only one) whether the polar ice-caps should be included (as solid water), it's hardly surprising that the reference books show some divergence. Despite this, a figure of "nearly 71%" for ocean in its ordinary sense of (sea) water, seems representative.

Now, according to Pythagorean ideas, first there is unity, then duality, which brings with it relationship of the halves to each other. As an example, we might take cell division. On the Earth's surface, as cooling proceeded, "unity" must once have existed in the sense of all-land. If the Pythagoreans were correct in their belief that due proportion or *harmonia* based on numbers permeates the natural world, should we expect to find equal shares of surface area going to water and land, or ocean and continent, instead of arbitrary-seeming numbers like 71% and 29%?

It turns out that, in effect, the watery share *is* based on 2, not on 2^{-1} — the reciprocal of $2 = 1/2$ — but $2^{-1/2}$ [24] that is, the square root of $1/2 = .707$ to three decimal places, and so nearly 71%.

Land's share of the globe resembles, instead of $2^{-1/2}$, $12^{-1/2} = .289$ or about 29% (cf. 12-BR table at Appendix A).

The proportion of land to water is then .41, similar to $36^{-1/4} = .408$.

---

[24] Recall that the positive form of this number, $2^{1/2}$, represented the scandalous hypotenuse of the right-angled triangle which did not fit the Pythagorean system of rational numbers (c.f. "What-Was-His-Name with the Thingamy?").

The alternative figures are: continents, up to 41%, oceans 59%, the ratio being .69. Notice that land's proportion to water .41 has become continent's absolute share, also .41.[25]

The world ocean is believed to have had its paradoxical origin in volcanic activity, which released water from rock in the form of vapour. So the present extent, as distinct from dispersion of the continents, should be what remains of the original area "after the flood".

As an analogy consider a circle of radius $= x$, just touching which at three points is drawn on the inside an equilateral triangle (one with its sides and angles all the same). Another circle is drawn inside the triangle, followed by a *square* inside the second circle. Further circles and regular polygons, each with one side more than the previous one, are drawn alternately. Contrary to expectations, this process cannot be continued indefinitely, but effectively reaches a limit — the polygon is now virtually as smooth as the circle. Interestingly, this occurs when the radius of the "last" circle reaches approximately $x/12$ (12^{-1}).

Change to three dimensions and we can see that with spheres and regular polyhedrons a limit will likewise be reached when the radius has decreased to $x/12$ [26]

It is one thing to figuratively fill a hollow sphere to the innermost 1/12th of its radius and quite another to cover a sphere which, if it had the size of a cricket ball, would need only a thin film to represent the depth of the world's water.

Nor does the merger between roundness and angularity in the first case have an analogue in the second. The seas merely conceal the irregularities of the land-forms below and it can be argued it is only a contingent insufficiency of supply which has restricted the concealment process.

In fact, land's share may fall to less than 29% through reamalgamations. Still, it's intriguing that 12 occurs both times, along with probably the "scaling effect" next most important after doubling or halving — the square root : square relation, as of $12^{-1/2} : 12^{-1}$.

---

[25] This sort of "ratio shift" seems to occur often.

[26] Kasner and Newman (1949). Were the Pythagoreans aware of the application of 12 in these geometrical experiments? Their idea of perfection was 10 (the *dekad*), the sum of the natural numbers 1, 2, 3, 4.

In geological theory all is physical, as physical as the spewings of volcanoes or grinding, rifting or sliding of tectonic plate boundaries.

So if we switch from the horizontal to the vertical we find that mountains are the product of either plate movements, causing continents to collide, as India with Asia, whence the Himalayas, or volcanic action, whence Aconagua, South America's highest peak. Throughout their life mountains are subject to the negative process of erosion.

The highest rises in seven continents in our own age are as follows:[27]

	Metres	Feet		
Everest (Asia)	8,848	29,028	$12^{-1/2}$	= .2887
Aconagua (S. America)	6,960	22,834		
McKinley (N. America)	6,194	20,320	$24^{-1/2}$	= .2041
Kilimanjaro (Africa)	5,895	19,340		
Elbrus (Europe, Caucasus)	5,642	18,500	$24^{-1/2}$) Av $36^{-1/2}$)	= .1853
Vinson (Antarctica)	5,140	16,864	$36^{-1/2}$	= .1667
Jaya (Oceania, Indonesia)	5,030	16,500	$36^{-1/2}$	= .1667

Above on the right are shown correlates from our 12-BR table for the heights in feet of five of the seven mountains. The two remaining peaks, Aconagua and Kilimanjaro, can also be fitted to the same table, but to numbers from later columns (cols.) which has the effect of "devaluing" the present correlations, which are with the cols. headed 12, 24 and 36 only (see 12-BR table). The correlation of only these five shows a strong association with 12-based numbers.[28]

---

[27] Sources: *Encyclopedia Americana* (1994), *Encyclopaedia Britannica* (1994), *World Almanac* (1999).

[28] Poisson $p < .002$

The metrical figures can be correlated this time with the *first* column of the adjacent 7-BR table (see Part I), either with a table number or the average of two consecutive numbers ($p < .05$).

But wait — two special cases must be noted, which blur these findings. The long-time height in feet of Everest, before it was altered to 29,028 feet, was 29,002, a mnemonic windfall for generations of schoolchildren, with its finicky "2". Satellite measurements now indicate a figure of 29,864 feet or 9102.6m, though so far this has not gained general acceptance.[29]

Then also Elbrus, ambiguously located near where Europe and Asia meet, might properly be outed in favour of Mount Blanc, France's snowbound peak.

Supposing we make these changes, we have:

	Metres	Feet		
Everest	9102.6	29,864	$132^{-1/4}$) Av. $120^{-1/4}$)	.29864
Aconagua	6960	22,834	$84^{-1/3}$	.22834
McKinley	6194	20,320	$24^{-1/2}$	.2041
Kilimanjaro	5895	19,340	$144^{-1/3}$) Av. $132^{-1/3}$)	.1936
Vinson	5140	16,864	$36^{-1/2}$	.1667
Jaya	5030	16,500	$36^{-1/2}$	.1667
Mont Blanc	4807	15,771	?	

Notice that the top two numbers (feet) now match our 12-BR table to *five* decimal places. Chance could not be expected to include two such correlations in 500 sets of data, let alone one set.[30] This, however, assumes only these two out of seven instances are "successes"; so the overall correlation is "thin". Lowering the "criterion" to include five/seven gives $p < .05$ by binomial test. The metrical data can be correlated as before with p also $< .05$.

---

[29] *World Almanac* (1999), p. 452.

[30] Poisson $p < .002$

Table 4.1

Part 1. Ratios Based on Fractions of 7 (7-Based Ratios: 7-BR)

Base (b)	1/7	2/7	3/7	4/7	5/7	6/7	
b,32[1]						.0072	A
b,16				.0001	.0046	.0849	B
b,8			.0011	.0114	.0678	.2914	C
b,4	.0004	.0067	.0337	.1066	.2603	.5398	D
b,2	.0204	.0816	.1837	.3265	.5102	.7347	E
base	.1429	.2857	.4286	.5714	.7143	.8571	F
b,1/2	.3780	.5345	.6547	.7559	.8452	.9258	G
b,1/4	.6148	.7311	.8091	.8694	.9193	.9622	H
b,1/8	.7841	.8550	.8995	.9324	.9588	.9809	I
b,1/16	.8855	.9247	.9484	.9656	.9792	.9904	J
b,1/32	.9410	.9616	.9739	.9827	.9895	.9952	K
b,1/64	.9701	.9806	.9868	.9913	.9948		L
b,1/128	.9849	.9903	.9934	.9956	.9974		M
b,1/256	.9924	.9951	.9967				N

[1]Note: Bases (b) and exponents shown on left. Exponents shown on same line as bases for neatness of layout.

Table 4.1

Part 2. 7-Based Ratios (7-BR) in Order of Size

.0001 (4B)[1]	.3265 (4E)	.8694 (4H)	.9827 (4K)
.0004 (1D)	.3780 (1G)	.8855 (1J)	.9849 (1M)
.0011 (3C)	.4286 (3F)	.8995 (3I)	.9868 (3L)
.0072 (6A)	.5102 (5E)	.9193 (5H)	.9895 (5K)
.0046 (5B)	.5345 (2G)	.9247 (2J)	.9903 (2M)
.0067 (2D)	.5398 (6D)	.9258 (6G)	.9904 (6J)
.0114 (4C)	.5714 (4F)	.9324 (4I)	.9913 (4L)
.0204 (1E)	.6148 (1H)	.9410 (1K)	.9924 (1N)
.0337 (3D)	.6547 (3G)	.9484 (3J)	.9934 (3M)
.0678 (5C)	.7143 (5F)	.9588 (5I)	.9948 (5L)
.0816 (2E)	.7311 (2H)	.9616 (2K)	.9951 (2N)
.0849 (6B)	.7347 (6E)	.9656 (4J)	.9952 (6K)
.1066 (4D)	.7559 (4G)	.9622 (6H)	.9956 (4M)
.1429 (1F)	.7841 (1I)	.9701 (1L)	.9967 (3N)
.1837 (3E)	.8091 (3H)	.9739 (3K)	.9974 (5M)
.2603 (5D)	.8452 (5G)	.9792 (5J)	
.2857 (2F)	.8550 (2I)	.9806 (2L)	
.2914 (6C)	.8571 (6F)	.9809 (6I)	

[1]Note: references to Part 1 give the column (denoted by the number, which is the numerator in the particular fraction of 7) and the row (indicated by the letter).

Ocean depths support the relevance of numbers as such (per se) to our understanding of Earth's salient physical features. The maximum depth in feet of each ocean is as follows:[31]

Pacific, Mariana Trench	36,080	$60^{-1/4}$	= .35930
Atlantic, Puerto Rico Trench	27,741	$48^{-1/3}$	= .27516
Indian, Java Trench	24,069	$72^{-1/3}$	= .24037
Arctic	17,965	$36^{-1/2}$) Av.	= .17875
		$144^{-1/3}$)	

$p < .05$

Air ... Thin Air

The air we breathe contains mainly nitrogen (N_2) and oxygen (O_2), together with water vapour in variable concentrations. Atmospheric gases whose proportions are regarded as constant include as well as N_2 and O_2, Argon (Ar), followed by a motley of minor ingredients, vaguely reminiscent of the additives in our daily bread.

It is surprising to learn that despite latter day exploitation of our planet, particularly by wholesale deforestation and conspicuous consumption of fossil fuels, the level of free oxygen has evidently not declined or that of carbon dioxide (CO_2) risen above what to commonsense seems a negligible average of .032 of 1% (or .00032).[32]

The proportions by volume of the top three "constants" are:

Nitrogen	.78084.	H1, G9 (Av.)	= .7808
Oxygen	.20946	F11	= .2119
Argon	.00934	C21	= .00957

The letter and number references shown above are to our *e*-BR table (Appendix B). Taken together, these correlations are non-significant (n.s.) though the *p* for N_2 alone is .05.

As well as in their proportions and properties, these gases are diverse in terms of origin. Nitrogen is regarded as a product of "outgassing", for example during volcanic eruptions. Its lion's share of the atmosphere follows the elimination in past ages of rivals carbon dioxide, which was consumed by weathering reactions, and water vapour, which condensed to form the oceans.

---

[31] Averaged from the same sources as in the previous example.
[32] .00032 is similar to the *e*-BR,C1, which rounds up to .00034.

Two major sources are given for oxygen: 1. oxygen released by a redox process (coupling oxydisation and reduction), involving buried unoxydised organic carbon and oxydised forms of carbon, and 2. the advent of land plants about 400 million years ago.

For argon, the most abundant of the "noble" gases (distinguished by their chemical inertness), the source is decay of radioactive potassium, which is then released by outgassing.

"Sources" in geology are complemented by "sinks", and a continuing concern of "green" parties is that the sinks for CO_2 sources may become blocked.

Consider then the following ratios of abundance by volume:

$$O_2/N_2 \; = .2682 \qquad F5 \;\; = .2689$$
$$Ar/O_2 \; = .0446 \qquad E11 = .0449$$
$$Ne/Ar \; = .0019 \qquad D11 = .0020$$

Note that another noble gas neon (Ne), next in abundance after argon but 500 times rarer, has been included here to show the cohesive pattern of these four gases ($p < .05$). Our empirical ratios are related as follows (parallelling the e-BR table programme):

$$\text{The square root of } .0019 \; = .0439, \text{ similar to } (\approx)\ .0446$$
$$\text{The square root of } .0446 \; = .2112 \text{ and}$$
$$.2112 / (1\text{-}.2112) \;\; = .2677 \approx .2682.$$

The number near which the "buck" stops in this chain of numbers — F5 in the e-BR table — is an important derivative of e as it is the smaller (divisible, complementary) factor of its reciprocal (e^{-1}). See also Figure 4.1.

Incidentally, the atomic weight of N_2, 14.0067, has reciprocal $(1/14.0067) = .07139$, which is near the *square* of F5 = .07233.[33] It should be noted that "atomic weight" is the ratio of an element to carbon 12, the principal isotope of carbon, whose assigned atomic mass is 12 exactly. Carbon then joins the pattern.

This pattern is evidence for a scaling factor in the composition of the Earth's atmosphere, whereas a physical model incorporating origins and maintenance as briefly noted implies *continuity* with no particular points on the "number-line" being preferred.

---

[33] 3/4 gases noted here have atomic weights whose reciprocals are near e-BR ($p < .05$).

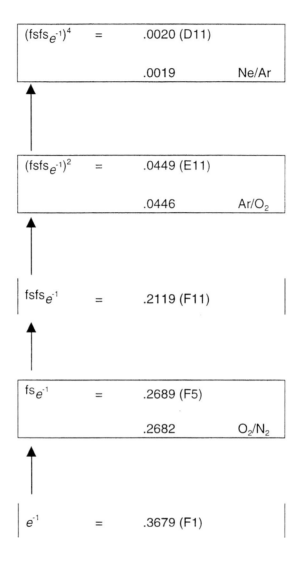

FIG. 4.1. Diagram showing the ratios between the abundances by volume of the four leading atmospheric gases fitted to derivatives of the natural log base e; $p < .05$. Abundances from *The New Encyclopaedia Britannica* (1994).

Note: $fs_{e^{-1}}$: smaller (divisible, complementary) factor of $1/e$; fsfs: smaller factor *of smaller factor*.

F1, F11, etc.: references to table of e-based ratios (e-BR) — see Appendix B.

Ne: neon; Ar: argon; O_2: oxygen; N_2: nitrogen.

A New Scaling Effect in Radioactive Transformation Times?

Of the four elements of Empedocles, water, air, fire, and earth, we have now glanced at all but the third, whose utility and potential menace have in our age to compete with the lure of atomic power and hazards of nuclear radiation.

An enduring image from the commencement of the nuclear age is of Marie Curie, the Polish-French physicist, and her cauldron with its up to 10 kg of pitchblende residues on the boil. Tons of the dust-brown ore, rail-freighted to Paris from the Joachimsthal mines in Bohemia and still mixed with pine needles passed through that cauldron and the various containers used in a sustained fractional crystallisation process. Four years of toil passed before the precious proceeds had attained the minute amount of $1/10^{th}$ gm — enough to satisfy the sceptical chemists of the existence of the new wonder-element of *radium*, with its fluorescent blue glow in the dark.

The discovery of radium in 1898 by the husband and wife team of physicists Pierre and Mme Curie followed the recent discovery by Becquerel of the radioactive property of uranium. These discoveries earned Marie and Pierre a share with Becquerel of the 1903 Nobel prize for physics. Radium was for a period the leading weapon against cancer.

Radium-226[34] is an emitter of alpha particles, which are similar to the atomic nuclei of helium (the lightest element after hydrogen). Through this radioactive process it changes into the radioactive gas radon-227. Radium itself is the decay product of thorium-230. These and various other "nuclides" are members of the radioactive transformation series based on uranium-238.

Besides uranium-238 two other naturally occurring series are known. These are uranium-235 and thorium-232.

Alpha particles have various energy levels, which can be measured by their "range", that is distance travelled through a

---

[34] 226, etc: mass numbers.

uniform medium. These particles have relatively low penetration — only .01 of that of beta particles (electrons), which some decay products emit in radioactive transformations.

The "half-life" or "half-period" (T) of a nuclide is the time period during which any atom of that substance has a 50 : 50 chance of "firing". There is an inverse relation between T and particular energy, that is emitters of high energy particles are short-lived and vice versa. (For alpha emitters this is known as the Geiger-Nuttall rule.)

T vary for different nuclides from (less than) < 1 millionth sec to (more than) > 1 billion years.

Radium has T of approximately 1600 years, its "parent", 80,000 years, its "daughter", 3.2 *days*.

Nuclides later in a series are generally shorter-lived and the largest swings relate to earlier transformations.

What may not be immediately clear is that the transformation of different "generations" is a concurrent process, so that in a sample of, say, U-238 a state of "radioactive equilibrium" exists between different products. The "numerics" of the proportions of such products would therefore make an interesting comparison with the atmosphere. The present evidence, however, has to do rather with the averaged ratios between T of daughters and of parents.

From what has been said about the variability and astronomical span of these T the last thing we might expect to find is scaling effects anyway comparable to those applying to the atmosphere. That said, a point concerning method should be mentioned.

When, as is generally the case, the daughter's T is smaller than the parent's, the ratio is of course < 1, but in reverse cases the ratio may balloon to a large number, which, if included in the average, produces an imbalance. To correct this the log (log e) is substituted in all cases. The most interesting of our results are now noted:

U-238, U-235, Th-232, Mean of antilog of each series' mean
log e = .10915, similar to $84^{-1/2}$ = .10911.

$p = .01$.

For the same grouping Mean of each series' mean log e = -2.5155. Antilog = .08082,[35] similar to C6 in the e-BR table = .08159 to five decimals.

p = .07.

The scaling effect mentioned in our subheading refers to the following pairs, for which the antilog calculated as in the just-preceding example are:

> U-238 and U-235 .1349 ≈ e^2 = .1353
> U-235 and Th-232 .0498 ≈ e^3 = .0498
> p : low.

As can be seen from the above, the averages for these pairs of series correspond to the "workhorse" numbers represented by consecutive powers of the natural log base e^{-1}.

This 2 : 3 scaling effect transfers to a similar 8 : 12 ratio of powers of a derivative of e shown in our table at F12, when the ratios of T are calculated from the separate antilog, as follows:

> U-238 and U-235 Mean of antilog of mean log = .14922
> U-235 and Th-232 Mean of antilog of mean log = .05724

The corresponding numbers based on F12 are .14876 and .05737.

It's a far cry from the mysterious "central furnace" conceived of by the Pythagoreans to the new millennium dream of replicating on Earth the nuclear fusion, which was, is, and will be in progress at the centre of our Sun. Is, not Pythagoras, but ... what-was-his-name? ... *Prometheus*, about to become our inspiration?[36]

---

[35] By a remarkable chance (?) the ratio of the Moon's synodic period to the Earthly year is .0808̲4, virtually the same (p of correlation with the e-BR, C6, also .07). Note: synodic period : eg, from one full moon to the next.

[36] Prometheus: Greek god and bringer of fire.

References for Chapter 4

CURIE, E., *Madame Curie* (Tr. V. Sheean; London: Heinemann, 1939)

Encyclopedia Americana International Edition (Danbury, Connecticut, 1994)

The New Encyclopaedia Britannica (15th ed., Chicago, 1994)

KASNER, E. and NEWMAN, J., *Mathematics and the imagination* (London: G. Bell, 1949)

The McGraw-Hill Encyclopedia of Science and Technology (8th ed., vol. 5, New York, 1997)

The World Almanac and Book of Facts 1999 (Mahwah, New Jersey, 1998)

Green Quiz Question No. 4

The city of Hamburg's figure is like the first two digits — not counting zeroes — of the *8th power* of the bigger factor of 1/*e*.

Where do you find this number in the table (Appendix B)? Give the letter and column number.

How many hectares of P'n'G has Hamburg got?

Extra clue: don't round up.

CHAPTER 5
QUANTUM CRICKET: A QUICK LOOK AT THE NUMBERS

FEW CRICKET fans probably stop to question if what you see on the surface is necessarily what you get if you delve beneath the statistics.

Statistics Ordinary

Each innings, each match produces its own figures. To get a "handle" on them averages are worked out. Records, made or broken, are entered or relegated to history.

Numbers have "moreness" or "lessness", but not *identity*. A notable exception is 100, which is singled out of the ruck, along with half that figure.

A hundred serves as a target for a batsman, a partnership, or a team and in the career of a bowler, as a milestone.

When they come, centuries bring excitement to a game and some critics might argue there aren't enough centuries to go round.

Could there be, though, amid the throng, other numbers which have escaped the spotlight? Numbers, which happen more often than, by the law of averages, they ought to do?

If "preferred" numbers do exist in cricket (or any sport) this has important implications. It means there are *numerical constraints* on the statistics. Not exactly in the "nervous nineties" sense but, by a sort of quantum leap in the argument, somewhat as energy levels on the scale of the atom can take only certain values (hence *quantum* physics).

Statistics Extraordinary

Mathematically, numbers can be grouped into types, according to what "base" is the generator. 100 (10 x 10) is the square of the base of our ordinary number system. Other numbers might be part of a pattern within this system. For a possible clue to what sort of numbers could be lurking in the shadows, let us turn to mathematics.

Records and Limits

Records in the sense of maxima and minima, like run-of-the-mill figures, come in a range of sizes — seemingly in almost any size. The concept of *record*, though, parallels the key mathematical concept of *limit*, so here is a ready-made bridge between a "mind-game" played out on the field and one played out, ultimately, in the mind.

The best-known mathematical model for growth or decrease to a limit is the constant $e = 2.718$ approximately. Does this arbitrary-looking number have a surreptitious role in record-making?

First it is necessary to do some simple pocket calculator operations, which take their start from e.

Successive steps in this process produce numbers which together form a table of derivatives.[37] Replicas or, most often, near-replicas of these numbers — all decimals less than 1 — have been found by the author in a variety of contexts.

Win Ratios in Test Cricket

A country's performance can be gauged by its ratio of wins to matches played. Heading the list is Australia with .411, followed by W. Indies (.385), England (.348), Pakistan (.243), S. Africa (.220), India (.161), New Zealand (.137), and, lastly, Sri Lanka (.054). A nondescript assortment, it seems. Look, though, at the top order:

Australia	.411	
	Average	.398
W. Indies	.385	
	Average	.366
England	.348	

The averages shown for (arithmetically) nearest neighbours approximate to derivatives of e very close to the base. These are $(1-1/e)^2 = .400$ and $1/e = .368$ and can be found in the e-BR table (Appendix B) at E2 and F1.

---

[37] See table of e-based ratios (e-BR) at Appendix B.

It turns out that all countries can be fitted to *e*-based numbers, either by averaging or one-to-one.

This pattern can hardly be accounted for by chance, as the probability (*p*) of this is only .01 by binomial test.[38] It is evidence, rather, for a numeric factor in cricket.

Whether the present set of win ratios, as they evolve, will continue to reflect *e*-based numbers, only time will reveal.[39]

Consistency as the Ratio of Highest to Lowest Scores : the Number 12

At grassroots level an essential part of winning games is putting runs on the board. But one big score doesn't guarantee success. For instance, the home side's first innings on the Adelaide leg of the recent (1994/95) tour of Australia by England's team yielded 419 runs, which is not far short of the highest total of the whole series. But the visitors still won this game through consistency in exceeding 300 each time they were at the crease.

Consistency in scoring can be very roughly estimated as the ratio, single highest/single lowest total in all matches. By this reckoning, lowly Sri Lanka came out on top with a ratio near 5 : 1. The average ratio for all countries was 14 : 1.

The ratios, average *highest score* to average *lowest score*, in home and away matches separately, were : Home matches 10.84, Away matches 13.23; mean or average *12.03*. (Data from *Wisden Cricketers' Almanack* 1993, pp. 164–227.)

The same number 12 is another remarkably adaptive constant, though less well known than *e*. Its usefulness also extends far beyond the number itself to derivatives, namely roots of 1/12, 1/24, 1/36, etc. In the present context, *lowest : highest* innings ratios for separate countries reflected these numbers.[40]

---

[38] Data from *Wisden Cricketers' Almanack* 1993, p. 164, including all tests up to August 9, 1992. For table of correlations see Chapter 6, "Quantisation Effects in Test Cricket".

[39] Written in 1995. Updating to August 31, 1998, again shows a relation to *e*-BR. Probability (*p*) is at or below .01. See Chapter 6, "Quantisation Effects in Test Cricket".

[40] A table of 12-based ratios (12-BR) is found at Appendix A.

Trans-Decimal Correlations: Some Examples

A still "curiouser" phenomenon is when a decimal fraction, be it a 12- or other based number, somehow loses its decimal point and turns up as a batting, etc, total or average total.

Take the average total scored in century innings by each country's master batsmen (those with 15 or more centuries to their name, a century being, of course, an innings worth *at least* 100 runs). These averages fit *e*-BR table numbers or means between adjacent numbers in the size-ordered table supplement (see Appendix B) as follows:[41]

Pakistan	155.8	E8, D2	mean	= .1549
Australia	143.8	F19		= .1443
England	142.5	D9, F19	mean	= .1426
New Zealand	142.4	D9, F19	mean	= .1426
South Africa	142.3	D9, F19	mean	= .1426
West Indies	140.8	D9		= .1409
India	135.4	E1		= .1353

$p < .05$

Note: E8, D2, etc: *e*-BR table references.

Then there are the record Australian partnerships in Ashes tests. Those for wickets 2 to 6 still show D. G. Bradman ("The Don") and can be correlated with 12-BR. The figure for the 2nd wicket (with W. H. Ponsford, Oval, 1934) is 451 ($4\sqrt{1/24} = .452$), for the 3rd (with A. L. Hassett, Brisbane, 1946) it is 276 ($3\sqrt{1/48} = .275$). The *p* of the five correlations is less than .01.[42]

The scores in the drawn Sydney test of the 1994/95 series were England, 309 (see below) and 255d. ($3\sqrt{1/60} = .255$), Australia 116 ($\sqrt{1/72} = .118$) and 344 ($4\sqrt{1/72} = .343$). Notice how the "quantum leap" in Australia's batting is reflected in the square : square root relation between the "strange" correlates, as the square root of $\sqrt{1/72}$ is, of course, $4\sqrt{1/72}$.

From across the board, highest individual innings for each country resembled *e*-based numbers minus the decimal point. Take Gary Sobers' (W. Indies) long-time (1958–1994) world record 365, not far short of $1/e$ (.368). (Brian Lara's record-

---

[41] Data from Test Cricket Lists (1996), including tests up to August 1996.
Note: this example has been added to the original article and *e*-BR table numbers are given to four decimal places.

[42] See Table 2 in Chapter 6, "Quantisation Effects in Test Cricket".

breaking 375 invites comparison with 3/8ths = .375, also E9 in the e-BR table — Appendix B.)

The list extends to bowling (most wickets) and most catches by a fielder: A. R. Border with 135, similar to $(1/e)^2 = .135$.

Perhaps strangest of all, Lance Gibbs' (W. Indies) world record most balls in a career, 27,115, is near 10,000 e (27,183).

The Numeric Factor in Cricket

In the foregoing and other similar cases, averages, totals, or ratios have patterns, which can be "decoded" with the aid of tables.

It is irrefutable that systematic mathematical relationships are reflected in cricket, though how this comes about is not obvious, at least from the ordinary perspective. From the mind-bending perspective of quantum physics the "impossible" is the norm, so perhaps it is this area of knowledge which might supply further clues.

As to whether the "numeric factor" is a cause for optimism or pessimism, numbers can be traps or targets, it seems. It's a matter of temperament, I guess.

(Year of writing: 1995)

Postscript

Returning to the 1994/95 (Sydney) Ashes test, from the extended table of 12-based ratios (12-BR), see Appendix A), we can see that .2554, .1179, and .3433 cluster symmetrically in the adjacent cols. headed 60 and 72. England's match-opening .309 is accounted for as near the average of .2554 and .3593 $(60^{-1/4}) = .307$ to three decimal places.

At August 31, 1998, Border still held the fielder's record with the (numerically) ordinary total of 156. Kapil Dev (India) had surpassed Gibbs with 28,741 balls. If treated as 2.8741 x 10,0000 in line with Gibbs' total (see above), 1/2.8741 = .3479 to four decimal places, comes near the salient 12-BR, $24^{-1/3} = .3467$. (See also Table 3 in Chapter 6, "Quantisation Effects in Test Cricket").

Although the updated figures for each country's highest individual innings and most wickets in a career seem not significant (statistically), the combined totals (runs plus wickets) can be fitted to the column headed 24 in our 12-BR table (see Appendix A) with $p < .01$.

The mean total is 631.6, very nearly $1-e^{-1} = .6321$, digitally. Also the standard deviation (*SD*), a measure of the average difference, up or down, from the mean, is 135.0, corresponding to e^{-2} (the square of $e^{-1} = .1353$). These close derivatives of e in conjunction[43] is another extraordinary example of the "numeric factor" in its "trans-decimal" form.

References for Chapter 5

DAWSON, G., and WAT, C. *Test Cricket Lists: The Complete Book of Test Cricket From 1877* (3rd ed., Noble Park, VIC, The Five Mile Press, 1996).

ENGEL, M. (Ed.) *Wisden Cricketers' Almanack* (Merrow, Guildford, Surrey; 1999).

ENGEL, M. (Ed.) *Wisden Cricketers' Almanack* (Merrow, Guildford, Surrey; 1993).

Green Quiz Question No. 5

Tokyo's figure is like the *square* of the bigger factor *of the bigger factor* of $1/e$. How many hectares of P'n'G has Tokyo got, give or take one? Where is this number found in the table (give letter plus number location)?

---

[43] As it happens, this pair is symmetrical with the pair of numbers representing the means of the top win ratios (see earlier section), which, it is recalled, were: instead of $1-e^{-1}$ and e^{-2}, e^{-1} and $(1-e^{-1})^2$.

CHAPTER 6
"QUANTISATION" EFFECTS IN TEST CRICKET

"THE ESSENTIAL fact is that an atom can be found only in discrete energy levels corresponding to the various electron orbits ... energy [does not] vary continuously,"[44]

"Quantisation" in the Macroworld

In that branch of atomic science known as quantum mechanics, discrete quantity (*quantum*) is the name of the game, but "quantisation" is not a generally recognised aspect of the macroworld.

Effects suggestive of quantisation were found by this author first in published data from, mainly, experiments on human vigilance. Structure/order was based on common fractions, particularly the series 1/12, 1/24, 1/36 ..., and sequential factors of 1/*e*. These factors were dividend and divisor, summing to unity (ie, complementary, divisible factors). Tables were compiled which included roots and/or powers of all bases.

Here, similar effects in test cricket are described, based on data (statistics) mainly from *Wisden Cricketers' Almanack* (1993).

Trans-Decimal Effects

A paradoxical finding, believed to be new when first referred to by the author,[45] is that numbers from the game of cricket (whether scores and averages or career totals and match attendance) and other real world contexts, whole numbers as well as decimal fractions, often resemble the *digit sequences* of decimal fractions, based on the 1/12 sequence, other fractions, or the 1/*e* sequence.

---

[44] Prigogine and Stengers (1990)

[45] Richardson (1995) The *e*-based ratio (*e*-BR) table reprinted here as Appendix B first appeared in that journal article.

The Numeric Factor

There is abundant evidence that mathematics, standard or "strange", impacts on the macro-world in the novel sense of, as it were, supplying from a "reservoir" of "preferred" values, *targets* for the actual (empirical) numbers which are obtained by counting or measuring.

This means that outcomes depend on (to stay with cricket) not only skill, luck, leadership, teamwork, etc., but on a *numeric* factor, and can often be "decoded" with the aid of tables.

Mathematical Constants: *e, 12*

In sport, "barrier" (the four-minute mile) and record parallel "limit" in mathematics, but a possible relation between records or barriers and mathematical constants appears to have been neglected. Probably the most important constant known to be associated with growth or decline to a limit is *e*, the base of "natural" logarithms (as distinct from "common" logarithms, based on 10), Its value is approximately 2.7183 (1/2.7183 = .3679). An apparently neglected *constant* is the number 12 which, it is interesting to note, is the total given for the known particles of matter.

In geometry, a circle around or within which regular polygons (triangle, square, pentagon ...) are sequentially drawn, alternately with circles, ceases to grow or contract when the radius has reached approximately 12x or 1/12th of the original.[46]

Quantisation Effects Based on 12

Previous research by the author had shown the importance of roots of 1/12 (and multiples), particularly those in the series 2, 4, 8 ... and 3, 6, 12 .... For a clear example from test cricket take the highest innings total against all comers (average for 8 countries) divided by the lowest innings total against all comers (average for 8 countries). The ratios are:

Home matches	= 10.84
Away matches	= 13.23
Mean	= 12.03, almost exactly 12

[46] Kasner and Newman (1949), pp. 310ff.

Broadening the sample[47] to include the average record totals (high and low) for each country against each opponent had surprising results: the *lowest* : *highest* ratios were now:

Home matches:	.2041	similar to	$\sqrt{1/24}$	= *.2041*
Away matches:	.1669	similar to	$\sqrt{1/36}$	= .1667

This remarkable quantum or scaling effect has low p (= .01)

Quantisation Effects Based on *e*

The question was, is there evidence of discrete differences, otherwise quantisation or proportionality, in the all-time or historical ratios of test matches won played by all countries?

Table 6.1 Test Matches Won/Played, as Derivatives of 1/*e**

Country	England		W. Indies		Australia
Won/Played	.348	(*M* .366)	.385	(*M* .398)	.411
Correlate		1/*e* (*a*)	$[1 - (1/e) = b]^2$		
Nominal Value		.368		.400	

Country	S. Africa		Pakistan
Won/Played	.220	(*M* .231)	.243
Correlate		(*a*).(*b*)	
Nominal Value		.233	

Country	New Zealand	India
Won/Played	.137	.161
Correlate	(a^2)	(b^4)
Nominal Value	.135	.160

Country	Sri Lanka
Won/Played	.054
Correlate	$[(ab)^2]$
Nominal Value	.054

*p .01 by binomial test.

Note: all tests up to August 9, 1992, included, as given by *Wisden Cricketers' Almanack 1993*.

Correlates shown can be found in cols. 1–4 of the *e*-BR table (see Appendix B).

Table 6.1 is a slightly different version of the one in Chapter 1, "The Numbers Show".

---

[47] Based on tests up to August 9, 1992, as given by *Wisden Cricketers' Almanack* (1993).

As shown in Table 6.1, all countries fit a cohesive pattern based on e. In some cases the average for paired countries with similar win ratios has been substituted for the separate figures. Close inspection of this pattern strongly suggests that it is not due to chance. To test the probability (p) of this a binomial test was used. For this test a "success" could be either a near "hit" on a table number or a near hit by the average for two countries with similar ratios on a table number. The total of "trials" took account of this extra option. The p of a success p (x) was the highest p for any separate correlation. As there were 8 "successes" from 13 trials, with p (x) $\leq$ .23, the p of these correlations being due to chance is (less than) < .01.

The average win ratio for all countries can be calculated either as the mean of the separate ratios or as total wins / total games, as follows:

Mean win ratio = .245
Total wins/total games = 724/1193 = .607

Note that .607 is approximately $\sqrt{1/e}$, further evidence of the role of e in relation to the outcomes of matches. (See also next section re wins and draws.)

Examples of Trans-Decimal Correlations

A simple way to realise a discrete range of natural numbers could be to go up or down by equal steps, for example, by 10's or 12's. Discreteness found in empirical data from the macroworld depends on a very different "programme". This was briefly noted by the author in a 1995 paper on the numerics of human vigilance. An example from test cricket showed the highest innings total by Australia at home and in each opponent's country resembled mostly 8th roots of 1/12 or multiples of 1/12.

Probably Australia's arch rivals in cricket have been England and the West Indies. The pattern of highest scores in Ashes tests is as follows:

Aus vs Eng in England	Lord's, 1930	6d-729	$8\sqrt{1/12}$	= .733
Eng vs Aus in England	Oval, 1938	7d-903	$24\sqrt{1/12}$	= .902
Aus vs Eng in Australia	Sydney, 1946/47	659	$6\sqrt{1/12}$	= .661
Eng vs Aus in Australia	Sydney, 1928/29	636	$5\sqrt{1/12})$ M	= .635
			$6\sqrt{1/12})$	

The p of these convincing 12-based correlations is < .01. (See also table of 12-based ratios — 12-BR — at Appendix A.)

Highest totals in meets between Australia and West Indies include a square root : square scaling effect (p of totals $< .05$).

To return to our all-time win ratios (Table 6.1), total wins are linked as follows with total draws:

| Total wins | 724 | similar to | $12\sqrt{1/48}$ | $= .724$ |
| Total draws | 467 | similar to | $6\sqrt{1/96}$ | $= .467$ |

Note: symmetrical change in base and root number by a factor of 2. [48]

---

[48] Writing on the "last day of the old millennium" (December 31, 1999) it is possible to confirm that at August 31, 1998, the updated win ratios for nine countries could again be related to e-BR. The exact correlation with $96^{-1/6}$ and $48^{-1/12}$ is replaced by a weaker one with $72^{-1/32}$ and $36^{-1/6}$, but the average win ratios support the e-connection as follows:

Mean win ratio	.2465	$\approx$	F22	$= .2465$
Total wins/total games				
(872/1423)	.6128	$\approx$	F9	$= .6127$

p of ratios $< .01$.

The constant e is yet again reflected in the ratio, total wins/total games for the sub-period 1946–1995 (*Wisden Cricketers' Almanack*, 1996) = 608/1046 = .5813 $\approx$ F3 = .5820.

The letter plus number references shown are to the e-BR table. A check with the size-ordered supplement (Appendix B) shows a parallel shift of one table number from near F16 (1992) to F22 (1998) and from G1 (1992) to F9 (1998), which can be seen as quantum increases. Then also F3 (1946–1995) next precedes G1.

Further Examples of Trans-Decimal Effects

Highest partnerships for Australia in "Ashes" tests against
England resemble 12-BR. Wickets 2 to 6 still show Bradman's
name (see Table 6.2).

Table 6.2: Strange Correlation with 1/12-Base Roots of Australian Record Partnerships in Tests vs England

Wicket	Partnership	Runs	Correlate	Nominal
2	W. H. Ponsford & D. G. Bradman	451	$4\sqrt{1/24}$	.452
3	D. G. Bradman & A. L. Hassett	276	$3\sqrt{1/48}$	.275
4	W. H. Ponsford & D. G. Bradman	388	$4\sqrt{1/48}$	.380
5	S. G. Barnes & D. G. Bradman	405	$4\sqrt{1/36}$	.408
6	J. H. Fingleton & D. G. Bradman	346	$3\sqrt{1/24}$	.347

Partnership data from *The Australian* newspaper, November 25, 1994
$p < .01$

Batting records for all tests, world-wide, support the
quantisation hypothesis, as, for example, highest individual
innings for each country could be correlated with e-based
numbers ($p < .01$). The world record of 365, held by G. S. Sobers
(W. Indies) from 1957/58 till 1994, approaches $1/e = .368$ in our
usual digital sense.

Most runs in a career for each country resemble roots of 1/12
and 1/24 ($p < .05$).

From bowling, most wickets in a career also receive a "tick", as
do runs conceded by each country's top wicket taker, from
I. T. Botham of England to Sri Lanka's S. L. Ratnayake, which
came generally near an e-BR ($p < .01$).

Particularly intriguing are most balls. The top total, 27,115
(L. R. Gibbs, W. Indies) is approximately $e = 2.7183$ x 10,000.
Utilising this possible clue, a decimal point was inserted after the
first digit and the reciprocal (.369) substituted. The same
transformation was used in each case and was justified by the
results, as a cohesive structure parallelling the e-based factoring
process referred to earlier was disclosed (see Table 6.3).

Table 6.3: Record Career Totals of Balls Bowled, as Scaled-up Reciprocals of Derivatives of 1/e

Country	Bowler		T'form	Correlate	Value
W. I.	L. R. Gibbs	27,115	.3688	$1/e$	.3679
India	Kapil Dev	24,967	.4005	$(1 - 1/e)^2$	.3996
N. Z.	R. J. Hadlee	21,918)M	.4568	$\sqrt{\text{fsfs}}_{1/e}$	.4606
England	D. L. Underwood	21,862)			
Pakistan	Imran Khan	19,458)M	.5186	$\sqrt{\text{fs}}_{1/e}$	*.5186*
Australia	R. Benaud	19,108)			
S. Africa	H. J. Tayfield	13,568	.7370	$\text{fl}_{1/e}$	.7311

Note T'form: transform = $1/[x/10,000]$, where x = total of balls.

fs, fl: smaller, larger factor. The correlates shown can be found in the e-BR table (Appendix B) at F1, E2, G11, G5, and F6.

Discussion

These examples comprise only some of those which were found. Though only weak and/or non-significant effects were apparent in a number of cases, and further research might consider these differences, the total picture is unequivocal: along with talent, hard work, concentration and all the rest, performance is associated with particular *numbers*. It is surprising to think that the vigilance lapse which cuts off a century innings in full flight may, in a sense, originate in something as abstract as a root of some multiple of 1/12.

Quantisation effects themselves call for an explanation of their origin and possible function. In the perspective of quantum theory it is perhaps not so surprising that these effects, although only crudely analogous to what takes place in the atom, do occur in the macroworld, in this case the human-scale world of cricket. For, according to "quantum cosmology", the universe is itself a quantum effect. But although the possibility of quantum effects in the macroworld has been raised by scientists, at issue appears to be quantum "uncertainty", not quantisation. (See Davies, 1992)

Apart from quantisation — the role of fixed, discrete values, instead of a continuous spectrum of energy values — one other main principle or rule of the atomic microworld appears to particularly lend itself to an explanation of what are here referred to as quantisation effects in test cricket. This is the principle of "non-locality".

Its twin, *locality*, applies to essentially localised events — an apple falls from a tree. Quantum mechanics is *non-localised* and particles carry traces of their previous interactions so that what happens to one particle (its fate) is *correlated* with the fate of its partner.

As "memory", at some fundamental level, certainly well below human consciousness, is surely a prerequisite for our numerical effects, quantum memory traces are suggestive.[49] Another evident need is "communication", which, in quantum theory enables particles which have become separated to maintain symmetry.

Seeing that "memory" and "communication", to which "computation" must surely be added, evidently entail the use of "resources" (dissipation of energy), we may ponder the possible function of our numerical phenomena. It would be wasteful if order existed only for order's sake.

Although the focus has been on cricket, many areas share the same features. Most of the evidence so far concerns human performance or affairs. Particularly those concerned in these areas are urged to take note of the "unreasonable effectiveness" of, for example, numbers referred to as 12- and *e*-based ratios to represent empirical data.

References for Chapter 6

DAVIES, P., *The cosmic blueprint: new discoveries in nature's creative ability to order the universe* (New York, 1989).

DAVIES, P., *The mind of God: science and the search for ultimate meaning* (London, 1993).

KASNER, E. and NEWMAN, J., *Mathematics and the imagination* (London, 1949).

PRIGOGINE, I. and STENGERS, I., *Order out of chaos: man's new dialogue with nature* (London, 1990).

RICHARDSON, N., Vigilance as a table of numbers, *Perceptual and Motor Skills* (1995, 80, 67-84)

Green Quiz Question No. 6

Milan is like Tokyo squared, as its number is near the square *of the square* of the larger factor *of the larger factor* of 1/*e*.

How many hectares of P'n'G has Milan, give or take one?

Where is this figure located in the table (give letter plus number reference).

---

[49] Non-locality might have particular relevance to, for example, the Hitler-Roosevelt (Nazi-Democrat) correlation of election results in November, 1932 (see Chapter 11, "The Last Elections of Weimar").

CHAPTER 7
THE ASHES WAR

DESPITE ENGLAND'S lacklustre performance in recent times, the biennial clashes between the "mother country" and her republican-minded commonwealth Down Under are still regarded by many fans in both countries as the crown of the cricketing calendar. While the current Australian advantage is reflected in the over-all figures, with 114 wins to England's 92, who is to say the home country of cricket may not some day level the score, even if overseas-bred players, including Australians, have to be enlisted to top up native talent?

The start of the modern era can probably be traced to the resumption of test matches following WW1, with Bradman waiting in the wings. For our numeric purposes we focus on the period from 1920–1921 (first post-war England tour of Australia) to 1997 (latest Australian tour of England).

It is said that a test match, or even a test series, is decided by the events of the first day. If so, a key measure or statistic should be the average score by each nation on the first day of each series in which that nation has first "knock". As a more readily accessible figure, we take instead the total for the first innings.[50]

A complication is that an innings terminated by a declaration seems not the same as one tested to "destruction". Three declarations by each side are on record.[51] Three one-off commemorative matches, not played for the Ashes trophy, raise another query. As does a game at Trent Bridge, Nottingham, which was washed out with only 32 runs on the board.

We deal with these "anomalies" by calculating averages (1) excluding (2) including the ambiguous items, and (3) including all but the Ashes-less commemorative games.

---

[50] Data from McCann (1994), *Test Cricket Lists* (1998), *Wisden Cricketers' Almanack 1998.*

[51] Plus one declaration by Australia in a commemorative game.

The resulting averages or means are as follows:

	England	Australia
1.	266.6	331.1
2.	278.6	353.3
3.	269.9	362.1

England's figures include two which are (digitally) near F5 in our e-BR table (Appendix B) = .2689, the mean of both (266.6 and 269.9) being 268.3. We now recall that the score by Australia, when batting first in the first test match of our period (Sydney, 1920), was about the same, that is, 270.

A likely explanation for effects of the "numeric factor" appears to involve the phenomenon of *resonance* (see discussion in Chapter 12, "Home Runs, Strange Numerics, and Form in the Event World"). A question, then, is, could resonance from the "270" (near F5, the smaller factor of e^{-1}) persist for seven decades?

The figure for Australia (mean of 331.1 and 362.1) is 346.6, digitally the same as $24^{-1/3}$ = .3466, to four decimals.

The means of the three means for each country (1, 2, and 3) are : England 271.7, Australia 348.8, with a small shift in both figures.

If we seem to have met figures (or, rather, digit sequences) like these before, this might be because the top line-up of win ratios (see Table 1 in Chapter 6, "Quantisation Effects in Test Cricket") showed: England .348 and England, W. Indies, mean .366, bearing in mind that .366 is near .368 (F1) which has F5 (.269) as its smaller factor.

The *sums* of the means for England and Australia are remarkable as both the *inclusive* criteria give figures near F2 $(1-e^{-1})$ = .6321, as follows: (2) 631.9, (3) 632.0. By these criteria, then, for the seven decades of our study, the runs scored by each team, when it batted first in an Ashes series, cannot be thought to centre on or have average, depending solely and simply on the combined effect of "real" factors. Rather (as mathematical usage might have it) the average total depended also on the solution of the equation $x = (1-e^{-1})-y$, where y is the opposing team's average. Given, that is, the decimal point from $1-e^{-1}$ is moved three places to the right.

For comparison, the mean sum of each test-playing country's highest individual innings and most wickets in a career (as at 1998) was 631.6 (see Chapter 5, "Quantum Cricket").

The *e* effect extends to the ratio between the England and Australia means. The average *ratio* is .7797, near H1 (the 4th root of F1 or e^{-1}) = .7788. The ratio between the overall means (means of 1, 2, and 3) is .7780, still nearer H1 in our table. Compare this figure with the ratio of Ashes tests won by our contestants: England 92, Australia 114, ratio .81. It seems that first innings runs are not a bad predictor of, at least, match outcomes.[52]

Were we a bit rash to imply that the complement of e^{-1}, $1-e^{-1}$ = .6321 (F2) served as an "attracter"[53] for the average sum of both countries' first innings scores, when batting first? Not if other statistics, associated with the means, are taken into account. These are the standard deviation (*SD*) and coefficient of variation (*CV*).[54] England's *SD* by criteria (2) and (3) are as follows:

2.   160.4
3.   161.0

These figures correspond to D2 (the 4th power of F2) = .1597. The *CV* for Australia are:

2.   .4054
3.   .3918

These figures correspond to E2 (the square of F2) = .3996. The value for F2 implied by these four digit sequences is .6322, only .0001 off the actual .6321 to four decimal places.

It's true that other combinations of "criteria" could be used — excluding only the "32" or only the declared innings, etc (see above) — which would give different averages. Averages depend, in any case, on the particular period and evolve over time. There is no finality in our figures. Nevertheless, as they stand, they strongly suggest that, for this period (1920–1997) and by these criteria (1, 2, 3, and, especially, 2 and 3) average first innings scores by teams batting first in Ashes tests, and their sums and ratios, were closely associated with *discrete numbers* based on the mathematical constant *e*.

---

[52] In the present sense of teams batting first and matches won.

[53] Attracter: roughly, a state to which a dynamical system is "attracted", eg, the lowest point in the swing of a pendulum to which no driving force is being applied.

[54] See Glossary.

In the next chapter, (8) "The Bodyline Campaign", we find further evidence of "e-BR" as well as "12-BR".

Postscript

Updating our figures to include England's 1998/1999 tour of Australia, when the home side batted first in the first (Brisbane) game, we have (with England's figures as before):

1. England	266.6	Australia	339.2	
2. England	278.6	Australia	358.8	
3. England	269.9	Australia	367.7	
Mean	271.7	Mean	355.2	~ 3*3 = 45

Australia's means of 339.2 and 367.7 closely fit E3 and F1 in our table. These are the square of the quotient $e^{-1}/(1-e^{-1}) = .3387$ and the reciprocal of $e = .3679$, these numbers being adjacent in the size-ordered table supplement (Appendix B). This is indeed a striking quantum effect. At the same time, the new ratio of wins, $93 : 117 = .795$ (G2) deviates from the new ratio of means, the new ratio of overall means being .7649.

Green Quiz Question No. 7

There's a city east of Adelaide that South Ozzies sometimes feel they're in its shadow. M—'s hectares of P'n'G have a long description; they're like the *4ᵗʰ power* of the *bigger* factor of the *smaller* factor *of the smaller factor* of 1/e.

Where exactly in the table do you find this number? Give the letter an' column number.

How many hectares of P'n'G has M— got, give or take one?

CHAPTER 8
THE 'BODYLINE' CAMPAIGN

NO EPISODE in the history of test matches between Australia and England — it may be in the history of international cricket — has achieved such notoriety as the 'Bodyline' series of 1932/33, played in Australia. No competition has so threatened to reduce, not only the body of cricket, but its spirit, to ashes. No series has tested so nearly to destruction goodwill between the governing bodies of two cricketing nations. The fascination of the 'Bodyline' series grows with the realisation that probably no other Ashes series so transparently evidences the 'numeric factor'.

To appreciate the events and numbers of 1932/33 some background is essential. When WW1 interrupted play in 1914, the trophy was held by England. The first post-war meeting (1920/21) in Australia had the unhappy outcome for the tourists of a 5-0 obliteration unprecedented in these contests (McCann, 1994, p. 63). Still in 1921, Aussie dominance was rubbed in by a 3-0 win in Blighty. Came 1924/25, yet another dose of humiliation was administered to the Poms when they went Down Under and down 1–4.

The roles were reversed in 1926. Then it was England playing at home who gave the Australians a taste of their own medicine, winning back the Ashes by the narrowest of margins, 1–0. 1928/29 told a different story — an England win 4–1. This five test series included a game at Brisbane remarkable for its, at least, five 'firsts'.

It was 1. the first game of the series; 2. the first test played at Brisbane; 3. the first test played in Australia in which an innings was declared closed — England's second at 8–342 (notice this figure as we will shortly return to it); 4. the first test — an England victory — won by the (still standing) record margin of 675 runs; 5. moreover, or most of all, the first test played by D. G. Bradman, otherwise 'The Don' or Sir Donald Bradman, as the celebrated Australian is now known. Bradman's opponents in that game included both Douglas Jardine and Harold Larwood, completing the trio at the centre of the 'Bodyline' series.

The solo challenge presented by "The Don" to England's custodianship of the Ashes was not evident from his debut scores of 18 and 1, though followed by a century, and again a century at the two Melbourne games.

At the next (1930) meeting, won 2–1 by Australia, it became painfully clear to England that in D. G. Bradman (on his first England tour) Australia had a run machine that tilted the odds in their favour, almost as in the recent trenches war the Lewis gun had tilted the odds against the Lee-Enfield rifle. With a century at Nottingham, a double century at both Lord's and the Oval, and a triple century at Leeds,[55] "The Don" alone accounted for 974 of Australia's series total of 2886.[56]

The question for England then was, Could the Bradman factor be contained? This would be put to the test in England's 1932/33 tour of Australia. Unfortunately for the spirit of cricket, the man chosen to captain the tourists was D. R. Jardine, a lawyer by training, with an animus towards Australia and Australians, particularly Bradman, and a fixed intention to win at whatever cost to the harmony of the game. To secure this objective Jardine would apply "fast leg theory" — "short fast bowling aimed at the body with a ring of fieldsmen in close on the leg side" (McCann, p. 76); stubborn resistance at the crease, or the arrival of Bradman, would cause Jardine to throw the ball to one or other of his pacemen and "with a hand clap over his head" to "call up his shoal of short legs" (Le Quesne, 1983, p. 147).

The crisper term adopted by the Australian press for "fast leg theory" was "bodyline bowling". Jardine's principal enforcer, H. Larwood, ex-coal miner, hence a "player" in the then class conscious England team, did not arouse the ire of the home crowd as did *gentleman* Jardine, the "Iron Duke". On one occasion, when the gesticulating figure on the field may have been in the spectators' good books, was heard the mild rebuke, "Leave our flies alone, Jardine. They're the only friends you've got!" In fairness to the "Iron Duke", he took on the tour against his will

---

[55] Bradman's 334 at Leeds was his career highest test score and remained the record for an Australian until 1998, when Mark Taylor equalled it against Pakistan.

[56] 2886 is — digitally — near $12^{-1/2} = .2887$; 974, still the record for an individual batsman, is near $12^{-1/96} = .9744$.

under paternal pressure, whereas "fast leg theory" was not in breach of the rules at that time. And so to the "Bodyline" series.

The first day, December 2, 1932, at Sydney augured well for the home side, but proved deceptive. S. McCabe leading the resistance in the absence of Bradman through illness, began his great innings of 187 n.o., despite which England went on to win the first test by 10 wickets and the series by four games to one.

In the second test at Melbourne Bradman contributed an unbeaten century in the second innings but it was 'Tiger' O'Reilly with *10 wickets* for the match who bowled Australia to their sole victory.

Had the planned containment of Bradman succeeded? Although he adapted to "fast leg theory" by stepping outside the leg stump and playing to the lightly guarded offside, and although his legendary speed meant he was hit only once (on the forearm) by a bodyline delivery, his 396 runs at 56 for the series, compared to 974 at 139 in 1930, testify to the relative effectiveness of the 'theory'. To keep perspective, "The Don's" average topped that for any other Australian.

The crisis came in the third (Adelaide) test. This game notoriously exposed the Jardine style of offense and led to the exchange of "forthright and bitter" cables between the respective cricket authorities. When in the first innings by Australia (batting second), their captain (not yet Bradman, but W. M. Woodfull), who had already been hit over the heart in a preliminary game, received a similar disabling blow, Jardine's "Well bowled, Harold!" created fury among the spectators.[57] Another Australian, wicket keeper W. A. Oldfield, received a fractured skull. Woodfull from the team massage table rejected England manager Pelham ("Plum") Warner's attempted peace-making: "There are two teams out there, but only one of them is playing cricket" — another declaration now part of the game's history.

Our chief concern is with numbers and we wish to see if the on-field drama is reflected in outstanding numerical features. Now, in this same (Adelaide) game for the first time in the series England won the toss and went in to bat. England's first winnings total was 341, similar, we recall, to their inning's total in the historic

---

[57] Recently reported medical research shows a single blow to the chest is enough to stop a healthy heart cold — if a certain area is hit at a specific time. "Bodyline" melodrama might have turned to "Bodyline" tragedy.

declared innings at Brisbane (1928), which was 342. Were England unconsciously (?) "revisiting" their Brisbane triumph of the previous tour — as if a touch of magic of the "cargo cult" kind could restore to them the bounty of 1928–29, including a scaled down Bradman run rate? [58] But how to explain that not only England, but more particularly Australia, also iterated close to the same number?

Take, for example, the fourth and decisive test at *Brisbane*, where Australia, batting first and about to lose the Ashes, joined in the "numbers game" with a score of *340* in this innings. Moreover, the *average* first innings score by Australia when batting first in the bodyline series — as was the case in 4/5 games — was 340.8, virtually the same figure as England's first innings total at Adelaide, as just seen. There is a parallel with the 1948 England tour by Bradman's "Invincibles", which opened the post-WW2 phase of the "Ashes War". Then the average England first innings score when batting first (also in 4/5 games) was 269.0, similar to Australia's 267 in 1920 and near England's *average* first innings score when batting first from 1920/1921–1997 (cf. Chapter 7: "The Ashes War"). In such cases some kind of resonance appears to be involved.

To pick up the tale of numbers around 340–341, if we take the average first innings by *both* Australia and England in the Bodyline series (mean of 10 innings), the figure is 342.9, near $72^{-1/4} = .3433$.[59] We therefore have:

Team	Game	F. I.	Series, Mean F. I. When Batting First	Series, Mean F. I.
England	3rd	341	(of 1) 341.0	
Australia	4th	340	(of 4) 340.8	
Both				(of 10) 342.9

Note: F. I.: first innings

---

[58] Compare, as a possible attempt to return to the past or "freeze time", "Babe" Ruth's career total of 714 home runs, which had the same digits as the first three of his team, the New York Yankees' (the 'Twenty-seven' Yankees') win ratio in its record year, 1927. This was exactly 5/7ths or .714 to three decimal places (see Chapter 12: "Home Runs, Strange Numerics and Form in the Event World").

[59] For simplicity, and as these most clearly evidence the numeric factor, as we have found, we restrict discussion to the figures for first innings.

When we compare the 10 first innings scores by both teams with our 12-BR table (Appendix A), the quantum effect is unmistakable, as follows (scores and correlates only):

$$360 \approx 60^{-1/4} = .359 \qquad 524 \approx 48^{-1/6} = .525.$$
$$228 \approx 84^{-1/3} = .228 \qquad 169 \approx 36^{-1/2} = .167$$
$$341 \approx 72^{-1/4} = .343 \qquad 222 \quad ?$$
$$340 \approx 72^{-1/4} = .343 \qquad 356 \approx 60^{-1/4} = .359.$$
$$435 \approx 12^{-1/3} = .437 \qquad 454 \approx 24^{-1/4} = .452$$

The probability (p) of these correlations occurring merely by chance is, by binomial test, $< .01$.

What of the average first innings figures for both sides, regardless of which had "first knock"? These are, England 368.8, Australia 317.0. These numbers resemble the reciprocal of e ($e^{-1} = .368$) and the reciprocal of pi ($\pi^{-1} = .318$), e and π being perhaps the most important mathematical constants.[60] They imply values for e and pi of 2.711 and 3.155, totalling 5.866, compared to the actual total of 5.860. To end this brief look at the numbers of "Bodyline", how strange that the passions which came to the boil in this series did not prevent (but even facilitated?) "harmony" at the numerical level.[61]

Green Quiz Question No. 8

Another Orstrailin city, noted for its sunshine, starts with a B. This one's total of P'n'G is like the square of the last one (see Green Quiz Question No. 7).

What is the location of B—'s figure in the table at Appendix B? Give the letter and column number.

How many hectares of P'n'G, give or take one, does B— have?

---

[60] Compare Hitler and the Nazis' shares of votes in four elections held in 1932, the year preceding the Nazi takeover in Germany. (See Chapter 11, "The Last Elections of Weimar", in which "Unmeasure for Measure").

[61] Cf. Discussion in Chapter 12: "Home Runs, Strange Numerics, and Form in the Event World".

CHAPTER 9
RESONANCE FROM A CAPTAIN'S KNOCK

IN BRADMAN'S first series as captain, for the first and still the only time in test cricket, a team came back from two tests down to win the series.[62]

Summary of Ashes series 1936–37

First and second tests won by England; third, fourth, and fifth won by Australia, with D. G. Bradman (capt.) making the major contribution, including two double centuries and one century. Bradman's figures in these games show "quantisation" or proportionality based on the constant e, as follows (note: "near" means digitally near):

1st test Brisbane, December, 1936

First innings	38	near D20 = .038
Second innings	0	

2nd test Sydney, December, 1936

First innings	0	
Second innings	82	near C6 = .082

3rd test Melbourne, January 1937

First innings	13	near C3 = .013
Second innings	270	near F5 = .269

4th test Adelaide, Jan–Feb, 1937

First innings	26	near C2 = .025
Second innings	212	near F11 = .212

5th test Melbourne, February 1937

First innings	169	near F13 = .167

Note: alphanumeric coding gives e-BR table reference

p of correlations < .05.

Bradman's three innings of ≥ 100 are closely related numerically, though this is not obvious without reference to our e-BR table (see Appendix B). Let us first set the numerical scene and then proceed step by step.

The post-WW1 era of Ashes tests was inaugurated by Australia's innings of *267* at the Sydney Cricket Ground (S. C. G.) in 1920; whereas England's first innings scores, when

---

[62] Record attendances add to this series' uniqueness: 350,534 for the 3rd match at Melbourne and 943,000 for the rubber.

batting first against Bradman's "Invincibles" in 1948,[63] when tests were again resumed after a war-time break, would average *269.0*; also, the average total by England, batting first in Ashes series from 1920–21 to 1997, would be *271.7*.

Step 1   To those numbers around 269 we can now add the Don's *270* at Melbourne in 1937. Recall that (point) .269 is one of the factors of the mathematical constant *e*, or, rather, of its reciprocal (1/*e* or e^{-1}). This factor is the base of col. 5 (F5) of our *e*-BR table. Here "factor" means not multipliable but divisible, complementary factor (so that F5 plus its complement F6, .731, = 1). F5 divided by F6 gives F1 (e^{-1}) = .368. *e* is familiar to mathematicians, scientists, and engineers but its (or rather its sequential factors') serviceability for the *identification* of numerical data is apparently not well known.

     Our *e*-BR table is based mainly on sequential factors of e^{-1} and partly on 1-e^{-1} and its factors. These factors depend on a simple repetitive procedure, which amounts, if you like, to tracing the "pedigree" or "lineage" of e^{-1} and 1-e^{-1}.

Step 2   A look at our *e*-BR table (Appendix B) shows one of the immediate "antecedents" of .269 (F5) is .212 (see F11 = .2119), the same, if rounded up to three places and the decimal point removed, as "The Don's" second innings total in the 4th test.

Step 3   *e*-based numbers or ratios (*e*-BR) include numbers arrived at by multiplication of complementary factors, and the product of F11 and F12, .212. (1 - .212) is .167 (F13). This is similar to Bradman's 5th test score of 169.

Step 4   To summarise, take the 4th test figure of 212 and add a decimal point. *Divide* .212 by (1 - .212 = .788) and the quotient is .269. ≈ (is similar to) .270 or (without the decimal point) 270. *Multiply* .212 by (1 - .212 = .788) and the product is .167 ≈ .169, or (without the decimal point) 169. A simple binomial test shows the probability (*p*) of drawing numbers as close as these three to table numbers by chance is less than 1/20 ($< .05$).

---

[63] As previously noted, England batted first four times out of five.

Problem   As the *e*-BR table is transparent in its make-up — a logical construction based on *e* — what is the origin of its connection with empirical numbers — numbers occurring in the real world? Does the real world tap the same logic?

Then again the sequence of Capt. Bradman's scores suggests resonance between (at least) the factor F11 and the number F5 and between the product F13 and the factor F11. (See Fig. 9.1 and the discussion in Chapter 12: "Home Runs, Strange Numerics, and Form in the Event World")

FIG 9.1. Resonance from a Captain's Knock:
Bradman's scores (centuries) are sequentially related in terms of digital "look-alikes" derived from the mathematical constant e^{-1} (see text). There is an effect of echoing or "cascading".

Postscript: The Australian Team of the Century

"The Don's" nomination as captain of the Australian "Team of the Century" (*The Advertiser*, Adelaide, January 19, 2000) is tribute to his place in the natural order.

It's interesting to note the near square-root : square (digital) relation between the *average* of the batting averages and the *average* of the bowling averages for this team:

Batting (mean of eight, including A. R. Border, "12th man")	51.48
Bowling (mean of six, including "pinch bowler" G. S. Chappell)	26.52

Note, then, $.5148^2 = .2650$
and $\quad\quad .2652^{1/2} = .5150$

Also, compare .2652 with Bradman's authority-reassertive 270 in the 3rd test of the 1937–38 series (see above), these numbers bracketing F5 = .269.

References for Chapters 7, 8 and 9

DAWSON, D. and WAT, C., *Test Cricket Lists: The Ultimate Guide to International Test Cricket* (Noble Park, Vic: The Five Mile Press, 1998)

DOUGLAS, C., *Douglas Jardine, Spartan Cricketer* (London: Allen and Unwin, 1984)

ENGEL, M. (Ed.), *Wisden Cricketers' Almanack* (Merrow, Guidford, Surrey: John Wisden and Co., 1999)

HAIGH, G. (Ed.), *Wisden Cricketers' Almanack Australia* (South Yarra, Vic: Hardie Grant, 1999)

LE QUESNE, L., *The Bodyline Controversy* (London: Secker and Warburg, 1983)

McCANN, M., *Cricket's Ultimate Ashes Test* (Sydney: The Five Mile Press, 1994)

ROSENWATER, L., *Sir Donald Bradman; A Biography* (London: Batsford, 1978)

WHITINGTON, R. S., *G. Hele: Bodyline Umpire (Adelaide: Rigby, 1974)*

Green Quiz Question No. 9

Copenhagen must be one of Europe's greenest cities. Its figure is similar to the square of the bigger factor of 1-1/*e*.

Where do you find this in the table (Appendix B)? Give the letter and column number.

How many hectares of P'n'G has this city got, give or take one?

CHAPTER 10
NUMBERS FOR AN AUSTRALIAN STATE

Bigger than Texas

IF AUSTRALIA is at the bottom of the world — there are two views on this — South Australia (SA) is at the bottom of Australia. Although only the fourth ranking Australian state or territory in area, SA exceeds in size the largest of the 48 contiguous American states, Texas (See also below re Texas).

The establishment of SA as a British colony in 1836 owed much to Edward Gibbon Wakefield, a Quaker of London. His plan for it was formulated at London's Newgate Gaol, where he spent the years 1827–1830 for the abduction of heiress Ellen Turner to cross-Channel Calais. While he lay at Newgate, did Wakefield dream perchance of Provence, or of the lower part of a far more distant continent?

The gifted Wakefield was an exploiter — of a young girl's devotion to her father (allegedly faced with financial ruin from which only Wakefield could rescue him) or of his own compassion for unfortunates like his fellow prisoners at Newgate. They should be assisted to a better life in a new type of colony, not based on convict labour, and self-funded through the sale of Crown land at a fixed price. Therein lay the appeal of the Wakefield Plan, among others to the "land jobbers", as those speculators were known. Somewhere along the line Wakefield himself would no doubt prosper. The colony of South Australia was formally established in 1836 but Wakefield never set foot there and ended his days in New Zealand in 1862.

To get a "handle" on this state of South Australia let us explore some representative figures with the aid of our tables of numbers. Significant correlations with these numbers give us a new way of looking at data.[64]

---

[64] It is important to remember, however, that numerical effects may be "artifacts" — of criterion, processing, etc. — rather than truly reflect what is there to be counted or measured.

FIG 10.1. An Unsettling Experience?
The area of South Australia "alternately expanded and contracted, from
the Wakefield Plan to the present time".

Conventional accounts or reasons may not be the whole story. In some cases no explanation may exist, as when "Why is ... ?" receives the answer "Because that's the way it is!" Such a case is, Why is the area of SA 984,377 square kilometres / 380,070 square miles?[65] Why *is* it the way it is?

Historical reasons *partly* explain these figures: All the land of SA was originally included in New South Wales (NSW). The colony sought by the Wakefieldians extended from the Southern

---

[65] Sq. km. from South Australian Yearbook, 1997. Most of the data on SA are from this source, with permission.

Ocean to the 20th parallel. Owing to opposition by the House of Commons, the South Australia Act of 1834 and Letters Patent of 1836 cut the area to about half, with boundaries "On the North the twenty sixth Degree of South Latitude, On the South the Southern Ocean — On the West the one hundred and thirty second Degree of East Longitude — And on the East the one hundred and forty first Degree of East Longitude". Except the western these boundaries define the present state. The truncated area "up for grabs" covered 802,508 sq. km. or 309,850.1 sq. miles. Banal seeming figures but notice that 309,850.1, treated as (*point*) .3098501, resembles $108^{-1/4}$ = .3102016 (See 12-BR table, Appendix A).

The western and eastern boundaries of the new colony followed the Wakefield Plan but the reason for the selection of 132° and 141° is not given in that document. The western boundary might evidently have been 135°, as only this much of Australia was claimed by the British Government in 1788. However, in 1824, to enable a base to be set up on the north coast of Australia (which eventuated as Fort Dundas on Melville Island), the land between 135° and 129° was formally claimed. In 1829 Western Australia (WA) was founded with 129° as its eastern border. Therefore, when SA arrived on the scene in 1836, a 3° wide corridor separated these neighbours. This state of affairs continued until 1861, when, after long resistance from NSW, "No Man's Land" between 129° and 132° was added to SA. The land to the north of SA — now the Northern Territory (NT) — was also (in 1863) added and much later (in 1911) taken away from SA. Such were the events which alternately expanded and contracted the state from the Wakefield Plan to the present time.

How unsettling! — perhaps the state should be re-named *Terra Nonfirma!* — What is the area of SA again?

The point is, the area of this state in sq. km. is 984,377 and 984,377 is near a "main sequence" derivative of e^{-1},[66] that is $e^{-1/64}$ = .984496 (L1 in the *e*-based ratio [*e*-BR] table — Appendix B), if you ignore the difference between an integer and a decimal fraction. The sq. miles figure is 380,070, which is similar to both

---

[66] *e*: the natural log base. Exponents in the doubling series, 2, 4, 8 … and 3, 6, 12 …, referred to here as "main sequences", applied to *e*- or 12-etc. based numbers (*e*-BR, 12-BR …), often correspond to actual (empirical) numbers.

G19 = .379860 [67] and $48^{-1/4}$ = .379918. In the last case the p is less than .02. Recalling the original sq. miles figure resembles $108^{-1/4}$ ($p <.10$), a sizeable question mark can be placed against chance as the origin of these correlations.

Hang on! This is all a bit much. Decimal fractions that are like whole numbers, "main sequence" derivatives of e^{-1} no one ever heard of. What next? No, but surely, if some politico-geographical quantity, chopped and changed around in the corridors of power, seems to keep approximating mathematically special numbers, whether the favourite e or a dark horse descended from 12, this *is* just a matter of chance? Certainly no one could have intended it. What would be the point?

Before accepting this "common sense" opinion, let us check out the other Australian states and territories. Surprisingly enough, the sq. miles figure for NSW, 309,700, is almost identical to SA's original 309,850.1, both (similar to) ≈ $108^{-1/4}$ = .3102016 (see above). The other states with large areas, Queensland (Qld) and WA, plus the NT, have sq. miles figures resembling e-BR, as follows: Qld 666,800 ≈ H7 =.665889, WA 975,300 ≈ L7 = . 974906, NT 519,700 ≈ G5 = .518594. These numbers, treated as decimal fractions, have a simple pattern: $.5197^2$ = .2701 and .2701 . [1 - .2701] = .1971 and $.1971^{1/4}$ = .6663 ≈ 6668;[68] also $.6663^{1/16}$ = .9749 ≈ 9753.

While the figures for all states and territories together are apparently non-significant (n.s.) in a statistical sense, that for SA gains credibility as a problem within a larger problem. Time now for a brief stopover in Texas, whose capital Austin is a "sister" city of SA's Adelaide.

The total area including inland water of Texas is 268,601 sq. miles. This number resembles the smaller (complementary, divisible) factor of e^{-1} (F5 = .268940). The p of this correlation is less than .04. The land area is 261,914 sq. miles or 678,354 sq. km. The latter in turn resembles a root (the 4th) of the smaller factor of F5, shown in the e-BR table at H11 = .678505. The p of this correlation is .04 (The alternative measures — sq. km. for

---

[67] Tables prepared by the author (See Appendixes A, B and C) show only 4 decimal places but where extra digits are available these are given in the text where appropriate.

[68] Where the sense is clearly "near the digit sequence of", this is no longer spelled out.

total area and sq. miles for land area — do not have obvious correlates).[69]

Whatever, just another couple of lucky shots?

Coastlines and Other Strange Distances

A basic *linear* measure for every Australian state has regard to coastline. Both SA, with approx. 3,700 km. and Australia, with 10x (an order of magnitude) as much at 36,735 km. have coastlines similar to e^{-1} (F1 = .36788). The *p* of these correlations is .23 and .06 respectively.[70]

So?

Another linear measure takes stock of road systems. As of June 1996 SA had 2,753 km. of national highways, including the Stuart Highway to Darwin, the Princes Highway to Melbourne and the Eyre Highway to Perth. The state figure for arterial roads was 9,560 and for local roads 83,020. Road systems which have evolved from need and the availability of funding and political influence should not amount to any special number of units — km. or miles. Yet the over-all total of 95,333 km. is near a main sequence derivative of *pi* (π), that is $\pi^{-1/24}$ = .95342. As well the *mean* of the three classes (national highways, etc.), 31,777.1, is near the reciprocal of *p i* (π^{-1}) = .318310 ($.317771^{1/24}$ = .95336, close to the over-all total of 95,333). Certainly a remarkable "coincidence".

Remarkable enough is the "coincidence" that the line drawn by nature on the map of SA, the coastline, is like e^{-1}, while the average total extent of the three classes of road built in this state is like π^{-1}, *e* and π, as previously noted, being possibly the most important of all mathematical constants.

Local roads in SA are mainly unsealed (gravel-topped or just graded) in the ratio sealed/unsealed = .2023 $\approx 24^{-1/2}$ = .2041. The ratio for arterial roads is 23.9 $\approx$ 24 ($23.9^{-1/2}$ = .2046 $\approx$ .2023). Arterial and local roads together have 23,147 km. sealed and

---

[69] Note 1) $.678354^4$ = .211751 and .211751 / [1-.211751] = .268635 $\approx$ 268,601, disregarding the decimal. 2) Interested readers might attempt to derive the sq. km. figure for SA, 984377, from either the sq. miles figure for total area or sq. km. figure for total land area of Texas.

[70] Coastlines are a well-known example of a measured quantity being an artifact of the method of measurement. The classic reference is B. Mandelbrot, "How Long is the Coast of Britain?". Certainly not too much should be made of the SA figure for coastline. The strange thing is that the Texas coastline is also similar to e^{-1} (F 1).

69,433 km. unsealed, similar to F4 = .23254 and H4 = .69443 respectively ($.23147^{1/4}$ = .69362). The p of these correlations are .19 and .04. *Is* there a numeric factor in the road system of SA?

Going Interstate

Since National Highways connect SA with the other states and territories, what of the distances between Adelaide and the other capitals?

In most cases the traveller interstate has the choice of rail, sea or air as well as road. If we average across the available modes for each city (in km. as given in the South Australian Yearbook [SAYB] 1997) and check with the tables we find there is a correlation with e-BR (binomial $p < .01$). Two examples are: Adelaide - Melbourne 778.5 ≈ H1 (.7788) and Adelaide - Hobart 1,359.5 ≈ E1 (. 13534). Readers can see from the e-BR table (Appendix B) that .7788 and .1353 represent $e^{-1/4}$ and e^{-2} respectively (Note, $.13595^{1/8}$ = .77924).

Various factors can be put forward to narrow the choice of location for a proposed capital. One obvious one is the best natural harbour, as in NSW, Sydney. Except for air transport, where the great circle route should be the basic model, so much still depends on contingency, however — for road and rail routing, the terrain — that there is no prospect of simply referring the "why" of correlation to natural (physical) causes as ordinarily understood.

Going Overseas

Are strange distances specific to Australia, if not SA — a Down Under effect? Suppose we swap Adelaide, the hub of multimodal routes radiating to other Australian cities, for Port Adelaide, which dispatches and receives vessels to and from the world?

It turns out that the distances (km.) to the 28 principal overseas ports listed in the SAYB 1997 can also be fitted to the e-BR table in more instances than could reasonably be expected ($p = .01$).

Examples where the correlate is from one of the leading table columns (cols.) are as follows: Santiago 13,653 ≈ E1 = .13534 (cf. Hobart 1,359.5 — smaller by a factor of 10) and both Naples via

Suez (15,940) and Rio de Janeiro (15,901) $\approx$ D2 = .15966. The best fit is for Yokohama 9,780 $\approx$ D21 = .09783.[71]

Change the mode to air and arbitrarily take as point of departure/arrival the first and last given world cities in a table of also 28, showing the air distances (miles) between each and every other (World Almanac 1998). The cities are Bangkok and Washington, D.C. Sufficient of the 27 distances for each can be correlated with 12-BR (Bangkok) and e-BR (Washington), with p depending on the test (range, cutoff), but for Bangkok the p might be as low as < .002, as to leave no reasonable doubt of an association.

Some interesting cases:

Washington/London 3,674 $\approx$ FI (e^{-1}) = 3679. Washington/Chicago and Washington/San Francisco have an exact (to 4 decimal places) square root: square relation, as follows: Washington/Chicago 596 $\approx$ E16 = .0595; Washington/San Francisco 2,441 $\approx$ F16 = .2441, with $.0596^{1/2} = .2441$.

Also, Washington/Berlin 4,181 and Washington/Stockholm 4,183 straddle G17 (.4182), which (see e-BR table) is a factor of G11 = .4604. Now Washington/Tokyo 6,791 ($\approx$ H11 = .6785) implies for G11 a figure of .4612 ($.6791^2 = .4612$) $\approx$ .4604. Washington/Berlin and Washington/Stockholm then share a factor: number relation with Washington/Tokyo, but for a difference of two powers (one step in the main sequence 2, 4 ...).

Defying the common sense assumption that cities are randomly distanced from each other, according to whatever their respective positions on the globe "happen" to be, in the present sample at least inter-city distances have an order of their own. More accurately, an order which (with many variations) they share with diverse other data.

Popular Numbers for a Population

Our question, Why is the area of SA 984,377 sq. km. / 380,070 sq. miles? has led us from the rump of the island continent to the world at large. But this world of strange distances is not the world we know. Is there another world, ruled by proportionality — a kind of Pythagorean *harmonia* — *behind* the "real" world? If so,

---

[71] The observant reader will notice that Adelaide – Melbourne 778.5 was not treated as .07785, as might be thought consistent with Adelaide – Hobart 1359.5 as .13595. Even if the change is made, however, the p of correlation with e-BR including cube and 6th roots is still < .01. In general, however, the aim is not so much methodological rigour as fair presentation of the abundant evidence.

is the relatively small population of the vast state of SA also represented in this "other world"?

The estimated total population of SA at June 1995 was 1,473,966. This is close to the mean of two fractions table numbers, 1/7 and $(8/9)^{16}$, mean = .1473789 (see Appendix C). Granted the disparity between an integer and a decimal fraction and the odd coupling of a proper fraction and a power of a different proper fraction, the fractions table is systematic and these numbers are adjacent in the size-ordered version. The p of the correlation is < .01. Also, the state's share of the national population was .08164 ≈ $(2/7)^2$ = .08163 (p = .04).[72]

During the period from Federation in 1901 to the year following the end of World War 2 — 1946 — the population of SA grew from 359,330 to 640,418. The first figure resembles $60^{-1/4}$ = .359304 (p < .01). The estimated total at the end of each subsequent five-year period (1906–1946) can be fitted to the e-BR table (p < .05). This implies a numeric factor in the population total from 1901 to 1946.

When growth rate is targeted, say the increase from one estimate to the next, proportional to the former, the five-yearly (quinquennial) increases from Federation to 1991 can also be related to e-BR (p < .05). The longest high growth period followed WW2:

1947–51	.1614	D2 = .1597
1952–56	.1589	D2 = .1597
1957–61	.1363	E1 = .1353[73]
1962–66	.1269	D3, E1, mean = .1250.

(The alphanumeric coding gives the table references.)

---

[72] For neutral or negative evidence there is the population of Adelaide.
  1,080,972 (≈ $84^{-1/2}$ = . 109109).

[73] From the latest figures in the SAYB 1997 the proportional increase in the indigenous population of SA at 1991 vs. 1986 was .1370 and at 1994 vs. 1991 was .1339. The mean .1355 is also near E1 (.1353).

Although this was the Baby Boom era the population rise did not depend solely on higher birth rate, but also on net gain from migration. Thus compound annual growth for SA averaged 2.78% from 1947 to 1966, compared to 0.76% for 1933–1947, but crude birth rate (births per 1000 of population) for 1946–1965, 22.77, was not greatly above that for 1926–1945, 17.64. It is interesting to compare the average crude birth rates for SA and the other lower ranking states (in terms of population) for 1946–1965:

Qld	23.81	$72^{-1/3} = .2404$
SA	22.77	$84^{-1/3} = .2283$
WA	24.16	$72^{-1/3} = .2404$
Tas	25.25	$60^{-1/3} = .2554.$

The p of these correlations is $< .05$. These states have, then, birth rate differences which, although small, appear to be "quantum" for this period. If the Baby Boom in these states was in response to post-war conditions, including return from war service and a buoyant economy, this evidence suggests response was at the same time measured.

Runaway or Measured Response to Marriage Breakdown?

In recent years the number of divorces has increased annually in SA while the number of marriages has fallen. A newspaper report (Adelaide *Advertiser* dated 9/6/98) stated that the ratio of divorces to marriages for 1996 — given as 54% — was the highest in Australia and had risen to that figure ("one in two") from "about one in three" a decade ago.

A former family counsellor cited in the report pointed to the bad reputation earned by marriage from a "skyrocketing divorce rate", whereas a psychologist stated, "Economic pressures, unemployment, higher expectations and changing roles all impacted on marriage today and were elements behind divorce".

Using data also from the SAYB 1997 we can compare ratios for the years 1986 and 1992–1996 with our tables. For 1986 the ratio was $3,776/9,878 = .3823$ and for 1996 it was $4,300/8,011 = .5368$. The 12-BR table shows $.3823 \approx 48^{-1/4} = .3799$ and $.5368 \approx 12^{-1/4} = .5373$. The years 1992–1995 "marry" less well with 12-BR but the six years together give p of correlation (with 4th roots only) $< .05$.

Another measure we can use is the 1986 ratio $\div$ the ratios for later years. These ratios of ratios can be correlated with fractions based on the number 7, for example .3823 (1986)/.5368 (1996) = .7122 ≈ 5/7 = .7143. The p of these correlations is also <.05.

There is a parallel then with the Baby Boom, where proportionality was suggested by the crude birth rates for South Australia and three other states. In the present case the step-wise progression is over time instead of between states, but also implies a measured rather than runaway response to changing attitudes and conditions.

Measured Response to Mortal Disease

If it seems to be splitting hairs to distinguish between a change in the divorce/marriage rate from "one in three" to "one in two" and a change from one derivative of (e.g.) 12 to another derivative of 12, there is, alas, little comfort to be drawn from the notion that the Grim Reaper has his own "quota system".

That mortality from diseases also obeys proportionality is shown by the following examples from South Australian data for 1994. The leading killers in a sample of seven, each contributing 10% or more to the entire toll, together with the death rates per 100,000 of resident population and the correlates for these rates were:

Diseases of the circulatory system	$358.66 \approx 60^{-1/4}$	$= .359304$
Malignant neoplasms	$210.02 \approx 108^{-1/3}$	$= .20999$
Ischaemic heart disease	$202.47 \approx 24^{-1/2}$	$= .20412$

(p of sample of 7 < .01)[74]

"Disproportion" in the Employment Market

Economics is the "dismal science". According to SA premier John Olsen's Employment Statement 98, "Unemployment remains a blight in this community [and has been] persistently higher [here] than the national average since the mid sixties". Some specific and general factors which dim or brighten the employment picture in this state include: loss of employment in manufacturing due to import tariff reductions vs. increasing

---

[74] Ironically, the rate for circulatory diseases is close to — in our usual digital sense, though 1.000 times (3 orders of magnitude) less than — the total population of SA in 1901 (See above).

importance of service industries, including particularly information technology; the financial burden from billion dollar misadventures by the failed State Bank vs. government incentives to enterprises setting up in SA; payroll tax vs. training schemes ... the list goes on. Driven this way and that by complex forces, what chance of the employment market in SA casting up an orderly set of numbers? Little enough it would seem, if the only agent of order *is* chance. What can be made of the statistics in our numerical sense?

The raw statistics for 1992–1996 show rises in the total of employed males and, particularly, females, rises in the total of males not in labour force, falls in the total of unemployed males and of females not in labour force, and fluctuation in the total of unemployed females. Our first positive finding is of a probable correlation with e-BR of the six figures (integers) obtained by averaging the totals in each category ($p < .05$).

The ratios between the female and male averages are: employed females/employed males $= 278,100/364,900 = .7621 \approx G3 = .7629$; unemployed females/unemployed males $= 28,440/46,140 = .6164 \approx H19 = .6163$; males not in labour force/females not in labour force $= 160,600/286,300 = .5610 \approx F21 = .5593$. This time the correlation is quite convincing ($p < .01$).

Let us now see how males and females fared in terms of (1) employment and unemployment rates (2) participation rates.

(1) Unemployment rates do not seem to have a clear pattern, therefore we focus on employment rates: average total of employed males/average total male labour force $= 364,900/411,040 = .8877 \approx G12 =$ also .8877; average total of employed females/average total female labour force $= 278,100/306,500 = .9073 \approx J11 = .9076$. As can be seen from the e-BR table, G12 and J11 are roots of the larger and smaller factors of F5 and are closely linked through the complementarity of their bases (.7881 and .2119, totalling 1.0).

(2) The average participation rates for the same period (1992–1996) have a different close connection with each other. "Participation rate" means total labour force/total civilian population aged 15 years and over. The average rates were: males .7192, females .5170. Correlates are found at H5 and G5, being related as square root and square ($.7192^2 = .5172$). As readers may already have noted, the participation rates and employment rates

are themselves related as table cols. 11 and 12 contain the factors of col. 5 (p of 4 rates < .01).[75]

The sequential *fractionation* of the SA population, first into those (males, females) in the labour force and those not in the labour force, then of those in the labour force into those in employment and those unemployed, parallels the sequential *factoring* procedure embodied in the table, both the employment rates and their correlates being found "downstream" of the participation rates and *their* correlates (See also Table 10.1).

Table 10.1 Labour Market in SA 1992–1996 as a Pattern of Sequential Factors of e^{-1} (Reciprocal of Natural Log Base).

	Males		Females
Fraction of			
Average Population			
in Labour Force	as H5	($H5^2 = G5$)	as G5(a)
		($G5^2 = F5$)	
		($F5/F6 = F1$)	
		($F1 = e^{-1}$)	
		($= .3679$)	
Fraction of			
Average Labour Force			
Employed	as G12	($G12^2 = F12$)	as J11
		($J11^{16} = F 11$)	
		($F11/F12 = F5$)	
		($= .2689$)	

(a) Alphanumeric references to *e*-based ratios (*e*-BR) table (Appendix B) show correlates for actual proportion of (eg) female population who are (eg) in labour force.

For all the complexity of the economic and other "real", including personal factors influencing who is in or out of employment or in or out of the labour force, there are then simple numerical patterns in these data. But these patterns can hardly be thought to be due to any single or combination of "real" factors as such (per se)[76] — rather to some organizing principle or numeric factor.

These patterns give a new context for the problems of women claiming equality of opportunity in face of obstacles of which the

---

[75] Recall that the over-all area of Texas and its land area also have a number : factor relation based on cols. 5 and 11.

[76] I.e. assuming continuity, rather than discreteness, in the distribution of outcomes of these factors.

"glass ceiling" is no doubt only the tip of the iceberg. For example, a proposed law which linked the participation rate for women to that for men in a markedly inferior ratio would probably never get off the ground. Yet from 1992 to 1996 it seems there was effectively such a restriction. Or was it just a mutually beneficial balance? In any case, what would it have taken to upset this balance?

"Disproportion" in Remuneration

What of the remuneration of employees, particularly in relation to the equal pay for women issue? The raw statistics show average (1) ordinary time only and (2) total weekly earnings of full-time adults, and (3) average weekly earnings of all employees. Averaging the six quarters from November 1994 to February 1996 for males and females gives six figures (one for each category for each sex). Comparison of these with the 12-BR table shows a probable correlation ($p < .05$), as did comparison of the labour force five year averages, but with the e-BR table. These and similar correlations are remarkable, it cannot be repeated too often, if only because the data are whole numbers (here persons, dollars) but the correlates (table numbers), decimal fractions < 1.

Despite, for example, the "equal pay for work of equal value" principle and the Sex Discrimination Act of 1984, a submission by the Federal Department of Industrial Relations to the Human Rights and Equal Opportunity Commission in 1992 referred to an earnings disparity of nearly 20% between the average total weekly earnings of female and male fulltime non-managerial employees. This was attributed to a number of factors, including clustering of female employees into particular relatively low paying industries and occupations, relative unavailability of promotion, industry training, shiftwork, etc., and relative lack of unionisation.

For the six quarters in our sample, we may calculate 18 female/male earnings ratios, which can be regarded as the outcome of numerous factors, including those just mentioned. The majority of these ratios, like the averaged earnings figures, can also be fitted to 12-BR ($p < .05$).

Most striking is the transition from ratio of total earnings to ratio of all employees' earnings. In each case the correlate shifts to near the square, as, for example, from near the 16th root to near the 8th root.

Taking 1995 alone, the averaged female/male ratios are: ordinary time earnings .8691, total earnings .8266, all employees' earnings .6716. The last two figures have a near sq. root : square relation, with .8266 $\approx$ $96^{-1/24}$ = .8268 and .6716 $\approx$ mean of $96^{-1/12}$ and $96^{-1/11}$ (= .6720).

The ratios between these ratios approximate to a pattern of 12^{-1} roots: .8266/.8691 = .9511 $\approx$ $12^{-1/48}$ = .9495 and .6716/.8266 = .8125 $\approx$ $12^{-1/12}$ = .8130.

The important mathematical relation sq. root : square which was found between the participation rates for males and females, averaged for 1992–1996, recurs then in the comparison of the 1995 female/male ratio of total earnings of full-time employees with the female/male ratio of earnings of all employees for that year. In this case, the sq. root : square form is the more remarkable for its association with the extraordinary number $12^{-1/12}$.

Although we should never drop our guard against the possibility that numerical effects may be specific to the reporting system, processing methods, etc., our findings certainly suggest there is more to the employment and earnings picture than might be supposed from typical discussions.

Keeping a Sense of Proportion about Road Safety

South Australians are highly motorised, with approximately 935,000 vehicles on register in 1995 for an estimated population of 1,474,000. The totals by vehicle type (passenger, light commercial, etc.) can be fitted to leading cols. of the *e*-BR table in most cases ($p < .05$).

Snapshot of a quantum car market: the top three makes by sales totals in the first half of 1998 were: Holden 5,421 $\approx$ $72^{-1/7}$ = .5428, Toyota 4,250 $\approx$ $72^{-1/5}$ = .4251, Mitsubishi 4,078 $\approx$ $36^{-1/4}$ = .4082 ($p < .05$) (Data from Adelaide *Advertiser* dated 7/7/98). This shows pattern is not, of course, restricted to "main sequence" numbers, but notice that $72^{-1/7}$ and $72^{-1/5}$ bracket $72^{-1/6}$.

The top totals (by suburb of registration) of infringement notices issued to speeding motorists in 1996/97 can be correlated with the *e*-BR table (p as low as .002) (Data from Adelaide *Advertiser* dated 28/5/98). These include No. 3 Morphett Vale 8,485 $\approx$ I5 = .8486 and No. 4 Happy Valley 7,201 $\approx$ H5 = .7201, which have the by now familiar sq. root: sq. relation $(.8485^2 = .7200 \approx .7201)$.

We wish to see if crash rates for SA also reflect fixed numbers. The SA Police Annual Report 1996/97 gives figures for 1986/87 and 1996/97. A "casualty road crash" is a road crash where one or more persons are injured and treated by a doctor (includes fatalities). The figures for casualty crashes trend downwards from 1986/87 to 1991/92, due almost entirely to decreases for the metropolitan (metro) area, then fluctuate in a fairly narrow range.

The report refers to "the decrease in casualty crashes from 1989/90 to 1991/92 [which was] largely attributed to the influence of speed cameras". These cameras were trialled in 1990 and became operational in 1991 (R. A. McColl, Traffic Research and Intelligence Section, 26/8/98, personal communication).

From Appendix 13 of the report the crash ratios 1991–92/1989–90 and 1991–92/1990–91 can be calculated for the metro area, country and state. These are: metro area .8197 and .8602, country .8252 and .9394, state .8211 and .8796.

The ratios for the state correspond to the main sequence numbers $24^{-1/16} = .8199$ and $60^{-1/32} = .8799$. The metro and country ratios fit e-BR $(p < .01)$.

The metro ratios for other years vs. 1991/92 can be correlated in almost all cases with e-BR $(p < .01)$.

Although the raw totals do not appear to be significantly related to numbers tables the ratios between each year's country and metro totals can in most cases be linked to 12-BR, mainly 4th roots/powers $(p < .05)$.

The over-all mean annual totals for metro and country areas, treated as usual as decimal fractions, have an approximate factor and number relation as follows: country $1,770.1 \approx E14 = .17835$, metro $5,320.3 \approx E6 = .53445$.

Then $.1770^{1/2}$ / $[1 - .17701^{1/2}] = .72630$ and $.72630^2 = .52751 \approx .53203$ (sequential factoring being the basis of the e-BR table).

The moving average (cumulative mean) of the annual total of crashes from 1986/87 to 1991/92 follows numbers in the leading cols. of the e-BR table $(p < .01)$.

The mean annual total of fatalities for the state from 1986/87 to 1996/97 is calculated to be 204.3. This is similar to $24^{-1/2} = .2041$. The mean cumulated to earlier years supports an association with 12-BR.

Alternative figures, for calendar years, are given in the SAYB. Here a road traffic accident is one involving a fatality or the hospitalisation of injured persons. A sharp drop in accidents precedes and follows the year 1991 (first year of camera operation), leaving this year isolated between level periods or plateaus, as follows: 1988–1990 mean accident total 2,128.0, 1991 total 1,733, 1992–1994 mean total 1,360.3. These figures correspond to F11 (.2119), F17 (.1749) and E1 (.1353) with p .21, > .50 and .11 respectively.

The 1991 total declined to .8144 of the previous 3-year average and the post-1991 3-year average declined again to .7849 of the 1991 figure. These ratios correspond to H20 (.8148) and I19 (.7851), with p .18 and p .19.

The post-1991 average has the ratio of .6393 to the pre-1991 average. Correlates are $36^{-1/8}$ ($6^{-1/4}$) or H13 (both also .6393) with p (H13) < .02. This correlation gains support from the ratios between the same periods with regard to fatal crashes, persons killed, and persons injured, as follows: fatal crashes .8059 ≈ H14 (.8061), persons killed .8150 ≈ H20 (.8148), persons injured .6237 ≈ G8 (.6223). The p of these (4) ratios is < .01.

The point is, on the present evidence, the annual statistics for various categories of accidents in SA do not take just any value subject only to the current trend. Instead, there is a tendency for (integer) event totals to match the digit sequences of (decimal fraction) derivatives of some constant (e or 12). This tendency is weaker for single years and stronger when several years are taken together. In one example, the average annual state total of fatalities from 1986/87 to 1996/97, 204.4, is close to the sq. root of 1/24 ($24^{-1/2}$= .2041). Such correlations are unconventional but justified by simple tests, where the p may be < .01.

The ratios between different years or periods show strong numerical effects. Clearly certain proportions are "preferred" by whatever process governs frequencies. For example, with 1991/92 or 1991 (when speed cameras became operational) the reference year, data for other years or periods show preferred proportions to the reference year.

Although, almost by definition, accident rates *should* not be orderly, it appears that they do have a pattern, but based on numbers not generally known.

Equally with those for other types of events which show numerical patterns then, explanations of accident data to be completely valid must take account of pattern or form (e.g. sq. root : sq. relations) in the data. Even if the solution is to show such patterns or forms are artifacts.

Speed is not of course the only risk factor to which drivers are exposed, or expose others. Another is alcohol, even when this has not been consumed by drivers driving, but by pedestrians, who may however be drivers trying to escape the police blitz on drink-driving. This was the explanation offered by Mr John Spencer, Manager of the Safety Strategy Section of Transport SA in a newspaper report of a five year study from 1992 by the Office of Road Safety, which found pedestrians involved in serious road accidents were more likely to be drunk than the drivers whose vehicle struck them.

During the five year period 33% (1/3) of 435 ($\approx 12^{-1/3} = .437$) pedestrians killed or seriously injured who were tested for blood alcohol levels had a blood alcohol reading over the legal limit of .05, compared to 25% (1/4) of drivers. In the upper level of .15 and over the figures were 23.2% ($\approx$ F4 = .233) and 14.8% ($\approx$ C12 = .149). On average 29 ($\approx 36^{-1} = .028$ or $12^{-1/2} = .29$) alcohol affected pedestrians were killed or seriously injured each year.

Of intoxicated pedestrian casualties 79% ($\approx$ H1 = .78) occurred in the metro area, 72% ($\approx$ H5 = .72) of the fatalities and serious casualties occurred in a 60 km. zone (source Adelaide *Advertiser* dated 15/7/98).

Although this example could not be tested because of imprecision of the figures it is typical of the very many cases which show positive association with numbers tables.

... And About House Fires

An insurance company's study of fire claims during 14 months to March 1998 found 28.6% of reported fires in SA started in the kitchen (generally from cooking oil or fat catching fire through inattention), 23.8% externally (often because of faulty barbecues), 16.7% in bedrooms and also 16.7% in lounge rooms (Adelaide *Advertiser* report dated 22/6/98). These figures (which total 85.8, leaving 14.2% unattributed) correspond to D6 (.286), F 10 (.237), and F13 (.167). The *p* is < .01. It seems clear that the combination of flammables and high temperatures can explain the large number of kitchen etc. fires but not their relative frequencies, which evidently depend on some previously unrecognised "numeric factor".

Getting the Measure of Production

SA's population represents over 8% of the nation's but the state gross product amounts to 1% less than this. The figures for 1992/93, 1993/94, and 1994/95 are ($m) 30.058, 31.863, and 33.225. The mean 31.7153 is near π^{-1} (.318310, close to the 1993/94 figure), and recalls the mean of the state's three road systems (31,777.1 km.). The standard deviation (*SD*) 1.5887, treated as .15887, (rather than .015887, as would keep consistent decimal point placement) is similar to D2 (.15966), and the coefficient of variation (*CV* = *SD*/mean) .05009 similar to $F1^3$ = .04979. Here again we find quantum effects associated with the key constants π and *e*.

Returning to the raw totals we find these approximate to $120^{-1/4}$ (.30214), $96^{-1/4}$ (.31947), and $84^{-1/4}$ (.33032). Taking pairs at a time, the mean of 30.058 and 31.863 is 30.961 $\approx 108^{-1/4}$ (.31020) and that of 31.863 and 33.225 is 32.544 $\approx$ mean of $84^{-1/4}$ and $96^{-1/4}$ = .32489.

As to rate of increase, the 1993/94 figure is .0601 above 1992/93, .0601 being similar to the mean of 12^{-1} and 24^{-1} = .0625. The 1994/95 figure is .0427 above that for 1993/94, .0427 being similar to 24^{-1} = .0417.

So gross state product advanced annually broadly as (the digit sequences of) 4th roots of the reciprocals of multiples of 12 and proportional increases parallelled the baseline of the 12-BR table.

The largest industry in SA is manufacturing, which contributed 17.5% of state product for 1992/93. The summary data, number of establishments, number of employees, wages/salaries total ($m) and turnover ($m) for that year, correspond to *e*-BR (*p* < 01).[77]

Rural industries accounted for 4.4% of state product for 1994/95. The number of agricultural establishments included in the Australian Integrated Agricultural Commodity Census for that year was 15,952 ($\approx$ D2 = .15966, *p* = .06). These operated on land totalling 56,101,000 hectares ($\approx$ F21 = .55927, *p* = .16). This represents approx. 56.8% of the total area of SA (.568 $\approx$ mean of F21 & F15 = .568, *p* = .11).

---

[77] Provided the data are treated as decimal fractions without regard to the number of digits.

One rural product for which SA is well known is wine. The state is responsible for approx. 45% of Australian output and a high reputation in overseas markets is claimed.

For the five years 1990/91–1994/95, the average yearly production (tonnes) of grapes for wine-making was 309,867.6, almost a repeat of the 1836 area of the state in sq. miles (309,850.1, or NSW's present area — see above. The correlate, $108^{-1/4}$, incidentally, fills the "blank" in the series of 4th roots correlated with gross state product.

The average total area (hectares) in production of (bearing) grapes for all uses was 24,390.4 ≈ F16 = .24397 $(p = .07)$. The average total area not yet bearing was 3045.4(?). The combined total of hectares was therefore 27,435.8 ≈ $48^{-1/3}$ = .275161. Recalling that the present area of SA is similar to $48^{-1/4}$ (see above), the basic statistics for viticulture in this state for the sample period "resonate" with stages in the state's development as a territorial entity.

A glance at the figures for the average output of wine grapes proves intriguing. Depending on whether the basis is bearing only or total hectares, the tonnage per hectare is 12.70 or 11.29. The mean is 11.99 ≈ 12 — an extraordinary result, which should of course be treated with a degree of caution.

As in the case of manufacturing, the number of employees, total of wages and salaries, and turnover of the wine and spirit industry can be correlated with e-BR. In the present case, for the years 1989/90, 1990/91, 1991/92 and 1992/93, the p is .01. (Number of establishments excluded as only 2 digits available.)

One noted fishery product of SA is abalone, a mollusc found in greatest numbers off the western Eyre Peninsula. The species exploited are greenlip and blacklip. Gross (in shell) weight taken and value for 1992/93, 1993/94 and 1994/95 yield several hits or near misses on table numbers, eg the value for 1992/93 ($1,000s) was 23,725 ≈ F10 = .23730, a difference of only $5,000 out of nearly $24m. The mean for 1993/94 and 1994/95 together was 25,004 ≈ 2^{-2} = .25. The mean *weight* for the three years ('000s kg.) was 841 ≈ $2^{-1/4}$ (.841), the standard deviation (SD) being 34.7 ≈ $24^{-1/3}$ (.347) and coefficient of variation $(CV = SD/\text{mean})$ .041 ≈ 24^{-1} (.042).

So too the catch of SA's marine and freshwater fisheries for the same period includes remarkable numerical specimens. The mean total for 1992/93 and 1993/94 together ('000s kg.) was

13,534 ≈ E1 (*.13534*). The mean for the three years was 14,266 ≈ 1/7 (.14286), the *SD* 1657 ≈ 1/6 (.1667). Correlations with *e*-BR of the marine and freshwater figures separately are probably significant ($p < .05$).

Most convincing, if tantalising, also in the case of abalone, are the supposable elements of an inapprehensible total pattern, glimpsed singly (FI0, E1 ...) like fins glinting on the surface momentarily, before vanishing from view.

For comparison, weight and value of the crustacean (prawn and rock lobster) catch for 1992/93–1994/95 appear to be of less numerical interest.

A Kind of Proportional Representation

A bit like employment, voting has two stages. A person may or may not participate in the labour force. He or she may or may not also be included on the electoral roll. Then again the person may or may not be employed, while the enrolled voter may or may not attend the polling station.[78]

It would be interesting, therefore, to see if the election data have structure comparable to the labour market (cf. "Disproportion in the Employment Market" above). Here we note only that between May, 1974, and March, 1996, there were ten federal elections for Senate and House of Representatives together. During this time the total number of electors in S.A. enrolled for both increased from just over 3/4 million to about 1 million. The ten totals can be correlated with (mainly) *e*-BR, with *p* below at least .05.

From March, 1973, to December, 1993, eight elections to the state Legislative Council and House of Assembly were held.[79] For these the elector totals also resemble table numbers (n.s.)

---

[78] Enfranchised persons (aged 18 years or over, etc.) are legally bound to enrol and vote, at least in federal elections.

[79] Note — from at least 1979 enrolment was for both state elections.

For the "lower" Houses the average totals of voters and of total votes for the periods given are:

Electors:	House of Representatives	891374	≈	H2	= .891661
	House of Assembly	854593	≈	G6	= .855020
	Mean of both totals	872983	≈	H3	= .873427
Votes:	House of Representatives	850346	≈	I5	= .84861
	House of Assembly	799879	≈	I13	= .79955
	Mean of both totals	825112	≈	F18	= .825125
	Mean of both means	849047	≈	I5	= .84867

p of chance : low.

Voter "turn-out" is the percentage or proportion of enrolled persons who vote. In House of Representatives elections this ranged from .9380 to .9697, approximately from J1 (.9394) to K1 (.9692) in our *e*-BR table. The mean, .9541, almost coincides with the mean of the same table numbers (.9543, $p = .03$)

"Informal", on the other hand, is the euphemism which, paradoxically, seems to administer the kiss of formality to ballot papers, including those defaced, left blank, etc. The average for House of Representatives elections is $4.14\% ≈ 24^{-1} = .0417$ ($p = .025$), *SD* $2.04\% ≈ 48^{-1} = .0208$ ($p = .16$).

In the federal election of 1996 and state election of 1993 the labor party fared badly vs. the liberals, gaining only a handful of seats in both lower houses and with substantially fewer first preference votes. Considering the ratio of each party's average number of first preference votes in electorates won to the average number for the winning party in all electorates, the ratios are:

1996 (House of Representatives)
Labor   .88220
Liberal   1.02356 or 1/.97698

1993 (House of Assembly)
Labor   .80421
Liberal   1.05292 or 1/.94974

The means for both houses are:
Labor   .84321 $≈ 60^{-1/24} = .84316$ ($p = .015$)
Liberal   1/.96326 $≈ 36^{-1/96} = .96336$ ($p = .11$)

The ratios between the parties' ratios are:
1996 (House of Representatives)   88220/1.02356 = .86189
1993 (House of Assembly)   80421/1.05292 = .76379

The mean of these ratios of ratios is $.81284 ≈ 12^{-1/12} = .81282$ ($p = .01$), a further instance of this remarkable number, here applied to differentiate the "quality" of elections won by both parties, whereas a recently encountered instance of the number 12 was as the tonnage per hectare of grapes for wine making. (See "Getting the Measure of Production" above.)

Quantum Crime

The following six-digit figures — which undoubtedly represent an enormous amount and range of unlawful behaviours — look neutral enough:

$$213,830 \quad 207,392 \quad 209,361 \quad 203,964 \quad 200,619$$

These are the total number of offences in SA for each year from 1993 to 1997, according to the Office of Crime Statistics in their report Crime and Justice in South Australia 1997 (Adelaide Advertiser dated 26/9/98). Resemblance to 12-BR has $p > .05$.

As the trend is mainly downward we can look for a pattern in the ratios 1997/each previous year. These, commencing with 1997/1993, are .9382, .9673, .9582, .9836. Reference to col. 1 of the e-BR table shows all except .9582 approximate to the main sequence roots of e^{-1} shown at J, K, and L (the root number doubling each time). The remaining ratio .9582 (.958244 to 6 decimals) $\approx 60^{-1/96} = .958247$ — a difference of only 3 millionths.

The average yearly total during the five year period is $207,033.2 \approx$ mean of $24^{-1/2}$ and $108^{-1/3} = .2070555$ (These are adjacent in the size-ordered 12-BR table). The SD is $5,057.3 \approx 60^{-1/6} = .50541$ and CV .0244 $\approx$ mean of 36^{-1} and $48^{-1} = .0243$. All three correlations have low p.

It appears that Adelaide's crime, at least in its statistical form, although massive in amount, is limited in the sense of being subject to the widely operating principle of proportionality.

Quantum Debt

Not included in the crime figures are the numerous instances of nonpayment of public school fees in SA. "Nearly $1 million ... remains outstanding for the 1997 school year" (Adelaide Advertiser dated 26/11/98). The three largest amounts owed by parents were to the high schools, Christies Beach $45,000, Aberfoyle Park $23,891, Reynella East $23,889, similar to $24^{-1/4} = .4518$, $72^{-1/3} = .2404$, and again $72^{-1/3}$. The ten biggest debts, including these, can be fitted in most cases to 12-BR ($p < .05$ or $< .01$, according to particular test).

"The Driest State in the Driest Continent"

For non-metropolitan South Australians, at least, the empty rainwater tank or dry storage dam is no novelty, for SA (it is often said) is the "driest state in the driest continent". It may seem captious to insist, on the contrary, SA is ahead of Vic. and Tas., at any rate, in what the hydrologist terms "ground water resources" (i.e., resources other than rainfall and surface water). In total resources SA lags behind all states and territories except tiny ACT. The leader is Qld., with 35,540 gigalitres (GL). Proportionally, the other states have (NSW) .5369, (Vic.) .3003, (SA) .0449, (WA) .4063, (Tas.) .3102. These ratios correspond to $12^{-1/4} = .5373$, $36^{-1/3} = .3029$, 24^{-1} .0417, $36^{-1/4} = .4082$, and $108^{-1/4} =$ also .3102 ($p = .05$).

To any readers who have struggled through the thicket of numbers comprising this chapter — congratulations. The author's more realistic hope is to convey an overall impression of the influence of numbers *as* numbers and of numbers as *structure* — on the physical features of the state of South Australia, the people who call it home, its economy, and the rest. Beyond this, it's hoped that readers with particular interests (which should include most) may find information bearing on that interest and, if this presents a challenge to accepted ideas and explanations, stimulation.

References for Chapter 10

GARDNER, P.M., *South Australian Yearbook No. 31: 1997* (Adelaide: Australian Bureau of Statistics, South Australian Office).

Government of South Australia, *Employment statement: presented by the ... Premier of South Australia on ... the occasion of the budget for ... 1998/99* (Adelaide).

JAENSCH, D. (Ed.) *The Flinders history of South Australia: the political history* (Netley, S.A.: Wakefield Press, 1986).

South Australian Commissioner of Police, *Annual Report 1996/97* (Adelaide).

The World Almanac and Book of facts 1998 (Mahwah, New Jersey).

Green Quiz Question No. 10

The table number for this big Canadian "mount" has a pedigree as long as your arm. The city's name is Montreal — if you didn't guess — an' to find its P'n'G figure you have to know your table.

To start with, find the smaller factor *of the smaller factor of the smaller factor* of 1/e. Then find the *bigger* factor of the *smaller* factor *of the smaller factor* of 1/e. The numbers you end up with should be side-by-side.

Next find the *product* of both numbers — that's easy 'cos it's right after them in the same row. It's the *square root* of the product that you want — just round it up an' that's your P'n'G figure.

Extra clue: South Australia

What is the letter an' column location of the number in the table — that's Appendix B, if you've forgotten.

How many hectares of P'n'G has Montreal got?

CHAPTER 11
THE LAST ELECTIONS OF WEIMAR

Hitler who?

THE HITLER of my early years was That Man. In that far off time, beyond the living memory of most, his was the brittle name of menace. Today, on repetition, exasperation also seems at home in the name, as may be appropriate.

Hitler was That Man and "It's That Man Again", with Liverpool comedian Tommy Handley, was to be war-time Britain's favourite radio show — a diversion from Hitler.

Nor was the seeming dissonance of *Herr* Hitler (the hit-*man*) or of *Herr Himm*ler[80] lost on juvenile wannabes.

But Hitler was the reason for trenches being started at the bottom of our street, left to fill with the winter rains, and then resumed. These were not intended for main services of the ordinary kind, but for air-raid shelters, whose urgency rose, fell, and rose again, as Hitler's territorial demands in Europe were asserted, fulfilled and renewed. In them later many a rumpled head nodded away the time between Göring's[81] night bombers.

Before the Blood-Dimmed Tide

Adolf Hitler, *Führer* of the Nazi party, became Chancellor of Germany on January 30, 1933. That evening his supporters paraded by torchlight through Berlin, but many Germans, Noah-like, feared that Hitler would unleash not only a river of light past the Chancellery on Wilhelmstrasse, but "a flood of sewage all over Germany and the world at large."

An early victim of the "cesspool of totalitarianism" was the existing form of government in Germany — the Weimar

---

[80] Heinrich Himmler, head of S. S. (*Schutzstaffel* — protection force)
[81] Hermann Göring, German air force (*Luftwaffe*) chief.

republic.[82] This had replaced the Second Reich, which met *its* demise with Germany's defeat in WW1.

Hitler's claim to the chancellorship was based on his party's strong showing, with 37.3% of the votes, in the general election of July, 1932. Despite a downturn in another general election in November, the Nazis remained by far the largest party in the Reichstag, as the Republic's parliament was still known.[83]

President *Marschall* Paul von Hindenburg had only reluctantly let Hitler be Chancellor on the supposition that his excesses would be curbed by a cabinet in which the Nazis were a minority; that the wild beast would not slip the chain.[84]

On the contrary, the new Chancellor's ice-cold, granite purpose was unfettered power. Almost immediately came his demand for fresh elections, which were set down for March 5. Days before this, on February 27, came the great fire which reduced the Reichstag building to a shell. Despite the propaganda value of this alleged Communist terror act and despite intimidation, the Nazi vote at 43.9% still fell short of a majority.

Even with that majority Hitler would surely have pressed ahead with his plans for a dictatorship (*Diktatur*). First the Chancellor must be empowered to rule by decree without Reichstag approval — a quantum gain in the erosion of parliamentary authority since Brüning's appointment to the chancellorship in March, 1930. After the gutting of the Reichstag (building) was to come the gutting of the Reichstag (assembly).

---

[82] "Flood of sewage" and "cesspool of totalitarianism" (Fischer, 1995, p. 263) seem to echo "flood of muck and filth" and "cesspool of the Republic" — Nazi-type put-downs of the *Republic* (cited by Lee, 1998, pp. 118, 121). When British Prime Minister, Neville Chamberlain, returned from Munich in 1938 with "Peace in our time", did he, in his time, tempt providence by capping a pledge Hitler had once given to his Storm Troops — "*National socialism* in our time?" (cited by Wheeler-Bennett, 1967, p. 454; emphasis and interrogation added).

[83] The Constitution, accepted by the National Assembly at Weimar on July 31, 1919, kept the title *Reich* (Empire) "to create an impression of continuity" (McKenzie, 1971, p. 73). The Republic's founders viewed their creation with mixed feelings; its first president, Ebert, "hated" the Republic. The Second Empire might be dead but had not been laid to rest.

[84] Dr. Heinrich Held, Bavarian Prime Minister's reason for lifting the ban on the Nazi Party after Hitler's release on parole from Landsberg prison fortress in December, 1924 (Bullock, 1955, p. 188). See "Mistaken Identity: the 'Bohemian Corporal' — Some Achieve Greatness".

The notorious Enabling Act ("Law for the Removal of the Distress of People and Reich"), which gave Hitler emergency powers ostensibly for four years, was placed before the Reichstag "of the day" on March 23. From outside the old Kroll Opera House, which made shift for a people's chamber, could be heard the chanted argument of the Stormtroopers, "We want the Bill — or fire and murder" (Bullock, p. 241), which rhetoric could not strike down. Then the Bill, whereby the Parliament effectively abolished itself and the Republic, was accepted by this Reichstag at its first and only meeting.[85]

The Thin End of the Wedge

Though the Germans who voted National Socialist were not solely responsible for the "collapse" of the Weimar Republic, they did constitute the thin end of the wedge which Hitler used to split away the Reichstag from the centre of power which he as Führer of Germany would personify.

A view long current among political analysts indicted the lower-middle class in Germany as the "culprit", or Nazi constituency. According to another, the "mass society" hypothesis, classless or unattached individuals are attracted to extremist parties like the Nazis.

Other investigators have cast their net more widely and found the Nazi support base was far more diverse than this. Childers (1983) from his major study concluded that the Nazis built a constituency across regions, in both town and country, and across both the social divisions and religious confessions. However, in a striking image, although "the party's support was a mile wide, it was at critical points an inch deep". Also it evolved and changed over time (pp. 3, 14, 268–269).

Can our numerical approach contribute, even in the most general way, to this debate? Is there evidence of a *numeric* factor in the terminal Republic's electoral process?

The Year of Elections, 1932

When we delve into the murky history of the dying Republic we discover that prior to the Hitlerian take-over a whole raft of opportunities was extended to the German people to make

---

[85] Already the Reichstag elected in July, 1932, in a procedural *comedy* at *its* first full meeting on September 12 had been dissolved almost immediately by an order obtained by Brüning's successor, von Papen.

political choices. In nine months (March–November, 1932) five general, or near-general elections took place, as follows:

March 13	Presidential election (Round 1)
April 10	Presidential election (Round 2)
April 24	Prussian Diet election[86]
July 31	Reichstag election
November 6	Reichstag election

By the end, in fact, the electorate, preoccupied with the "cancerous growth of unemployment", had grown "thoroughly tired of ... the whole democratic process" (Fischer, p. 236). Even Hitler's propagandist, Dr. Paul Joseph Göbbels, diarised about the electioneering success which did not bring power as dropping dead from winning elections (Fest, 1974, p. 332) — ironical in view of his and his family's suicide in 1945.

The year of elections, 1932, saw Hitler's greatest oratorical triumphs. It was a "heroic epoch", a "hell fought through", a "titanic battle of character" (Hitler, in Fest, 1987, pp. 331–332). Seeing his way to power by constitutional means, "Hitler *Légalité*" found elections grist to his mill; they gave scope for what Fest calls his "special brand of agitation" (p. 314). Nor, without prejudice to his "deserts", was Hitler one of those who "fears his fate too much [to dare] To win or lose it all"[87]

The 1932 Presidential Election

The fascinating personality clash between Hindenburg, the product of a 700-year-old military aristocracy, and Hitler, prophet of the 1,000 year hegemony of a German master race (*Herrenvolk*), makes this election of paramount interest.

---

[86] Prussia was almost two-thirds of Germany.

[87] From James Graham, Marquess of Montrose, "My Dear and Only Love" (in Knowles, Ed., 1997, p. 93). The full passage is:

He either fears his fate too much,

Or his deserts are small,

That puts it not unto the touch,

To win or lose it all.

If his lover played him false, the poet would merely "laugh and walk away". Hitler, whose "bride", according to a confidant, Otto Wagener, was Germany (Wagener, 1985, p. 33) ended, however, by willing destruction of the nation which had "failed him". A former Australian PM, of a quite different (trade union) political stamp, had a "love affair" with his people.

Hindenburg's seven year term as President was near its end. Chancellor Brüning, needing time to resolve international issues concerning reparations (exacted from Germany as the "guilty party" in the war) and disarmament, sought an extension of one or two years for the President. This required approval by two-thirds of the Reichstag but approaches to Alfred Hugenberg, Nationalist leader, and Hitler for support met with refusal.

The Candidates

Hindenburg had received an offer of unconditional endorsement by the Kyffhäuserbund ex-servicemen's association. In this topsy-turvy election, however, the right-wing Protestant monarchist's acceptance went to a non-party committee headed by Berlin mayor, Heinrich Sahm (The Sahm Committee), which collected three million signatures on petitions to the President to stand again. Hindenburg's support came, in fact, mainly from parties of the left and centre (Socialists, trade unions, Catholic Centre), while the right-wing parties which had voted for him in 1925 switched to Hitler — in name, at least, a socialist. Another ex-servicemen's organisation, the *Stahlhelm*, fielded its own candidate.

The four significant candidates were: (Hindenburg ("SPD", "*Zentrum*"), Hitler (NSDAP), Ernst Thälmann, ex-pugilist leader of the Communists (KPD), and Theodor Düsterberg (DNVP — Nationalists, Stahlhelm), the last-named dropping out after the first round.

Mistaken Identity: the "Bohemian Corporal"[88] — Some Achieve Greatness

Adolf Hitler, demagogue extraordinaire, a famous architect of destruction, abominated for his evil deeds, was of Austrian birth. The son of a senior (admin. grade) official in the customs service, he had been an aspiring artist cum down-and-out in Vienna, then in Munich an Austrian draft dodger. A "fanatic" about politics, he nurtured an obsessive antipathy towards Jews.

---

[88] Hindenburg's jocular (?) term for Hitler may have been a side-swipe at the leader's dilettante ("bohemian") life-style, though (wilful?) confusion of Braunau (Bohemia) with Braunau (Austria), Hitler's birthplace, is another possibility (see Fest, p. 781, note 16).

Hitler the Soldier

Though unwilling to fight for the Austro-Hungarian Empire with its majority non-German ("racially inferior") population, when war broke out in August, 1914, he immediately volunteered for the Bavarian army, serving first as an infantryman, then as a dispatch-runner with the rank of lance corporal (*Gefreiter*). Wounded on October 7,[89] 1916, and shortly before the Armistice, on another October day, but of opposite repute, October *13*, 1918, temporarily blinded in a British gas attack,[90] he had been awarded a Second, later upgraded to a First Class Iron Cross for bravery and zeal.

Hitler the Politician

After the war he had gained notoriety in Munich as a political agitator vehement against the "wrongs" done to Germany by the Treaty of Versailles (1919), against the (Socialist — SPD) "traitors" on the home front who negotiated the November, 1918, Armistice — the "November criminals" — against all those others, pacifists, revolutionaries ..., behind the "stab-in-the-back ("*Dolchstoss*") of the German army, against the Jews, against "Marxism"[91] ... the list is incomplete and the order arbitrary.

The Nazi party (from *Nazional Sozialische Deutsche Arbeiterpartei* [NSDAP] — National Socialist German Workers' Party) sprang from the former German Workers' Party, which Hitler had joined in September, 1919, as Committee member No. 7 (Bullock, p. 59). The new party's programme of 25 points — an aggregate of nationalism, anti-Semitism, and socialism — was announced by him in February, 1920, at the Hofbräuhaus Beer-Hall in Munich, to acclaim from an audience of "almost 2,000" (Hitler, pp. 332ff.) In December of that year he acquired the *Völkische Besbachter* newspaper ("Folkish" or "Racialist Observer"), whose name he retained.

---

[89] Hitler (1997), p. 173. Various examples of the number 7 in the life of Hitler or other contexts are mentioned in what follows. For other numbers which strangely echo see "The Strangely Intertwined Careers of Hitler and Roosevelt".

[90] Hitler's gassing is referred to by Fest on p. *77*!

[91] Marxism was the credo of the SPD.

Hitler the Putschist

The future dictator early became acquainted with General Erich Ludendorff (*Pour le Mérite* cross), war-time Chief-of-Staff and master strategist, who had himself, as the dominant partner, exercised joint dictatorial or near dictatorial powers with Marshal Hindenburg from 1916 to 1918. On November 8–9, 1923, it was, however, the corporal and the general who led the "Beer-Hall *putsch*", associated with Munich's Bürgerbräu Keller. The armed putschists hoped to compel the ruling nationalist (anti-Republican) clique in Bavaria to move against Berlin and set up a new national government, much as Benito Mussolini had gained power in Italy the previous year with his "March on Rome". However, expected support from the Army did not materialise and the column of marchers, headed by Hitler and Ludendorff, was stopped by bullets from a cordon of police (or police and military). Hitler went down, probably dragged to the ground by a fallen comrade.[92] Only Ludendorff, accompanied by his adjutant, continued marching until taken into custody. Though Hitler escaped from the scene, with at least a dislocated shoulder, his early arrest and that of many of his associates ended the *putsch* (only one of several attempted against the Republic in its early years).

Hitler the Felon

At his trial (February, 1924) for high treason Hitler turned the tables on his accusers, the former ruling triumvirate, which had lost office through its own involvement in plans for a coup, and received from the sympathetic court the minimum sentence of five years, with eligibility for parole after six months.

With convicted fellow-Nazis around him — Ludendorff was acquitted — he spent nine months only in lenient conditions at Landsberg fortress near Munich.[93] There he held aloof for the most part from party developments in the outside world — even resigning as leader in July, 1924, as an appeasement gesture to the authorities (Bullock, p. 115) — and commenced work on his

---

[92] Scheubner-Richter, who first suggested the *putsch*. Authors do not all agree on how Hitler "hit the ground", nor is it clear which side fired the first shot.

[93] His room was the only one available — No. 7.

autobiographical and programmatic "My Struggle" (*"Mein Kampf"*).[94]

In his absence, the now-banned Nazi party did not lie low in South Germany but, slipping out of Hitler's grasp, took the electoral road to Berlin. In alliance with ultra-nationalist groups in the north, as the National Socialist German Freedom movement, it contested the May 1924 Reichstag election and shared in a tally of almost two million votes. However, the following December election saw the total vote shrink to less than half. Among the remnants of the former Nazi party, feuding erupted.

Hitler Légalité

On December 20, 1924, Hitler was released, determined now to win power in Germany — to get his hands on the state, as Bullock puts the Nazis' frank intention — by legal means, that is, through the ballot box. He became known as "Hitler Légalité".

Yet violence was for the Nazis — as also for their arch-rivals, the Communists (KPD) or Reds — a veritable credo. It took the form of street fights, break-up of opposing party meetings or protection of their own by strong-arm methods.[95] On one occasion — November 4, 1921, at the Hofbräuhaus — a Nazi meeting, packed by hostile Reds, was cleared of the "enemy" by a smaller number[96] of Nazi toughs, almost all of whom, Hitler boasted, were covered with blood five minutes into the brawl (Hitler, pp. 458–460). Elements of the Nazi private army of "storm troops" (SA — *Sturmabteilungen*) received their baptism of fire in this "hall battle" (*"Saalschlacht"*: Flood, 1989, pp. 227ff).

"Kicking a political opponent to death was well within what Hitler meant by legality." (Bullock, p. 202, re the much later murder by Nazis of a Communist miner in Silesia.)

The ultimate source of Nazi violence was, in Bullock's view, what the historian calls Hitler's "verbal violence ... the extraordinary impression of force, the immediacy of passion, the

---

[94] Hitler's original title was: "Four and a Half Years' Struggle Against Lies, Stupidity and Cowardice" — for Hitler seemingly a re-run of WW1, also a more than four year struggle.

[95] One of Chancellor Brüning's speeches (at Königsberg in East Prussia) on behalf of Hindenburg's 1932 re-election campaign was disrupted by white *mice* cannily let loose among the audience by Nazis (Brüning, 1970, p. 537).

[96] "45 or 46" — see "Unmeasure for Measure".

intensity of hatred, fury and menace conveyed by the sound of the voice alone without regard to what he said." (pp. 64, 341)

Violence against the "enemy" was *exclusion* — especially of the Jew — and like the lightning attack in war (*Blitzkrieg*) had an extra *propaganda* value (p. 346). *Inclusion* had perhaps equal propaganda value and was achieved spectacularly at the annual party rally, first (1923) in Munich and later Nuremberg. Bullock refers to "the hypnotic effect of thousands of men marching in perfect order" (p. 347). These rallies were "the very heartbeat of the National Socialist movement". (Burden, 1967, p. ix)[97]

Hitler on parole made peace with the Bavarian government and, with the bans lifted from the party and the *Völkische Beobachter*, quickly brought together the nucleus of a new party. On February 27, 1925, he established absolute personal control as leader. At this meeting, held at that place of memories, the Bürgerbräu Keller, the "reformed" putschist vented his continuing resolve to destroy the "enemy", including the republican regime: "either the enemy passes over our bodies or we pass over theirs." (In Shirer, 1962, p. 119).[98] This led to extensive bans on his speaking in public from 1925 to 1927–1928 ("*die Verbotzeit*" — the "ban-period).

Capping the volcano and the improving German economy did not prevent the party membership from growing steadily from its end-of-1924 low. Regional groups were brought under Hitler's direction and by the end of the ban-period the party organisation ran throughout Germany as a shadow state ready to assume the functions of the existing state once the Nazis came to power. The change-over ("Everything Must Change") would be rapid: "to destroy the last remnants of the old state ... took but a few hours", Hitler afterwards boasted (in Shirer, p. 121)[99]

---

[97] The Nuremberg rallies excelled, inter alia, for their choreography, of which an interesting example from manoeuvres on the *Zeppelinwiese* in 1936 was reported: "It was odd to see the advancing infantrymen flinging themselves on the ground not naturally but in so many precise movements as on a parade ground." (In Burden, p. 133. Attributed to S. H. Roberts, "The House that Hitler Built"). Did this display — or "piece of revisionist symbolism", as Fest (p. 513) described a ceremony commemorating the failed "March on Munich" — finally rid Hitler of the spectre of November 9, 1923?

[98] Hitler's outburst was inspired by the enthusiasm of the crowd (Shirer), complicating the origins of Nazi violence as above.

[99] By *Gleichschaltung* (co-ordination, though subordination seems more apt) "the whole of the organised life of the nation was to be brought under the single control of the Nazi Party" (Bullock, pp. 245ff.). Thus in 1933 the states were brought under the rule of, generally, the local *Gauleiter*, other

"The Wooden Titan"[100]: Others Have Greatness Thrust Upon Them

Hindenburg's double-barrelled title, as given by an Oxford historian who had a "ringside seat" at the decline and fall of the Weimar Republic, was General-Field-Marshal Paul von Beneckendorff und von Hindenburg (Wheeler-Bennett, 1967, p. 3). The holder of *77* medals, including Prussia's highest military award, the Grand Cross of the Iron Cross with Golden Rays (pp. 149, 264), he was known more simply as *der alte Herr* (the old Gentleman). He was the virtual embodiment of the old German military tradition, being descended from the union of two ancestral houses with military records back to Teutonic Knights of the thirteenth century. To him, an ingrained monarchist, the Republic was a disagreeable fact he had learned to live with while still dreaming of the return of Kaiser Wilhelm from exile in so near Holland.

A Retrospect: the 1925 Presidential Election

The death of the Republic's first president, a former saddler/harness maker[101] who became leader of the Socialist Party (SPD), Friedrich Ebert, came suddenly on February 28, 1925, the day after Hitler's NSDAP re-establishment meeting (see above). Ebert had been nominated as President by the National Assembly at a time of national emergency; a successor was now to be appointed by popular vote.

In the first election on March 29, 1925, the most votes, but less than the absolute majority required by the Constitution, went to the nationalist *Reichsblok* candidate and Bürgermeister of Duisberg, Dr. Karl Jarres.[102] Fearing a win in the second round (runoff election), by the newly-formed *Weimarblok* of republican

---

political parties were eliminated, and Trades Unions were replaced by the Labour Front.

[100] Cf. Wheeler-Bennett's (1967) book title. Giant wooden statues of Marshal Hindenburg had been erected during the 1914–1918 war, including one in Berlin's Sieges Allee (Victory Avenue). Into these colossi, on payment of, it is believed RM 1, an iron nail could be driven. Receipts went to the German Red Cross. (Wheeler-Bennet, p. 79, except for donation amount.)

[101] C.f., Hitler, Ed's note on p. 237.

[102] Of special interest is the overall total of valid votes cast in this round, which shows strange "resonance" with the overall total in the second round of the *1932* presidential election (see "Order in Politics and Order in Numbers").

parties, the *Reichsblok* now sought as candidate the victor of the Battle of Tannenberg (1914) and national idol, Marshal Hindenburg. At 78 years of age Hindenburg preferred private life: "*Ich will meine Ruhe haben*" ("Leave me in peace.") Between Hindenburg and one Schmidt[103] Wheeler-Bennett reports an exchange full of foreboding, as in a Shakespeare tragedy: "The devil take you all!"; "I don't mind if he does, so long as we have you for Reichspräsident!" (p. 259). Having yielded to the blandishments of a retired *admiral* (Grand Admiral Alfred von Tirpitz — pp. 260–261), Hindenburg took little part in his own campaign. On election day, April 26, his share of the vote, 48.3%, was more than his nearest rival, Wilhelm Marx of the Centre Party, and sufficed in this round to assure his election.

The Campaign: Head-to-Head

The 1932 presidential election campaign opened quietly. Hitler, not yet a German citizen, had his eyes fixed on the chancellorship, not the presidency. He procrastinated. When Göbbels finally received the word that his leader would run, the campaign sprang to life as a "head-to-head" between Hitler and Hindenburg. The "Bohemian" acquired instant German citizenship by becoming a government councillor (*Regierungsrat*) for the state of Braunschweig (Brunswick) for one week.

Hindenburg, a citizen for all of his now 85 years, was against the whole idea of another election, let alone a campaign. His public appearances were limited to one, aside from which, in a broadcast speech, he declared that the broad masses of the nation wished him to stay in office to prevent a takeover either by the left or right. Brüning campaigned for Hindenburg.

Things Fall Apart ... Brüning

Captain Heinrich Brüning, Iron Cross, First Class, had commanded a machine-gun company in the war. At the end of March 1930, he had stepped into the void created by the collapse of Socialist Hermann Müller's coalition government. This, the Republic's last constitutional régime (with majority support in the Reichstag), was a casualty of the economic crisis resulting from the 1929 Wall Street Crash and ensuing Great Depression. With unemployment in Germany soaring — registered unemployed full-time workers alone would top six million by election time —

---

[103] Probably the legal scholar/political scientist, Carl Schmidt.

the problem was, how unemployment payments were to be funded. Should business or labour foot the bill? With the coalition partners in a state of deadlock, the Müller government had to resign.

Brüning was the selection of General Karl von Schleicher[104], also Iron Cross, First Class, the liaison officer between the Army (*Reichswehr*) and Government, who, together with other insiders (the Palace *Camarilla*)[105] had the ear of the President.

His own party, the *Zentrum* (Centre Party), having gained only 12.1% of the vote in the last (1928) Reichstag election, Brüning was to head a "presidential ministry", dependent on the confidence of the President, not the Parliament. For his part, Hindenburg would rely on the ill-defined emergency powers given him by Article 48 of the constitution to decree measures not acceptable to the Reichstag.

In practice, Brüning had unofficial support from the Socialists (SPD) and frequent use of Section 48 was tolerated by the Parliament.

The Issues

At issue in this election was a complex of agendas, open and covert.[106] On Hindenburg's side the primary ostensible aim was to block Hitler's rise to power. This was why the SPD supported Hindenburg instead of nominating their own candidate. Their slogan was, "Defeat Hitler! Therefore vote for Hindenburg." (Mommsen, 1996, p. 409). Although Hindenburg had included the Communists in the threat from extremists, Thälmann was not a serious challenger. Hitler stood for National Socialism, claimed to be the only solution for Germany; first Hindenburg must go.

A battle of slogans developed between the opposing parties. To the "enemy's" "We will stay at any cost", Hitler rejoined with, "We will overthrow you in any case" (Fest, p. 318). "He hath kept faith with you; be ye faithful unto him" provoked, "Honor Hindenburg: Vote for Hitler" (Toland, p. 262). "Only Hindenburg can save us from Hitler" (McKenzie, p. 224) met with "Old man,

---

[104] G: Schleicher: "creep", "sneak", "intriguer".

[105] Cabal or clique.

[106] For examples of covert issues see "A Sub-Text: the Postage Stamp Slur" and "Order in Politics and Order in Numbers".

you must step aside." "For freedom and bread" (Toland, p. 262) was a constructively worded Nazi slogan.[107]

The Re-election of Hindenburg

If the result had depended on the scale and novelty of each side's campaign, Hitler would have been "home and dry". His was a "masterpiece of organized agitation which attempted to take Germany by storm" (Bullock, p. 180), and included the use of films, gramophone records, and air-dropped leaflets, as well as a "sea of posters and banners" (Fischer, p. 237). Hitler and Göbbels toured Germany (in Round 2 by hired aircraft — "Hitler over Germany") on a "heroic" schedule of spoken propaganda, much of it targeted against Brüning's policies.[108] At grass roots level columns of brown-shirted S.A. men marched and sang.

Hindenburg's campaign, shouldered by Brüning and the Hindenburg Committee, which "marched" separately from the Sahm Committee, contrasted Hindenburg's "non-partisanship" with Hitler's "fractiousness". The SPD's contribution was massive in terms of rallies and street force (supplied by the *Reichsbanner*). After falling short by less than 1% of an absolute majority in the first ballot held on March 13, Hindenburg's vote increased in the second round on April 10 to 53%, the only absolute majority in the series of direct presidential elections of which this was the last.

A Sub-Text: the Postage Stamp Slur

Hitler's first meeting "in the flesh" with Hindenburg had been on October 10, 1931, at his own request.[109] Distraught from the

---

[107] Strangely, both Fest and Wheeler-Bennett start their accounts of the election campaign on "special" page numbers. These are the same (digit sequences of decimal fractions or the decimal fractions themselves) as we will find important in Unmeasure for Measure". Thus, Fest, on p. 318, similar to the reciprocal of *pi* (π^{-1} = approximately .318) and Wheeler-Bennett, on p. 368, similar to the reciprocal of *e* (e^{-1} = approximately .368).

[108] There was besides an "army of agitators" to "whip up the passions of the already tormented people" (Göbbels in Fest, p. 318). This again points to give and take of passion between, in this case, the second string of Nazi campaigners and the German voter.

[109] Ludwig (1935) presents Hitler's August, 1932, meeting with Hindenburg as his first, but more than compensates for this evident lapse in a brilliant passage contrasting, for example, "The man with the biggest moustache in Germany" with "the man with the smallest", or the legendary "president with his marschal's baton" and "the tribune of the people ... holding unseen

recent suicide of his niece and inamorata, Geli Raubal, he was ill-at-ease before the "Wooden Titan". His out-of-place monologue did not enhance his claim to be Chancellor — then only half as strong in Reichstag seats as it would be next year — but fuelled Hindenburg's immediate dislike. On the departure, empty-handed, of Hitler and his companion, then Nazi contact-man, Hermann Göring, thus the President to his entourage: "This Bohemian corporal wants to become Reichschancellor? Never! At most he could be my Postmaster General. Then he can lick me on the stamps from behind." (In Fischer, p. 234; attributed to Meissner and Wilde, 1958, p. 49). In another account, Hindenburg was more explicit: "Then he can lick my ass on the stamps." (Attributed to Ernst von Weitzsäcker; see Fest, p. 781, note 16).[110]

We may assume that Hitler heard at least a sanitised version of Hindenburg's remark, as "From [Hindenburg's] entourage [it] was subsequently leaked that the President was at most prepared to appoint this "Bohemian corporal" Postmaster General, certainly not Chancellor" (Fest, p. 302).

In the earlier part of his political career Hitler showed "grotesque respect for authority" (Stone, 1989, p. 31). Vestiges of awe might explain Hindenburg's jibe.

By an extra twist Hindenburg had been a major player in the propagation of the "*stab-in-the-back*" legend (*Dolchstosslegende*), the theory or myth that the German army had not been defeated in the field, but brought down by the treachery of left-wing politicians at home (Wheeler-Bennett, pp. 235ff.). In Hitler's hands this became a potent weapon against the *System*. Hindenburg's taunt may then have been meant to deflate Hitler by reducing etiology to scatology. Yet again, it may have been a patrician dig at Hitler's low rank war service as company runner (message-carrier).

Hitler was sensitive to ridicule (Fest, pp. 517–518) so the presidential campaign must have been envenomed for him by this loss of face vis-à-vis his arch-opponent.

Were the "insult and invective" heaped by him on Hindenburg during the campaign (Wheeler-Bennett, p. 369) repayment for lost self-esteem?

---

in his hand the secret key which would open to him the heart of his people" (pp. 347ff).

[110] In Chancellor Brüning's memoirs Hindenburg contents himself with "He can't be made a minister" (Brüning. p. 391)

FIG 11.1 Dissonant Dreams
Hindenburg ("The Wooden Titan"): "At most he could be my Postmaster
General";
Hitler: "Old man, you must step aside".

And was the dressing down he received at his August, 1932, meeting with Hindenburg — instead of the expected mantle of Chancellor — return payback by the President?

As *Führer* of Germany Hitler received fees from the Reich for the use of his portrait on German postage stamps, though this did not commence till 1937 or become fully established until 1941 (Von Lang, 1979, pp. 90ff.).[111]

By then the wheel had turned full circle.

---

[111] Stone, in his taut narrative, even has it that Hitler received no salary as Chancellor or *Führer* but Von Lang states his initial refusal of a salary was overcome by Treasury insistence.

The Remarkable Numbers of Weimar

By "numeric factor" is meant the tendency for numerical data, including whole numbers, from perhaps any area, to correlate with tables of decimal fractions developed from various bases. The bases include proper whole number fractions, 12 and multiples of 12, and sequential factors (divisible, complementary factors) of e^{-1}, the reciprocal of the natural log base e. These tables include roots and powers of the bases (see Appendixes A, B and C). Other bases might well prove useful.

1. All-Decimal Correlations

At first sight, such tables might be more likely to parallel ratios or proportions of some measure — "dimensionless numbers" — than quantities or totals expressed in whole numbers. With election data then we might first look at the percentages of votes received by candidates or parties, to see if these tend towards "preferred" (table) numbers, instead of being free from *numerical* constraints, as is conventionally assumed.

One convincing example concerns the (northern) autumn (November) Reichstag election of 1932. Upwards of 17 parties contested this, the last free general election of the Weimar Republic, six of which polled at least one million and accounted for almost 94% of the valid votes. The six, together with their shares of the valid votes and the correlates for these, are as follows:[112]

Nazis	.3309	$84^{-1/4} = .3303$
Social Democrats	.2044	$24^{-1/2} = .2041$
Communists	.1686	$36^{-1/2} = .1667$
Centre Party	.1193	$72^{-1/2} = .1179$
National People's Party	.0834	$12^{-1} = .0833$
Bavarian People's Party	.0309	$36^{-1} = .0278$
Total	.9375	

The probability (p) of these correlations with 12-based ratios (12-BR — see Appendix A) can be estimated by a binomial test, either

      1. a "coarse-grained" test, based on the total "window"; which is the product of the number of relevant table

---

[112] All election data from Mackie and Rose (1991).

numbers in the interval spanned by the data multiplied by the margin of error allowed; "relevant table numbers" would generally include only roots/powers in the doubling series 2, 4, 8 ... or 3, 6, 12 ... (or both) in cols. up to a certain multiple of 12; "margin of error" means the allowed difference of the empirical number from the table number, multiplied by 2 (as the difference could be plus or minus) plus 1 to cover the direct hit case. This gives a single p of success, $p(x)$, for ratios drawn at random from the same interval, or

2. a "fine-grained" test, where the p of each party's share is calculated from the interval between the nearest neighbours of its correlate in the reordered supplement to the 12-BR table and the margin of error allowed.

Then the p of our sample of party shares of valid votes is either 1. << .01 or 2. < .05 or < .01 (depending on whether or not the Centre Party's .1193 is treated as a success).

Republican candidates in the *1925 presidential* election had received shares of the valid votes which can also be fitted to 12-BR, as follows:

Round 1

Braun (SPD — Socialists)	.2904	$12^{-1/2}$ = .2887
Marx (Centre)	.1447	$48^{-1/2}$ = .1443
Hellpach (DDP — Democrats)	.0583	?

Round 2

Marx (Weimarblok)	.4531	$24^{-1/4}$ = .4518

Notice the "quantum" shift in the correlate for Marx's figure and the singular relation of (the Blok's) figure to the first round SPD figure, with doubling of both base and exponent. Amalgamation and chance alone surely did not produce these relations. The suggested "mechanism" is resonance. (See discussion in Chapter 12, "Home Runs, Strange Numerics, and Form in the Event World").

In 1932 also the first presidential election (round) did not produce an absolute majority. At the head of the poll stood Hindenburg. The other candidates, in proportion to Hindenburg's, received shares of the valid votes similar to e-based ratios (e-BR), as follows:

Hitler (NSDAP)	.6080	G1 = .6065
Thälmann (KPD)	.2672	F5 = .2689
Düsterberg (*Stahlhelm*)	.1371	E1 = .1353

The alphanumeric coding gives the *e*-BR table reference (see Appendix B). The *p* of these correlations is less than (<) .01.[113]

Recalling that *e*-BR are derivatives of e^{-1}, we can "recover" from the same proportions (ratios) the values they imply for that constant. The average of the three values is .3682 vs. F1 = .3679 ($p < .02$).

2. Trans-Decimal Correlations

Fitting to tables of decimal fractions ratios which are themselves decimal fractions seems straightforward, even if it would not normally be expected to succeed. Fitting whole numbers might be thought still less likely to succeed, because of the evident incompatibility of the different types of numbers. Yet evidence suggests "trans-decimal" correlations are no more rare than "all-decimal" correlations. The four nation-wide elections of 1932 yield first a weak example, then a strong one:

Total electorate:

March	Presidential Election	43.95 m
April	Presidential Election	44.06 m
July	Reichstag Election	44.21 m
November	Reichstag Election	44.37 m
	Mean	44.15 m

A look at our size-ordered *e*-BR table shows 44.15 comes digitally near F20 (.4407) and G7 (.4434). The mean of this pair of near neighbours (.4421) is located near the midpoint of the much larger interval between F14 (.4223) and G11 (.4604) = .4413. Considering the latter interval the *p* of the near hit of 44.15 on .4421 is < .07.

Means of Valid and Total Votes

The mean total of valid *and* "total" votes (including invalid votes) in each election ranges from 35.63 m to 37.77 m. The overall

---

[113] This table contains sequential factors, that is divisible pairs of complementary factors of e^{-1}; for example, F5/F6 = F1, with F5 + F6 = 1. The table could be further extended by continuing the factoring procedure, or a particular segment (subset) can be taken; the *p* then applies to that subset. In the present case the *p* is based on the first seven columns (cols.).

mean is 36.76 m. In this case further calculation is hardly needed as this figure nearly coincides digitally with e^{-1} (F1 = .3679).[114]

For further examples of "all-decimal" and "trans-decimal" correlations, see also "Unmeasure for Measure", "Order in Politics and Order in Numbers", and "The Voting that Men Do".

Unmeasure for Measure

1. Measure in the Response of German Voters to Hitler and the Nazis:

In Reichstag Elections

Recall that the Nazi party contested its first Reichstag elections — as part of an alliance — in May and December, 1924, while Hitler was at Landsberg. We wish to know whether support for the party in all Reichstag elections evidences the numeric factor. We find that if the totals of valid votes for the 1924 alliance and subsequently for the party, are divided by the Nazi total in the *March, 1933* ballot, the last semi-democratic election of the Weimar Republic, the *ratios* so obtained can be fitted to e-based numbers (e-BR), as follows:

May, 1924	.1110	D15	= .1114
December, 1924	.0525	E4	= .0541
May, 1928	.0469	B18	= .0462
September, 1930	.3710	F1	= .3679
July, 1932	.7959	G2	= .7951
November, 1932	.6794	H11	= .6785

p of ratios < .05.

Note that D15 (see May, 1924) is the 4th *power* of the larger factor *of the larger factor* of e^{-1} (F1) and H11 (November, 1932) is the 4th *root* of the smaller factor *of the smaller factor* of e^{-1} (F1). So exact symmetry exists in the proportions which the alliance's and Nazi party's figures (valid vote totals) in the first and last Reichstag elections prior to Hitler's coming to power in January, 1933, have to the March, 1933, total.

The mean of the December 1924 and May 1928 ratios is .0497, almost equal to $F1^3$ (the cube of e^{-1}) = .0498, so the proportions in the four elections from December 1924 to July 1932 shadow

---

[114] For the whole table the *p* is less than (<) .04; for cols. 1–7 only it is < .01.

roots/powers of e^{-1} or its complement $1-e^{-1}$ (of which G2 — see July 1932 — is the square root).

These correlations exemplify "measure", as do the following.

And in the Four Nationwide Elections of 1932

Including his or his party's vote in both presidential rounds (March, April) and both Reichstag elections (July, November), the electoral year 1932 went for Hitler as follows:

Valid Votes

March	11,339,446	D3 = .1147
April	13,418,547	E1 = .1353
July	13,745,700	E1 = .1353
November	11,737,400	D3 = .1147
Mean 12,560,273		

If we average March with November and April with July, the *means* are:

March, Nov	11,538,423	D3 =.1147
April, July	13,582,123	E1 =.1353

In each case (with or without averaging) these figures (whole numbers) can be related to our e-BR table with p at least $< .05$.

Proportions

March	.301194
April	.367725
July	.372690
November	.330903
Mean .343128	$72^{-1/4} = .343295$

p of Mean : low

The means for the same pairs as before are:

March, Nov	.316048	$\pi^{-1} = .318310$
April, July	.370207	$e^{-1} = .367879$

It turns out that the *sum* of March and November, .632097, is very nearly $1-e^{-1}$ (F2 = .632121 to 6 decimal places); p of this sum : low.

The overall total is 1.372512, extremely close to $2(e^{-1} + \pi^{-1}) = 1.372379$; p of this total : low.

We can infer then two different (quantum) levels of popular support for the Nazis in 1932, the party's proportions of valid votes corresponding to *pi* and *e*.

Summary

Overall mean of valid and total votes in the four elections of 1932:	36.76m	similar to e^{-1} = .3679
Mean of Hitler's, the Nazis' valid vote totals in March, November	11.54m	similar to $[e^{-1}/(1-e^{-1})]^4$ = .1147
Mean of Hitler's, the Nazis' valid vote totals in April, July:	13.58m	similar to e^{-2} = .1353
Mean of Hitler's, the Nazis' proportions of valid votes in March, November	.3160	similar to π^{-1} = .3183 *- .0023* *= .3160*
Mean of Hitler's, the Nazis' proportions of valid votes in April, July	.3702	similar to e^{-1} = .3679 *+ .0023* *= .3702*

In the April, 1932 presidential elections the role of the *e* constant is particularly important and merits close scrutiny, as follows:

The 1932 Run-off Election for President

In the 1932 run-off election for president Hitler received 36.8%, more exactly 36.77%, of the valid votes. This is very nearly e^{-1} (.3679) and digitally practically the same figure we found for the overall mean of the averaged valid and "total" votes in the four 1932 nationwide elections, including the run-off election. That figure was 36.76 *million*. (Cf. "The Remarkable Numbers of Weimar".) Let us call the Hitlerian correlation with e^{-1} Correlation 1.

A rough check on the probability (*p*) of this occurring merely by chance is based on the interval between the two nearest neighbours (one on either side) of .3679 in the size-ordered *e*-BR table (.3753 minus .3387 =) .0366. Then the difference between the actual and table figure (.3679 minus .3677) = .0002, multiplied by 2 (as the difference could be + or -), with .0001 added (to cover direct hits), gives .0005. This is divided by 1/2 the interval as above (being the reference interval applicable to F1) = .0183 and gives < .03, which is the *p* of Hitler's share of votes happening by chance to so nearly coincide with e^{-1}.[115]

Most surprisingly the Hitlerian digit sequence 3677, which extends to 36772, recurs in the figure for *total votes* (including

---

[115] This is a conservative result. If only cols. 1–7 are taken, the *p* is < .01.

invalid votes) in this election. This is 36,771,787. The first five digits, rounded up, are again 36772.

To see how unlikely this could happen by chance we can make the following simple calculation. The first five digits of the *valid votes* total are 36491 (after rounding). As 36772 minus 36491 is 281, supposing Hitler's share (ratio) could have taken any value from .36492 to .36772, the *p* of hitting .36772 is 1/281, that is <.004. Let us call this correlation No. 2.

It is easy to see these correlations are independent of each other. Just because one (empirical) figure is like e^{-1} doesn't mean the other should be.

To see immediately, without more ado, the extreme improbability of these results, if the "valid" and "total" votes figures are averaged, and the *mean* 36,631,274 is *squared*, the first *six* digits exactly match the first six of Hitler's valid votes total, as follows: $36,631,274^2$ = (first 8 digits) 13,418,502, vs. (Hitler's vote) 13,418,547. The difference is just 45 votes.[116] This correlation, No. 3, is not independent of the first two correlations, however.

Summary

Valid votes (V.V.)	36,490,761		
Hitler (H)	13,418,547		
H's ratio		$\approx e^{-1}$	
(first 5 digits)	36772	(first five digits)	36788
All votes (A. V.)	36,771,787		
H's *V. V.* ratio		$\approx$ A. V.	
(as above)	36772	(rounded up)	36772
V. V., A. V. : mean	36,631,274		
Square (first 6 digits)	134185		
H's V. V. total		$\approx [(V. V. + A. V.)/2]^2$	
(first 6 digits)		(as before)	134185

A Note on the Limit of a Function and the Limit of a People's Support for Hitler and his Party

A possible objection is: You are headlining the German people's measured response to Hitler and the Nazis and, at the same time, highlighting the role of the mathematical constant *e*. Isn't there a contradiction here? After all, Hitler's supporters were not voting

---

[116] The same number, or one shy of that given by Hitler for the stormtroopers who were blooded at the Hofbräuhaus (See above). Hitler's age at the time of the elections (43) falls in the same bracket.

for e^{-1}. Why should e or e^{-1} have *any* role in the Weimar Republic elections?

1. It is important to realise that e is not an exact number — nor is *pi* — but the limit of a function. The best known such function is $(1 + 1/x)^x$. When x is a large enough number this function reaches a value near e (approximately 2.7183). With a minus sign substituted inside the brackets, the value *decreases* to near e^{-1} (approximately .36788).

2. Consider, then, Hitler's valid votes total grew from 11.3 million in round 1 to 13.4 million in round 2 of the presidential election, 13.4 being (digitally) similar to the square of e^{-1} (E1 = .135 in the *e*-BR table). As a proportion of all valid votes Hitler's share increased from .301 to .368, the latter figure being similar to e^{-1} (F1 = .368).

Then the Nazi party's valid votes total, from base = 0 in 1920 rose to a peak 13.7 million in July, 1932, slightly more than the square of e^{-1} (e^{-2} or E1 in the table) in a digital sense.[117]

If, instead, September, 1930 — when the Nazis rode the unemployment wave to a startling 6.4 million votes — is taken as the base, in July and November, 1932, averaged together, the party's figure nearly doubled to 12.7 million and in March, 1933, increased to 17.3 million, almost e times the 1930 figure (6.41 x 2.72 = 17.4).[118]

The combination of (1) and (2) supports a link between the election data and the mathematical constant, e^{-1}. (For further evidence see "Order in Politics and Order in Numbers" and "The Strangely Intertwined Careers of Hitler and Roosevelt".)

2. Unmeasure in Hitler's Getting and Abuse of Power

If the natural log base is a measure and the approximate limit of popular support for Hitler at this critical time,[119] we may reflect

---

[117] As we have seen, the April and July averages, 13.6 million and .370, are closer to the *e*-BR (E1, F1).

[118] Like a second wave following the first, which crested in July. The July election was the 7th since the war, including the 1919 election for the Constituent Assembly, whereas 7 Reichstag elections came between the end of the war and Hitler's appointment as Chancellor.

[119] "Hitler's attitude" of saviour against Marxism, etc "was a last exaggerated expression of Europe's claim to remain master of its own history, and thus of history in general" (Fest, p. 755). An interesting comparison can be made with the 1932–1933 England cricket tour of Australia which ended just one month after Hitler reached his goal on January 30, 1933. The test match series played during this tour, the "Bodyline" series, is infamous by reason

that Hitler himself valued proportionality. This is seen already from his life-long interest in architecture. In geopolitics his thinking started with the disparity between Germany's population and land area. It was intolerable, he argued, that the *Herrenvolk* should be fenced in an area "absurd" compared to that of the American Union, Russia, or other geographic giants. (Hitler, pp. 586ff.) He could also keep a sense of proportion about *disproportion*, if credence can be given his reply to Roosevelt's plea of May, 1933, for world peace: "Germany knows that in any military action in Europe, even if completely successful, the sacrifice would be out of all proportion to any possible gains." (In Toland, 1981, p. 312.)

Yet, as Fest puts it, "Hitler's peculiar greatness is essentially linked to the quality of excess. It was a tremendous eruption of energy that shattered all existing standards." (p. 3). For examples, should we take the reckless grab for the soil and spoils of Russia, followed by a scorched earth policy in Germany which — if fully implemented — would have denied even the essentials for physical survival to the proven unworthy (read "defeated") German people themselves ("Sydney or the bush" become world domination or self-destruction)?

Or National Socialism, which was more than a political movement, more than a religion — rather "the will to a new creation of man" — the way to which passed over the bodies of millions?

Or, to return to our present theme, the explosion of energy, with Hitler and his henchmen barrelling along the highways or zooming across the skies of Germany between speaking engagements in an election campaign "such as the world has never seen before" (Göbbels on the 1932 presidential election campaign; in Fest, p. 318), to which, for all that, the German voter's response was moderate, measured, and in favour of Hindenburg?

---

of the England captain, Douglas Jardine's intimidatory tactics, contrary to the spirit of the game. Was this, in a sense, a belated attempt to bring the colonials to heel, Jardine being himself an Aussiephobe? What can be shown is that the average first innings run total for England in each test had digits similar to e^{-1} . That average was 368.8 vs. $e^{-1} = .3679$. The average for Australia was 317.0 near the reciprocal of *pi*; $\pi^{-1} = .3183$. So the same pairing of constants which pointed to discrete levels of support for the Nazis in 1932 occurred around the same time in top competitive cricket (See also Chapter 9: "The 'Bodyline' Campaign".)

Order in Politics and Order in Numbers

1. Order in Politics

For a people mangled by war and its aftershocks the Hindenburg Legend had shone like a beacon. Its namesake, then General Beneckendorff, was commanding officer of the German 8th Army in 1914 when it annihilated a Russian army in a great battle near the village of Tannenberg in East Prussia. Beneckendorff/Hindenburg was acclaimed as a national hero. The legend was a talisman which opened the path of duty as he followed it to the supreme military and civil offices. But wasn't the triumph of Tannenberg, on which depended the ensuing chain of achievement, no more than the birthright and service owed by a son of his proud lineage?

The story of Tannenberg (and the story behind the story), as told by Wheeler-Bennett from the German standpoint, makes gripping reading. At the outbreak of war General Beneckendorff was already retired after a career full of merit without renown. When a replacement was required for the demoralised high command of a numerically inferior army seemingly in danger of being overwhelmed by the Russian invader, the automatic choice for chief-of-staff was General *Ludendorff*, whose *Pour le Mérite* had come from capturing, almost single-handed, the citadel at Liège (Wheeler-Bennett, p. 13). To head the command, Beneckendorff's name was selected, partly because he lived at Hanover, on the railway line to the Eastern front ...

Contributing to the Russian *defeat* were (1) an event 10 years into the past, and (2) a non-event in the present. Here again we encounter a kind of resonance (or synchronicity — Jung).[120]

Hindenburg's first meeting with Ludendorff, the start of a highly successful wartime association, was at Hanover railway station, when the special train carrying Ludendorff drew in to take on board the waiting Beneckendorff.

> 1. In the story behind the story, during the Russo-Japanese war another railway platform — at Mukden in Manchuria — had witnessed one Russian general knock down another following recrimination over lack of

---

[120] The Battle of Tannenberg itself resonates with — was the "historic answer" to the slaughter by Lithuanian and Slav invaders of the Teutonic Order's massed knighthood 500 years before at Tannenberg. Present then were a Beneckendorff and a Hindenburg (p. 28)

support against an earlier Japanese attack. The aggrieved party who dealt the blow was General Samsonov, who 10 years on had reason to rue it.

2. In the greater conflict Samsonov, commander of the southern arm of the Russian force pushing into East Prussia, found he had been lured into a German trap. His only hope lay in assistance from the commander of the northern army — General Rennenkampf, still rubbing the bruise from Mukden.

Because help did not come, and because (Beneckendorff) held fast against unnerved Ludendorff's call (based on faulty intelligence) to break off the operation, Samsonov's army was smashed and its commander took his own life.

Hindenburg's contribution had been stability, to "shield, or reflect, the shining light of Ludendorff's genius" and he had "little or no part in the actual victory" (pp. 14, 27).

The extraordinary contingencies underlying the German victory and the momentous results of Hindenburg's part in opening the way to Hitler's *Diktatur* compel the question, What if … ?, which we may ponder.

Hindenburg, "a man of service [who] had little regard for reward" (p. xiii or *13*), though the people's father (*Vater des Volkes*), earned a reputation in some quarters for disloyalty to his friends and supporters. Göbbels in the Reichstag accused the (1932) candidate (meaning the Marshal) of the "party of desertion" (meaning the Socialists or "1918 criminals") of betrayal of the right when it elected him in 1925. Just Nazi propaganda, perhaps. Yet similar charges came afterwards from a retired naval officer who had served in the war, that is (1) "the Right elected him in 1925 and he betrayed the Right, (2) "the Left elected him in 1932 and he … has betrayed the Left" (p. xii).

As to (1) views differ. Wheeler-Bennett states Hindenburg's mandate in 1925 had been the destruction of Weimar and the restoration of the monarchy (p. 371), but Dorpalen (1964) argues there should have been no reason for the expectation that Hindenburg would defy the constitution, to which he had given his oath (p. 83). Mommsen refers to (republican) concerns that he would depart from the Constitution after 1925, but these proved unfounded (p. 238).

If Hindenburg betrayed the right after 1925, before the end of his first term, influenced by Schleicher and the Palace *Camarilla*, he had begun to make amends — by another "betrayal" of his election day constituency. Before the 1932 election, then, Hindenburg was already committed to policies at variance with both his official non-partisan campaign status and with his actual dependence on the Socialist vote, as follows.

A major concern of all parties was rearmament, pressed for by the *Reichswehr*, opposed by the SPD. In autumn, 1930, Hindenburg still hoped to teach France a lesson: "Give me 24 army corps and you'll see!" (Patch, 1998, p. 190)

Also on the President's confidential agenda was to return to government by the right wing, which would not obstruct the continuance of rearmament then proceeding clandestinely.

Before the election Hindenburg had given an undertaking to his former right-wing supporters that he would try to bring about "a healthy swing to the Right", so breaking his pledge of non-party allegiance" (Mommsen, p. 408).

Brüning's head was on the chopping block already. The crisis came when the Chancellor replied to Göbbels' unparliamentary attack on Hindenburg (for which he was temporarily expelled from the Reichstag) with a radio address in which he assailed the Nazis — a public burning of bridges to the right, which it was Brüning's secret commission to rebuild. In February, 1932. Hindenburg informed his aristocratic friends he would sacrifice the Chancellor if an opportunity emerged to forge unity on the right (Patch, p. 239).

Brüning's survival thus far had depended not solely on Hindenburg's confidence, but on an understanding between his Centre party and the SPD, based on mutual deterrence. If the Socialists toppled Brüning's government, the Centre party in coalition with the SPD in Prussia would topple the SPD government of Otto Braun.

The Chancellor received his marching orders or request for his resignation on May 31, 1932, *seven* weeks after his exertions had been crucial in securing Hindenburg's re-election. His fault — failure to open discussions with the Nazis and Nationalists (Hugenberg's party) with a view to forming a new coalition.

As for the German people, their predicament, had they known it, mirrored that of Russian General Samsonov's army at Tannenberg — where Hindenburg's nerve did not fail — a rabble, well and truly trapped, fleeing from the guns of General von François, vainly into the guns of Marshal von Mackensen.

It could be argued that it was because Hindenburg's nerve *did* fail in January, 1933, that after repeated refusals to endorse Hitler as *Chancellor*, he finally gave way, against his better judgment.[121]

Be this as it may, in 1932 the choice was, as it turned out, not between Hindenburg and Hitler, but between Hitler direct and Hitler courtesy of the President, as the candidate whose slogan was, "Only Hindenburg can safe us from Hitler", but was secretly committed to "a healthy swing to the Right", would redeem this pledge on January 30 of the following year, with a vengeance.[122]

Aspects of ignorance in the 1932 presidential election: mainly concerning what the German voter did not know.

Problem	Integrity of Reich
Solution	(SPD) General disarmament
Solution	(Wehrmacht, Hindenburg, Schleicher, Hitler) Rearmament
Problem	SPD obstructing already ongoing clandestine rearmament
Solution	(Wehrmacht etc) Exclude SPD from government, including especially in Prussia
Problem	Re-election of Hindenburg
Solution	(Brüning, Schleicher) Accept support of SPD
Problem	SPD support unwelcome to Hindenburg
Solution	(Hindenburg's campaign) Do not acknowledge SPD support
Problem	Instability resulting from party system of government; dependence on SPD support

---

[121] Mistaken Identity: the "Russian Prisoners".

There is a story that as Hindenburg watched the ecstatic parade of young Nazis in celebration of Hitler's becoming Chancellor, the old Marshal asked of an aide, "Did we really take all these Russians prisoners at Tannenberg?" (Charman, 1989, p. 3) The reason for this apparent misapprehension may have been senility or may not Hindenburg, with his "great insight" (Wheeler-Bennett) have received a belated premonition of the fate reserved for his people?

[122] "Things fall apart; the centre cannot hold; / Mere anarchy is loosed upon the world / The blood-dimmed tide is loosed, and everywhere / The ceremony of innocence is drowned." (From W. B. Yeats, "The Second Coming'" in Knowles, Ed., 1993, p. 306.)

Solution	(Hindenburg, Schleicher) Change to presidential system, relegating parliament to minor role
Problem	If plan for presidential system becomes known, support from SPD (at least) will be lost
Solution	(Hindenburg, Schleicher ...) Do not let plan become known
Problem	Brüning as "cunctator" (procrastinator: Schleicher); his failure to negotiate with right to widen coalition and bring order to right
Solution	(Hindenburg, Schleicher) Brüning must go
Problem	Brüning has essential contacts in SPD
Solution	(Hindenburg, Schleicher) Let Brüning stay till after Hindenburg re-elected
Problem	If Brüning finds out he may resign — as he, in fact, twice offers before the election, but is dissuaded by Hindenburg
Solution	(Hindenburg, Schleicher) Do not let Brüning know

2. Order in Numbers

The results of the 1932 presidential election already show *order*, that is numerical order, on the right (Cf. "Unmeasure for Measure"). Order on the left is also found, for example, in the valid vote totals for the Sahm Committee cum SPD candidate, Marshal Hindenburg, which, together with his 1925 total, can be seen to advance through our size-ordered e-BR table, landing on or half-way between the numbers, as follows:

1925 Round 2 14,655,641. F19, C12 Mean (first 4 digits) .1465
1932 Round 1 18,651,497. E14, E20 Mean (first 4 digits) .1863
1932 Round 2 19,359,983. E20   (first 4 digits) .1942

p of totals $< .05$.

Only one other candidate stood in both 1925 and 1932 — Thälmann for the Communists. Hindenburg and Thälmann together, despite the Marshal's actual SPD reliance, span the line (front, or range) of politics. Here are their vote totals or shares (proportions), *cumulated* over the election rounds they fought:

Hindenburg

1925	Round 2 14,655,641.	F19, C12	Mean (first 4 digits)	.1465
1932	Round 1 33,307,138.	E15,		.3337.
1932	Round 2 52,667,121.	G5, E6	Mean (first 4 digits)	.5265.

p of cumulative totals < .05.

Thälmann (Notice the leapfrog movement and consistent downward displacement of actual vs. table numbers):

1925	Round 1	.0697.	E5	.0723
1925	Round 2	.1333	E1	1353
1932	Round 1	.2645	F5	.2689
1932	Round 2	.3661	F1	.3679

p of cumulative shares < .05.

Returning to 1932, round 2, we find not only Hitler's, but Hindenburg's total has a (digital) square : square root relation with another total, in this case the electorate (Hitler's was with the mean of valid and total votes — cf. "Unmeasure for Measure"), as follows:

Hindenburg   19,359,983
Electorate   44,063,095, with $44,063,095^2$ = (first 4 digits) 1941

If the square of the mean electorate in both rounds is substituted, we have: $44,006,388^2$ = (first 4 digits) 1937. (See also "The Unnecessary Election?" below)

The *sum* of the mean electorate in 1925 and 1932 is 83,326,614, very nearly 5/6 = .8333. (or I4 in the e - B R table = .83332264). This remarkable near coincidence with fixed numbers by itself implies a strange order or cohesiveness from the first direct election for president (1925, round 1) to the last (1932, round 2), which extends to valid and total votes, as is next shown, after which overall symmetry in voter turn-out is shown.

We recall that Hitler's figure (proportion) in 1932 round 2 was (digitally) near that for total votes (cf. "Unmeasure for Measure"). The figure for total votes was 36,771,787, (digitally) near e^{-1} (F1) = (first 4 digits) .3679. We now find that *valid* votes in 1925 round 1 were 26,866,106, (digitally) near the smaller *factor* of e^{-1} (F5) = (first 4 digits) .2689. The p of chance is, in each case, < .03 or < .02, depending on whether the whole e-BR table, or only cols. 1–7 are taken.[123]

The means of valid and total votes for the same rounds are:

1932   Round 2 36,631,274, the first 4 digits being 3663
1925   Round 1 26,941,433, which, treated as F5, implies F1 = (first 4 digits) 3688

the mean of 3663 and 3688 being 3675, near F1 = (first 4 digits) 3679[124]

p of mean : near .05.

In an (e-based) numeric perspective the growth in voting during Hindenburg's first term has the form of a movement from the smaller factor of e^{-1} to e^{-1}. We will find similar growth in U.S. presidential voting during the period from 1920 to 1928 (see "The Strangely Intertwined Careers of Hitler and Roosevelt" below).

Turnout is the ratio total votes / electorate. Based on the sums of both rounds in each election, the figures are:

1925   .7323   near F6   = .7311
1932   .8483   near I5   = .8486

p of ratios < .05.

As these figures correspond to the larger factor of e^{-1} (F6) and the 8th root of the smaller factor of e^{-1} (I5) they are symmetrical and there was a quantum increase in turnout in 1932 compared to 1925.

---

[123] Even if only these two figures of the eight for total and valid votes in both rounds of both elections could be fitted to e-BR. the p by a Poisson test is near .01.

[124] Compare 3675 with 36.76, the overall mean of valid and total votes in 1932. (Sec "Unmeasure for Measure" above.)

The "Unnecessary" Election?

We can now see that the outcomes for Hindenburg and Hitler in the second round of the 1932 presidential election were also symmetrical, as follows:

Hindenburg (votes)		19,359,983
Electorate	44,063,095	
Square (first 8 digits rounded up)		19,415,563
or		
Electorate	44,063,095	
Electorate (round 1)	43,949,681	
Mean of both	44,006,388	
Square (first 8 digits)		19,365,622
Hitler (votes)		13,418,547
Total valid votes	36,490,761	
Total votes	36,771,787	
Mean of both	36,631,274	
Square (first 8 digits)		13,418,502

A rough test of p is to assume each candidate's vote total could have come anywhere in the interval between both. Then, with due account taken of the "error" observed, the p of each outcome is: Hindenburg .02 or .003, Hitler .002.

In a model for this election which assigns to the chief contestants (assumed equal favourites) vote totals corresponding — digitally — to the square of one or other of two overall statistics, either the total electorate or the total votes (in the present sense of the mean total), it appears that Hitler drew the short straw.

The Strangely Intertwined Careers of Hitler and Roosevelt

The 1929 Wall Street Crash and the Great Depression which followed had humbled the transatlantic colossus, casting an army of workers out of paradise in the new "Buddy, can you spare a dime" era. With similar economic problems, both Germany and the U.S. found radical and charismatic leaders.

For all their differences, a remarkable twinning of dates and careers is apparent in the biographies of Franklin Delano Roosevelt (F. D. R.) and Adolf Hitler (A. H.), as follows:

F. D. R.	born	(1882, January)	30
A. H.	appointed Chancellor	(1933, January)	30
A. H.	born	(1889, April)	20[125]
F. D. R.	inaugurated as President	(1933, March 4)	
	re-inaugurated as President	(1937, January)	20
		(1941, January)	20
		(1945, January)	20
A. H.	re-born as parolee on release from Landsberg prison	(1924, December)	20
A. H.	re-born as survivor of assassination attempt	(1944, July)	20
A. H.	"died" as survivor of the execution on his order of his *alter ego*, Ernst Röhm?[126]	(1934, June)	30
	died by suicide	(1945, April)	30

Not only were the careers of Hitler and Roosevelt as head or next-to-head of state inaugurated (A. H.) or reinaugurated (F. D. R.) on the same day of the month as the birth of the other, but both careers lasted approximately 12 years and covered almost exactly the same historical period.

We therefore wish to know, does "twinning" extend to these leaders' election figures?

The last free election in Weimar Germany was the Reichstag election of November 6, 1932, just two days before the election which brought Roosevelt to the White House.[127] The results were:

November 6, 1932	Nazis	.3309	$84^{-1/4}$	(.3303)
November 8, 1932	U.S. Democrats	.5742	$84^{-1/8}$	(.5747)

p of both ratios below at least .05.[128]

---

[125] Hitler was born *seven* years after Roosevelt.

[126] He had already survived the suicide (?) of his favourite niece, Geli Raubal, on September *18*, 1931.

[127] The mean of these election dates — November *7*. The Reichstag election anniversary on November 6, 1999, is at the time of writing the proposed date for a referendum in Australia on whether the Queen should be replaced as head of state by an Australian. Of a total of 347 delegates at a pre-referendum forum 73% voted Yes, 27% No. Interested readers are invited to check the 12- and *e*-BR tables for correlates for the three numbers.

[128] This does not take account of the important square : square root relation.

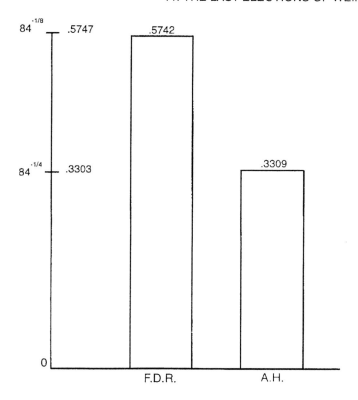

FIG 11.2. Strange bond between mutual admirers (soon to be enemies) Franklin D. Roosevelt and Adolf Hitler in terms of numbers; Democrat F.D.R.'s November 8, 1932. U.S. Presidential election share is near the *square root* of Nazi A.H.'s in the November 6 German Reichstag election, as is shown by doubling of the exponent of 84 (see left side of figure).

The extraordinary trans-Atlantic square : square root relation seen in Fig. 11.2 is similar to that between the republican candidates in the 1925 German presidential election (cf. "The Remarkable Numbers of Weimar") and if attributable to resonance, this must be resonance at a distance.

A different type of relation, factor : number, links the 1925 and 1932 German presidential elections. While the valid votes figure in 1925, Round 1, resembles a factor (F5) of e^{-1} (F1) (cf. "Order in Politics and Order in Numbers"), the valid votes figure in 1932, Round 2 (as well as the total votes figure, though not so nearly) resembles F1.

Remarkably enough, two U.S. presidential elections had previously (in 1920 and 1928) returned practically the same figures, as follows:

U.S. Pres. election 1920	Valid votes			
	(first 5 digits rounded up)	26754	F5	(.26894)
U.S. Pres. election 1928	Valid votes			
	(first 5 digits)	36790	F1	(.36788)

For comparison:

German (G) pres. elections

Round 1	1925	Valid votes			
		(first 5 digits)	26866	F5	(.26894)
Round 2	1932	Valid votes			
		(first 5 digits)	36491	F1	(.36788)

We note the period during which votes increased from near (always in the sense of the first five digits) F5 to near F1 is almost the same. The *mean* is 7.5 years. If 26754 and 26866 are treated as estimates of F5, the implied values (digits) for F1 can be calculated. Although matching of implied and actual digit sequences near F1 is for neither nation better than approximate, cross-matching gives close agreement, as follows:

U.S.	(1920)	26754	implies F1		
			(first 5 digits)	=	36526
G.	(1932)				36491
G.	(1925)	26866	implies F1		
			(first 5 digits)	=	36735
U.S.	(1928)				36790

p of cross-matching : low.

The average of the implied values for F1 is
(first 5 digits)   36631

The average of the given numbers (first 5 digits)
correlated with F1 is   36641

— a nearly exact agreement which would be striking even for figures not associated with an important mathematical constant.

A news item of unknown significance: as part of the German government's move back to Berlin, the parliament held its first meeting in the restored Reichstag on April 20, 1999, 110 years to the day from the birth of Adolf Hitler.[129]

The Voting That Men Do

When the campaign has ended, the poll closed, the count is official, and the post mortem has begun, while the people's representatives make their way to the parliament, what remains of the ballot itself — gone like the snows of yesteryear; but a memory; a set of numbers only, without residual energy, inert ... ?

We have already noted effects in these data suggestive of resonance. To return again to an example from the 1925 presidential election, in Round 1 the republican Socialist (SPD) candidate received a share of the votes similar to $12^{-1/2}$ (.289 or 28.9%) and in Round 2 the republican *Weimarblok* nominee, a share near $24^{-1/4}$ (.452 or 45.2%), the base and exponent of the correlate having doubled.

"Resonance" also seems to operate between presidential and Reichstag figures, as well as — transdecimally — between presidential and Hitlerian or Nazi figures.

Recall that in the "unnecessary" election of 1932, Hindenburg's votes total resembled (digitally) the square of the electorate. Dividing Hindenburg's total by the electorate gives then digits similar to those for the electorate, to which we shortly return. Meanwhile let us check 1925 for a comparable effect.

Hindenburg's total in 1925 — 14,655,641 — divided by the electorate — 39,414,316 — gives (to four decimal places) .3718. It doesn't work this time; however, we recognise .3718 as near enough the *Nazis'* share (proportion) of votes in the *July, 1932 Reichstag* election — .3727. If we substitute as divisor the mean electorate in both 1925 rounds, the quotient is *.3727; the same as* the Nazi figure.

---

[129] An all-American presidential tragedy which repeated itself after not quite 100 years was the assassination by gun-shot in 1865 of Abraham Lincoln, echoed by that of John F. Kennedy in 1963. A nest of strange coincidences in the details of these events includes (1) matching successors to the late President, both being Johnsons — Andrew and Lyndon — born 100 years apart in 1808 and 1908, and (2) matching assassins, John Wilkes Booth and Lee Harvey Oswald, also born 100 years apart in 1839 and 1939. (Rex Jory in the *Advertiser* newspaper of Adelaide, Australia, November 22, 1999).

Whereas, in "Unmeasure for Measure", we fitted the Nazi July figure of .3727 into a pattern of four Hitlerian or Nazi figures for the 1932 nation-wide elections, here, on the other hand, is apparent "resonance" from *seven* years before.

What, then, of the Hindenburg/electorate quotient for the March election (Round 1)? This time we reach a dead-end. Back to Round 2 and we now find the quotient of .4394 is close to the Nazi figure in the *March, 1933* Reichstag election : .4391.

We have now related both the July, 1932, and March, 1933 Reichstag elections (unfair as the latter was) to Hindenburg "shares" of the electorate. This leaves the November, 1932, Reichstag election, for which we need a correlate for the Nazi share of the votes, also, if possible, from the presidential data.

We recall that Hitler's share of the valid votes in Round 2 was (digitally) the same to five places as the total of all votes (including invalid). It turns out the November figure for the Nazis has the first four digits, 3309, near those of the mean total votes (including invalid) in all four rounds of the 1925 and 1932 presidential elections: 3306.

Also, the average votes total ("all votes") in the two 1932 presidential elections (rounds) has the first four digits, 3733, again near the Nazis' share (ratio) in July — .3727. So, of the four figures representing Hitler's or the Nazis' shares (proportions) in the elections of most interest to us, the national elections of 1932, only Hitler's share of the first presidential poll scarcely fits the pattern.

To be clear, links are evident between the *"total votes"* figure in one or more than one presidential polls (including both 1925 and 1932) and Hitler's and the Nazis' *proportions of valid votes* in at least three of the *1932* ballots.

Summary

Presidential election (Round 2), April 1925
    Total votes (millions) 30.57

Presidential election (Round 1), March, 1932
    Hitler (ratio of valid votes) .... .3012

Presidential election (Round 2), April, 1932
    Total votes (millions) 36.77
    Hitler (ratio of valid votes) .... .3677

Presidential election (Rounds 1 & 2), March, April, 1932
    Total votes (mean, millions) 37.33

Reichstag election July, 1932
    Nazi party (ratio of valid votes) .... .3727

Presidential election (Rounds 1 & 2), March, April, 1932
Presidential election (Rounds 1 & 2), March, April, 1925
    Total votes (mean, millions) 33.06

Reichstag election, November, 1932
    Nazi party (ratio of valid votes) .... .3309

p of correlations : low

We can see from this list how the correlate (presidential votes total) lags behind the current (Hitlerian or Nazi) valid votes ratio, catches up, then regresses as a moving average which includes previous "total votes" figures.

Does (to adapt Shakespeare) "the voting that men do live after them?"

There is a tide ...

Was the Nazi takeover inevitable? History is not science, where a single negative instance is sufficient to upset a theory (if a, then b). Identical circumstances, which might produce different outcomes, or be manipulated, do not occur in different societies or, sequentially, in the same society. You cannot step into the same river twice.

If inevitability cannot be *disproved*, neither, of course, can it be proved. Even in science it cannot be proved that (b) *always* follows (a); that (b) is inevitable. Most people would probably be content that the historical necessity of Nazism cannot be established.

Hitler himself, despite occasional doubts, believed it was his destiny to become the Führer of Germany. "I know I will not be President; I know I will be Chancellor ... I go the way that Providence dictates with the assurance of a sleepwalker."

The chroniclers of the Weimar Republic, for their part, have implicated various circumstances or persons in its collapse, for example, the economic crisis and the conservative advisers of the President (Bracher, pp. 169ff., Haffner, p. 153, Turner, 1997, pp. 164ff.)

From outside the compass of the normal came to the aid of Hitler according to Fest, the force of irrationality itself, with, in its train, the "five major elections, held largely by chance in the course of 1932, in which Hitler could employ his special brand of agitation" (p. 314).

The numeric profile of the Republic's last elections, which were cut from the same cloth as the 1925 presidential elections, brings an extra perspective to Hitler's rise to power.

If the "irrational" includes phenomena hardly due to chance, though not explicable by well-understood causes or principles, the foregoing evidence of quantisation or proportionality (though actually bordering on *rationality*, as *ratio* and *reason* are connected) adds weight to the suggestion of *irrationality*, in Fest's sense, as a "force" behind the scenes while the Weimar tragedy unfolded.

Recall that the number of Germans voting in presidential elections evolved during the first seven years of Hindenburg's presidency from (1925, Round 1) approximately 27.0 million, (digitally) near F5 = .269, to (1932, Round 2) approximately 36.8 million, (digitally) near F1 = .368 : from the smaller (complementary divisible) factor of e^{-1} to e^{1}.

And the Nazis' share of votes in Reichstag elections rose from base 0 (1920) to .373 (July, 1932), that is to just over e^{-1} (and votes total from 6.4 m in September, 1930, to 17.3 m in March, 1933, so increasing by a factor of approximately e).

And the proportion of votes for Hitler rose from (1932, Round 1) .301(?) to (1932, Round 2) .368, again approximately e^{-1}.

There is convergence of different measures at nearly the same sequence of digits, corresponding to e^{-1} .

An analogy is with the elaborate staging of an address by the Führer in beer hall or Nuremberg arena : the use of music, lighting, marching men, the whole Nazi ballyhoo (Bullock) — all to delay and accentuate Hitler's climactic entry.

Haffner refers to, but rejects a view put forward by English historians during WW2 that Hitler was "as it were, the predetermined product of the whole of German history" (p. 163). Here, we may think, is evidence that the seven year period between the election and re-election of Hindenburg as President — commencing from the death of Ebert immediately following Hitler's return to politics (when the rider has remounted, his saddler's work is done?) was pre-formed to contain the surge of support for the Führer to flood-tide level.[130]

The hand of "irrationality" is also apparent in the strange empathy or resonance between the Germans who voted a proportion of votes equivalent to $84^{-1/4}$ to the NSDAP on November 6, 1932, and the Americans who voted a proportion of votes equivalent to $84^{-1/8}$ to the Democrats on November 8, 1932. Neither time nor distance, it seems, is a barrier to this force.[131]

But the flood-tide of 1932 was a tide to nowhere. In his bid for the presidency Hitler had gained not even an ambiguous half-share of the votes (v) : v/2 but, with the crucial addition of a decimal point and shift of 2 from denominator to exponent, an unambiguous $.v^2$ of the votes. Though he had the largest party, Hitler had no automatic right under the constitution to become chancellor. The message of the numbers may be "Hitler in our hearts", but it is not "Hitler first in our hearts", not "Hitler for president", not "Hitler for chancellor".

This does not mean that providence, destiny, or fate did not intervene in the final phase before January 30, 1933, for example to fix the "chance" meeting between von Papen and a Cologne banker and Nazi sympathiser (Baron von Schröder), which led to the displacement of Schleicher from the Chancellorship, and Hitler's opportunity (Turner, p. 168).

Just as, years before, his failure as a revolutionary in the Munich *putsch* — when Scheubner-Richter received a fatal bullet which may have been aimed at the *upstart* leader — not, that is, Ludendorff — had first set Hitler on the legal path to power.

Perhaps Hitler *was* destiny's instrument for necessary change, if not destiny's dupe; what Hitler had to learn through bitter defeat and personal trauma was that destiny is the tool of no man.

---

[130] For comparison, valid vote totals in post-WW2 *Bundesrepublik* elections evolve smoothly through the region of F5 and F1.

[131] In a contemporary perspective this strange correlation might have been seen as a mark of solidarity of Nazism with a more general movement.

Innovation or Useless Information?

In a numeric approach, the first, essential step is *identification*. Data fitted to a numbers table are, in that sense, identified data. Knowing that a political party's tally of votes, (say) just below 30%, corresponds to $12^{-1/2}$ (.289) gives a new handle on that result. If another party has near $24^{-1/2}$ (.204), a pattern emerges based on numbers *as* numbers.

If, on the other hand, data are treated simply as points on the "number line", differentiated only by a certain number of percentage points up or down, any *internal* relation between them goes unnoticed. Then *external*, real-world factors — geographic, economic, social, etc. — fill the field of view, with loss of much potential information.

The numeric factor can be demonstrated in, apparently, any area often enough, with p low enough to validate its role beyond any doubt. What importance it loses by its on again-off again inconstancy it probably recoups from association with key events, record performances, or other extreme cases or limits (see other chapters for examples from cricket and baseball).

To return to our particular theme, election studies of the recent past (Hamilton, 1982, Childers, 1983) show movement away from the "centrist" position — that it was the German lower-middle class which supported the Nazis — to wider and more detailed research of the Nazi constituency, together with a relative discounting of "global" factors in general. A mass opinion change, manifested in a "realigning election" may not be the direct result of a big event, even where a suitable candidate is ready to hand, such as the economic catastrophe of the 1930s, which preceded Hitler's rise to power (Hamilton, pp. 5ff, 439–440).

Childers (1983) sought to identify the *Nazi voter* — "get a handle" on the Nazi constituency — by examining a combination of major "structural variables" for large urban and rural samples. For the urban sample (212 *Gemeinden* — towns and cities) there were 13 variables, including economic sector (industry, handicrafts, etc) and occupation status (blue collar, white collar ...). For the rural sample (266 *Kreise* — counties)[132] eight relevant variables were taken. The aim was to examine the relative effect of each variable on the National Socialist vote in

---

[132] 212 (towns), 266 (counties) resemble F11 and F5, with their factor : number relation. Cf. Chapter 9, "Resonance from a Captain's Knock".

Reichstag elections from 1924 to 1932 by means of a "multivariate regression analysis". The percentage of the total "variance" (a statistical measure of variability) in the N.S. vote in each election attributable to the structural variables taken together (given by the statistic r^2) was low for elections in the pre-depression period but at the apex of Nazi electoral success, July 1932, rose to 60% (urban) and 71% (rural). The low r^2 for pre-depression elections Childers relates to the party's then small constituency and considerable religious ("confessional") and social diversity (pp. 279–281).

The main point to note is that those who voted Nazi in the earlier elections, before 1928 or 1930, did not constitute a well-defined social aggregate — an identifiable sector of the electorate — but showed considerable diversity, whereas the party's later constituency had a more definite character or profile.

By contrast, such diversity can have been no bar to the cohesiveness we found in the sequence of proportions which the Nazi share of the vote in Reichstag elections before 1933 have to the party's share of the 1933 vote. These proportions, which correspond to tabled derivatives of e^{-1}, represent fixed amounts or quanta. In so seemingly unpromising circumstances[133] only some "global" *numerical* factor can surely account for this pattern.

When Hitler and Hindenburg came "head-to-head" in the 1932 presidential election, both drew scant satisfaction from the result. An irritant to Hindenburg was his heterogeneous constituency, which was below strength in right-wing supporters and included a large contingent of Socialist reinforcements. Its distribution was uneven, as was Hitler's — "a mile wide ... at critical points ... an inch deep". Yet the figures for the duo have a "global" symmetry, with one leading statistic (mean of valid and total votes) vouching for "Hitler in our hearts" and another (total electorate), "Hindenburg first in our hearts". (Cf. "The Unnecessary Election?") Here again we see social (real-world) diversity coupled with numerical unity or cohesiveness.

The "global structural factor" (in a literal sense) crucial to the Nazi success was the international economic depression following the 1929 Wall Street crash. This did not evoke a uniform political response but, for example, the election of a laissez faire Democrat

---

[133] Recall that the May and November, 1924, elections were contested by the Nazis as part of a coalition — an extra source of heterogeneity.

government by voters in the U.S., the election of a sequence of Labour, Conservative, and Liberal governments in the U.K., and the uplift of the Nazis to most favoured party in Germany (Hamilton, pp. 439–440).

Despite differing orientation, we found matching features in the careers of Roosevelt and Hitler and striking symmetry — a square root : square relation between their respective percentages of the vote (equivalent to $84^{-1/8}$ and $84^{-1/4}$) in the almost simultaneous elections (the German first by two days) which raised one to the highest office and briefly preceded the other's triumph.

One thing this trans-Atlantic correlation does is, in some sense, confirm the Nazi figure as an element in a pattern which spans several years as well as an ocean and is important enough to resummarise here.

In "Unmeasure for Measure" we found that the Nazi November, 1932, votes *total* was similar to D3 in our e-BR table and together with Hitler's or the Nazis' totals in the other three presidential or Reichstag elections of 1932 forms a pattern of e-BR with $p < .05$.

The same Nazi figure has a ratio to the Nazis' March, 1933, total similar to H11, while the May, 1924, figure has a ratio to that of March, 1933, similar to D15. These ratios, which, recall, apply to the first (May, 1924) and last (November, 1932) Reichstag elections prior to Nazi takeover, are exactly symmetrical in view of the make-up of the e-BR table.

The corresponding *proportion* of votes for the Nazis in November, 1932, is embedded in a multi-faceted pattern comprising the four nationwide elections of 1932. That proportion is = 3309, similar to $84^{-1/4}$ = .3303 (p near .10). The mean of the four proportions is .3431, similar to $72^{-1/4}$ = .3433 (p near .05).

The *sum* of the November figure and the first of the four, the .3019 of March is (to five decimal places) .63210, almost exactly $1-e^{-1}$ (F2 = .63212 to five decimal places). The p is conservatively estimated at below .01. Also, the April figure (Hitler's second round share of presidential votes), is almost the same as the complement of $1-e^{-1} = e^{-1}$.

In the indicated two-tier arrangement of the four 1932 proportions, the mean of the November and March figures approximates to π^{-1} and the mean of the April and July figures approximates to e^{-1}. This arrangement is consistent with the overall *sum* of 1.372512, extremely close to $2(e^{-1} + \pi^{-1})$, with difference of less than 1/10,000 (< .0001) from the correct figure = 1.372379.[134]

The November, 1932, Nazi proportion is also locked into a pattern not confined to the 1932 data but involving the 1925 presidential election data as well, that is the Reichstag election figure is similar to the overall mean total of all votes (including invalid votes) in the four rounds of the 1925 and 1932 presidential election taken together — if the overall mean is treated simply as a digit sequence and the Nazi proportion similarly. What makes this convincing is that Hitler's share of the valid votes in the April, 1932, presidential round, though a decimal fraction, has the first *five* digits the same as those for the total of all votes (including invalid votes) in this round, though this is a whole number.

Together with the "trans-Atlantic" correlation of the Nazis' November 1932 figure with the U.S. Democrats' figure, the evidence for the impact of the numeric factor on the Nazis' figure is compelling.

In the Weimar literature, the drop in support for the Nazis in November from the high point of July has been linked, for example, to Hitler's failure to support the government of von Papen, and his defence of the S. A. men charged with the murder of a Communist miner in the Potempa (Silesia) affair, followed by pragmatic Nazi support for the KPD inspired Berlin transport strike in the run-up to the election. (Stone, p. 52, McKenzie, pp. 277ff.)

However, from the evidence of the numbers the effect of these real-world factors was itself mediated by the numeric factor: that is, the *quantum* of the residual vote was not determined by real-world factors, assumed to produce their effect regardless of numbers as such.

If the effect of a real-world factor or combination of factors may have been fine-tuned or shaped by the numeric factor, it may be concluded that prior to investigation of the numerical features of a particular case, exactly what requires explanation remains partly unknown.

Other assumptions can be questioned. The concept of a voter taking his pick of the field in isolation from other voters, as if in a

---

[134] Mathematical note: π and e are exactly related by Euler's formula
$e^{\pi i} + 1 = 0$, where i is the imaginary number, the square root of minus 1.

vacuum, though possibly an essential "ideal voter" model, is incompatible with evidence of "coordination" on the national scale (however "communication" might be thought to occur).

Similarly; the "commonsense" view of political parties vying with one another in a scramble for votes stands in marked contrast to the November, 1932, Reichstag election results, which suggest less a free-for-all than a share-out — a harmony not found anywhere in the real world at the level of ordinary experience, let alone in Germany in 1932.

Finally, human freedom also seems at stake. We think of democratic elections as the opportunity for a people freely to choose their governors. But in the German Republic at the end of its tether in November, 1932, but still before the inauguration of the totalitarian state, "freedom" appears to take the form of conforming to a predetermined measure. In the case of the engine of change, the NSDAP, the measure (x) appears to be ironbound by the equation: $x = 2(\pi^{1} + e^{-1}) - (.301 + .368 + .373)$.[135]

References for Chapter 11

BRACHER, K. D., *The German dictatorship: the origins, structure, and effects of national socialism* (London: Weidenfeld and Nicolson, 1971).

BRÜNING, H. *Memoiren 1918–1934* (Stuttgart: Deutsche Verlags-Anstalt, 1970).

BULLOCK, A., *A study in tyranny**[136] (London: Odhams P., 1955).

BURDEN, H. T., *The Nuremberg party rallies: 1923–39* (London: Pall Mall P., 1967)

CHARMON, T., *The German home front: 1939–45* (New York: Philosophical Library, 1989).

CHILDERS, T., *The Nazi voter: the social foundations of fascism in Germany 1919–1933** (Chapel Hill, NC: Uni of North Carolina P., 1983).

DORPALEN, A., *Hindenburg and the Weimar republic* (Princeton: Princeton Uni. P., 1964).

FEST, J.C., *Hitler: a biography** (trans. R. Winston and C. Winston, London: Weidenfeld and Nicolson, 1987).

FISCHER, K. P., *Nazi Germany: a new history* (London: Constable, 1995).

---

[135] The figures in brackets corresponding to Hitler's shares of the presidential polls and the Nazi share of the July Reichstag election.

[136] Works mainly relied on for this chapter are marked *

FLOOD, C. B., *Hitler: the path to power* (London: Hamish Hamilton, 1989).

HAFFNER, S., *The meaning of Hitler* (London, Phoenix Grant, 1997).

KNOWLES, E. M. (Ed.), *The Oxford dictionary of phrase, saying, and quotation* (Oxford: Oxford Uni. P., 1997).

LANG, J. von, *Bormann: the man who manipulated Hitler* (trans. C. Armstrong and P. White; London: Weidenfeld and Nicolson, 1979).

LEE, S. J., *The Weimar republic** (London: Routledge, 1998).

LUDWIG, E., *Hindenburg and the saga of the German revolution* (London: William Heinemann, 1935).

McKENZIE, J.R.P., *Weimar Germany 1918–1933* (London: Blandford P., 1971)

MACKIE, T. T. and ROSE, R., *The international almanac of electoral history** (Washington DC: Congressional Quarterly, 1991).

MOMMSEN, H., *The rise and fall of Weimar democracy* (Chapel Hill, NC: ... 1996).

PATCH, W. L., Jnr., *Heinrich Brüning and the dissolution of the Weimar republic* (Cambridge: Cambridge Uni P., 1998).

SHIRER, W. L., *The rise and fall of the third Reich: a history of Nazi Germany** (London: Secker and Warburg, 1962).

SNYDER, L. L., *Hitler and Nazism* (New York: F. Watts, 1961).

STONE, N., *Hitler* (London: Coronet Books, 1989).

TOLAND, J., *Adolf Hitler* (New York: Ballantine Book, 1981).

TURNER, H. A., Jnr., *Hitler's thirty days to power: January, 1933* (London: ... , 1997).

WAGENER, O. (Ed. H. A. Turner, Jnr.), *Hitler: memoirs of a confidant* (trans. R. Hein, New Haven: Yale Uni. P., 1985).

WHEELER-BENNETT, J. W., *Hindenburg: the wooden titan** (London: Macmillan, 1967).

Green Quiz Question No. 11

If you found the right answer to Green Quiz Question No. 10, you'll have no problems with this one, 'cos Singapore's figure is just like the *square* of Montreal's.

What is the location of Singapore's figure in the table? Give the letter and column number.

How many hectares of P'n'G has Singapore got?

CHAPTER 12
HOME RUNS, STRANGE NUMERICS, AND FORM IN THE EVENT WORLD

About Numbers

Numbers as Barriers

IN ATHLETICS, swimming, etc., certain "marks" resemble barriers: a time out of reach (the four minute mile) or a crowd idol's record, which *must* not be broken ("Babe" Ruth's 714 career home runs — HRs). These particular "barriers" belong to history, but there is more to the Ruthian example than meets the eye, and 714 is our point of departure on a "mystery" tour of baseball. As our main interest is in the *numbers* of America's national pastime, a preliminary briefing re numbers is appropriate.

Numbers as Data and Numbers as Numbers

Just as air is a vital part of the environment, numbers are a vital part of data,[137] whether ball game statistics, experimental results in science, or the results of counting or measuring in a vast range of other areas of work or leisure. Data are valued for the *information* they contain which, like the nutrients in our food, is extracted by "crunching". But, unlike a course *al dente*, whose ingredients the diner recognises partly by the characteristic form of their resistance to grinding, the raw numbers pass through the blender anonymously.

In effect, numbers are treated as mere points on the number line — that imaginary line which stretches to infinity and has room for all the "real" numbers which have ever been, or can be. It is *data*, not *numbers*, which are brought into an average, or "analysis of variance", or an equation. Data, not numbers, are questioned as to

---

[137] Data. a handy term, almost always plural, for what is given; the evidence.

whether means are "significantly" (reliably) different, how "variance" is accounted for, or rate of change determined.

Identification of Numbers

What is lacking in all this is to check out the actual numbers at each stage before going on to the next. "Check out" means, first of all, *identify*.

Now, the data analyst must be rare who has no inkling of the differences which can exist between numbers, other than digit or decimal point differences: numbers can be odd or even, "rational" or "irrational", prime or (rarely) perfect, Fibonacci ... to name but a few kinds. Off our own route despite its name, a number can even belong to a *Ruth-Aaron* pair ... the list goes on.[138]

Yet the off-the-cuff response of a scientist, economist, or statistician to the suggestion that numbers be *identified* might well be — These *are* the numbers. These are our data. We *know* what the numbers are. Anonymous? You've got your terms mixed up, haven't you? It's people that are anonymous; a number is a number is a number.

To make things clear, identify is meant here in the following sense: to identify a number — any number — is to find the base or bases, of which there is some derivative which corresponds to that number. This is made easier by appropriate tables.

By Their Friends Shall We Know Them

The route which led this author to the conclusion that certain numbers crop up in data more often than is likely to happen by chance originated in some work on the reanalysis of published data from, mainly, experiments on human vigilance.[139] The "preferred" numbers belonged to three main groupings:
1. Fractions — proper, common (whole number) fractions (1/7, but not 8/7, and not 1.7/7.8) with denominator not more than 10 (≤ 10).
2. 12-based ratios (12-BR) — the series 12^{-1}, 24^{-1}, 36^{-1} ... (the reciprocals of 12, etc.).
3. *e*-based ratios (*e*-BR). The number *e* (2.718 approximately) is the base of "natural" logarithms. The bases in this table are

---

[138] We meet again with Ruth and Aaron frequently along the way; re Ruth-Aaron and other number types see Glossary.

[139] Richardson (1990, 1995).

mostly sequential factors of e^{-1} (the reciprocal of e). These are complementary pairs of *divisible* factors.

The systematic table made for each grouping includes roots/powers. "Roots" and "powers" are different ways of saying the same thing: 2 is the square root of 4 ($\sqrt{4} = 2$, as $2 \times 2 = 2^2 = 4$) or 2 is 4 to the power of one-half ($4^{1/2} = 2$). Instead of "power of", "index" or "exponent" can be used to refer to the superscribed 2 or 1/2. Where roots are concerned, here "root number" means the index, for example the 2 in a square root.

For (1) and (3) the roots or powers are in the series 2, 4, 8 ... , to which it would be useful to add 3, 6, 12 ... . These series comprise the root numbers / exponents which appear to be most "preferred". The 12-BR table includes consecutive powers in its range. Derivatives of other constants, such as the well-known *pi* might also be useful.

Data can be correlated with at least one of these tables[140] often enough and with probability (p) low enough to confirm the influence of an apparently universal, or near universal *numeric* factor.

The Numeric Factor

This includes the tendency for data to fit some number table or tables, together with typical relations among data, such as root : power or number : factor. It manifests in diverse areas.

The tables comprise decimal fractions less than 1 (< 1) but it is not only decimal fractions in this range which tend to resemble table numbers; the same applies to whole numbers (integers), if these are treated simply as digit sequences, and the table numbers similarly.[141] Such matchings are referred to as "trans-decimal" correlations.

Not unusually, a number can be equated with the mean of two adjacent entries in the size-ordered supplement to a basic table.[142]

Uses of the Numeric Factor

So ingrained is the "commonsense" idea that the numbers obtained by counting or measuring — in baseball, anything from home runs or the distance the ball travels to attendance at the

---

[140] Note: copies of the 12-BR, e-BR and fractions tables are included here as Appendixes A, B and C respectively. Experience suggests this is the most useful, though perhaps not most logical, order.

[141] This was first reported by Richardson (1995).

[142] Supplements follow tables as appended.

ballgame — are fully determined by "real" factors, that to suppose numbers have a mediatory, if not proactive role is seen as putting the cart before the horse, and the study of numbers is shrugged off as idle "numerology".

Yet it is easy to see that data which are related directly as powers, roots, etc, of each other, or can be fitted to the same table, to name only leading cases of numerical orderliness, cannot be completely accounted for (explained) by real factors as such (per se).[143]

"Real" factors in ballgames include talent, skill, fitness, morale, quality of opposition, the field, luck ... virtually the whole stock-in-trade of our typical sports writer or commentator.

Numerical effects of various kinds can, of course, come about by chance, but in many cases a "significance" test reasonably excludes chance as the cause.[144]

Evidence of a numeric factor should not be shied away from as a constraint on human freedom. The goal is to further the understanding of our world, including ballgames, and the numerical phenomena of baseball, which are about to be demonstrated by examples, need to be explained along with all the rest.

Areas on which the numeric factor impacts gain a new perspective, as when we trace the evolution of a key number — Aaron's HR total in the final period of his career is one example — through a table of numbers.

Unsuspected relations between baseball statistics for the same or different players or teams may be found.

Small differences between, for example, averages, which an ordinary "significance" test might adjudge within the range of random variation, may have the imprint of the numeric factor. This raises interesting questions for the theorist. (See the appendix to this chapter for examples.)

Most important, prediction must remain a possibility, where a regular pattern is recognised.

---

[143] That is, if the real factors are *continuous* in their effect.

[144] The probabilities (*p*) given here are based on binomial tests and represent the *p* of the particular effects occurring by chance. The *p* is not the absolute *p* of the numeric factor being involved, but relative to the particular table.

"Babe" Ruth's Home Runs Record

The extraordinary place of this record in the history of baseball[145] does not depend solely on its durability — from Ruth's retirement (1935) to Aaron's usurpation (1974) — but as much, or more on the personality of the "Babe". Leaving the identification of numbers for the moment, then, we turn to the identity of "Babe" Ruth. All aboard and "Fasten your safety belts!"

The "Babe"

Born on February 6, 1895, near the real and earnest waterfront of Baltimore in Maryland, George Herman Ruth received his familiar title as a rookie under the wing of Jack Dunn, owner-manager of the Baltimore Orioles.[146] The phenomenon who is better remembered as the star of the New York Yankees team has been characterised with fitting ebullience and flamboyancy by leading baseball historian, D. Honig. This is how Honig introduces the big hitter:

> If BABE RUTH had not been born it would have been impossible to invent him ... He was the greatest player on the greatest team in the greatest city. He was power. He was the Yankees. He was New York. He was baseball, [all of this] packaged into a booming, fun-loving perennially adolescent personality.

One Ruthian crowd pleaser (or teaser) when batting was to "call his shot". A possibly apocryphal story told by Honig concerns the 1932 World Series ...

The Yankees are pitted against the Chicago Cubs in Chicago. Only one strike remains in the 5th inning of Game 3, when a lemon insultingly rolls onto the plate, where stands the Babe.

He holds up two fingers, which some say point towards the bleachers, showing Rutheric readiness to engage in fruitful barter. If the question is a lemon, the answer has to be — the *apple*.[147]

And so Ruth's homeric response flies beyond the field of play into the lore of baseball, where it becomes part of the legend of "Babe" Ruth.

---

[145] Ruth's record of 60 HRs in one season (1927) is probably equally renowned.

[146] Oriole: a yellow-coloured passerine (perching bird) of the genus *Icterus.*

[147] Apple — baseball slang for the ball.

Ruth revolutionised a game which had previously set finesse above raw power. "He came crashing through baseball like a tidal wave across the placid face of a mountain lake."[148]

His "style of offense — the 'Big Bang' — brought to the 1920s 'Ruthomania'".[149]

The "Big Bang"

There is a blatant parallel between the Big Bang personified by the Babe (the Bambino, the Sultan of Swat) and the new cosmology then in the air, following the work of the Soviet meteorologist, Alexandr Friedmann and the Belgian cleric, Abbé Georges Lemaître, who independently showed that the universe might not be fixed size-wise but still expanding 10 or more billion years after the cosmic explosion — also the "Big Bang" — synonymous with its creation.

Comes the Hour, Comes the Man

Expansion in Twenties America was no theory but a roaring reality and "rushing along with the national energy was the world of sports", with Babe Ruth "the Hercules of all sport".[150] In a naming sense, which came first, the Big (Cosmic) Bang or the Big (Baseball) Bang, or whether these phenomena were named independently of each other, merits further investigation.

Babe Ruth's Home Runs Record Identified

Ruth's swag of 714 has the same digit sequence (same digits, same order) as 5/7ths = .714 to three decimal places. We can be reasonably sure of the fractional connection for a range of reasons, some of which are given now and others in what follows.

First off, it is surprising to find that Ruth's average *per game* (714/2503) is .2853, similar to 2/7ths = .2857.

---

148 Honig, p. 120, pp. 187ff.
149 Voigt (1983), p. 136.
150 Honig, pp. 120–121.

Going down the all-time (U.S. major leagues — ML) list,[151] we
have in places one to six:

Hank Aaron	755
"Babe" Ruth	714
Willie Mays	660
Frank Robinson	586
Harmon Killebrew	573
Reggie Jackson	563

From our fractions table (Appendix C) we note 573 is (always
in a digital sense) approximately *4/7*ths = .571 and 755 is near the
square root of .571 = .756.

Three of the six totals, then, come near 7-based ratios (7-BR —
see special table in Chapter 4: "The Great Globe Itself").

As the top three and next-to-top three totals have as medians
numbers similar to 5/7ths and 4/7ths respectively, what of the
means for the same groupings? They are 709.7 and 574.0. Despite
the shift away from our 7-BR, the values they imply for 7 (7.05
and 6.97) have the impressive mean of 7.01.

We need not stop there as the next *nine* continue the pattern,
except for a wobble half-way down. Grouped again in threes,
these are:

Mike Schmidt	548
Mickey Mantle	536
Jimmy Foxx	534
Willie McCovey	521
Ted Williams	521
Ernie Banks	512
Ed Mathews	512
Mel Ott	511
Eddie Murray	504

The group means are 539.3, 518.0, and 509.0. The correlates
are $6/7^4$ = .5398, (G5 = .5186 — see *e*-BR table at Appendix B),
and $5/7$ths^2 = .5102. The probability (*p*) of the now four 7-based
means is less than .05 by binomial test. The value for 7 implied by
these four is 7.006

---

[151] Source: *The 1999 ESPN Information Please Sports Almanac* (cut-off date
October 31, 1998), p. 126.

Moreover, five of the nine separate totals also resemble 7-BR, so that altogether 8/15 HR totals at the top of the table can be correlated with decimal fractions based on 7 ($p < .01$).

Wheels Within Wheels

Although Aaron is the U.S. ML leader, the world leader is Sadaharu Oh with 868 career HRs. If we top out the U.S. list with the Japanese baseball champion, cum martial arts practitioner, cum Zen philosopher, the first six become:

Sadaharu Oh	868
Hank Aaron	755
'Babe' Ruth	714
Willie Mays	660
Frank Robinson	586
Harmon Killebrew	573

From our fractions or 7-BR table, 868 approximates to $4/7^{1/4}$, the 4th root of 4/7ths = .869, so Killebrew, Aaron, and Oh form an orderly progression based on 4/7ths, with the root number or exponent changing by a factor of 2. These three numbers, together with Ruth's 5/7ths look-alike, imply for 7 a value of 7.01.

The means of the reformed first and second groups of three are 779.0 and 606.3, extremely close to $e^{-1/4}$ and $e^{-1/2}$, or, we can equally well say, the 4th and square roots of e^{-1}, the reciprocal of the natural log base, e (see H1 = .7788 and G1 = .6065 in the e-BR table). The values for e^{-1} implied by our means are .3683 and .3676, mean = .3679 = e^{-1} to four decimal places (see F1 in e-BR table and Fig. 12.1). As to the reason for these extraordinary relationships, chance, at any rate, is hardly a contender.[152]

---

[152] Not least extraordinary is the blending-in of the Japanese contribution. Oh's figures are from Sadaharu Oh and Falkner, 1984. Hickok, 1995, confirms Oh as the world leader. The possibility that other world players have career HR totals rivalling U.S. leaders cannot be excluded but would not be too damaging to our findings as the U.S. links with Japanese baseball are particularly close, eg, Aaron played (and won) a head-to-head HRs contest with Oh in Japan. Oh's rivalry with Aaron drove Oh's career until the American's retirement (Sadaharu Oh and Falkner, eg, p. 248).

There is also a strange parallel between the square root : square relation of Oh's to Aaron's figures and the similar relation between Roosevelt's Democratic party (presidential) and Hitler's Nazi party (Reichstag) votes, both in November 1932 (see Chapter 11, "The Last Elections of Weimar"),

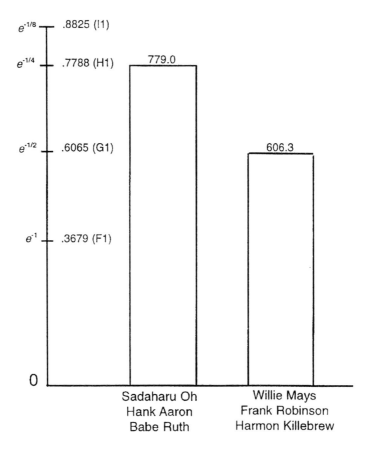

FIG 12.1. Career home run averages for two groups of leading players on an *e*-based ratio (*e*-BR) scale — an example of trans-decimal correlation with a table of numbers. Note: F1, G1 ... references to *e*-BR table (Appendix B).

which supports the relevance of an international aspect of the numeric factor.

After this auspicious start we wish to see how including Oh's figure is reflected in the subsequent reformed groups of three. This time a pattern extends over *five* "threes" and involves 12-based numbers (12-BR — see table at Appendix A) instead of 7- or e-BR , except for the middle group. The 15 players and their scores are:

Reggie Jackson	563
Mike Schmidt	548
Mickey Mantle	536
Jimmie Foxx	534
Willie McCovey	521
Ted Williams	521
Ernie Banks	512
Ed Mathews	512
Mel Ott	511
Eddie Murray	504
Lou Gehrig	493
Stan Musial	475
Willie Stargell	475
Dave Winfield	465
Mark McGuire	457

The means are 549.0, 525.3, 511.7. 490.7, and 465.7. The correlates are $36^{-1/6} = .5503$, $48^{-1/6} = .5246$, $5/7\text{ths}^2 = .5102$, $72^{-1/6} = .4903$, and $96^{-1/6} = .4673$. The value for 12 implied by the four "12-BR" is 12.06.

Whimpers

What pestle is to mortar, or matter is to anti-matter, the Big Bang is to the strike-out (SO), in which consists its counterpart or nemesis. The pitcher with the all-time ML record in SOs is Nolan Ryan with 5714, in our sense 4/7ths exactly to four decimal places. Recall Aaron's figure, 755, is near the square root of the same fraction, with $.755^2 = .5700$ and $.5714^{1/2} = .756$ approx.

So the same square : square root relation we found between Killebrew and Aaron's figures and between Aaron's and Oh's exists between Aaron's and Ryan's figures in their respective specialties.

The all-time SOs leader among pitchers active at end of 1998 season was Roger Clemens. His total was 3153. His rival in the HRs table is Mark McGuire with 457, also at end of 1998 season. Interestingly, these figures have a near $7:1$ ratio ($457/3153 = 6.899$).

The top of the SOs table[153] again shows structure based on trios. The first two trios are:

Nolan Ryan	5,714
Steve Carlton	4,136
Bert Blyleven	3,701
Tom Seaver	3,640
Don Sutton	3,574
Gaylord Perry	3,534

The means are 4517 and 3582.7. Their correlates are $24^{-1/4} = .4518$ and $60^{-1/4} = .3593$ ($p < .05$).

Summary of Evidence for Numeric Factor in Career HRs Table

In the all-time ML HR table, 8 of the top 15 figures are similar to derivatives of the number 7 ($p < .01$).

Four of the first five means of consecutive trios of totals also resemble 7-BR ($p < .05$).

A near square : square root relation links all-time HRs leader Aaron's figure with all-time SOs leader Ryan's.

A near $1:7$ relation links contemporary (active at end of 1998 season) HRs leader McGuire's total and contemporary SOs leader Clemens's.

Placing world record holder Oh's HRs total at the head of the ML table gives new trio means as follows: the first two almost exactly match the 4th and square roots of the reciprocal of e; four of the next five fit 6th roots of reciprocals of multiples of 12 in the range 1/36–1/96.

Although grouping could be carried out differently, it is clear that the individual totals are part of a larger structure.

[153] *The 1999 ESPN Information Please Sports Almanac*, p. 127.

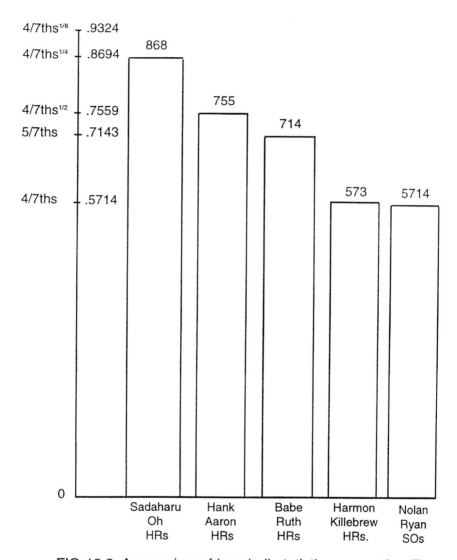

FIG 12.2. A new view of baseball statistics: proportionality ("form") based on the number 7 in the career figures for leaders in home runs (HRs, 4) and strike-outs (SOs, 1).

The 7-BR pattern made by the top individual career totals is as follows:

		5/7ths (.7143)	4/7ths (.5714)	
Sadaharu Oh	(HRs)		868	$.868^2 = .753$
Hank Aaron	(HRs)		755	$.755^2 = .570$
Babe Ruth	(HRs)	714		
Harmon Killebrew	(HRs)		573	
Nolan Ryan	(SOs)		5714	

The value for 7 implied by these five instances is 7.009 (see also Fig. 12.2). The home venue of the N.Y. Yankees and original showcase for the Big Bang, the Yankee Stadium, has been called "The house that Ruth built". Here, then, is another structure, for which Ruth laid the foundations. But, in a slightly more poetic vein, from what strange quarry came the stone to build it, and what strange conveyance carried it to the site?

The Numbers Behind the Numbers

The figures accredited to the all-time leaders in HRs are based on the explosive release of energy but themselves evolved over the years, generally about 20 for each player. *How* (numerical how) did each player's total arrive at its final value?

Aaron's Quest for the HRs Title

The player with the most HRs — or, as Honig tells it, "one-way bangers", "full crackers", or "irretrievables" — under his belt is baseball's equivalent of boxing's heavyweight title holder.

Henry Aaron ("Hammering Hank"; to his mates he was "Supe") of the Atlanta Braves almost took Ruth's title in 1973, instead ending the year with 713, one shy of parity.

With Ruth's divestiture imminent, the nation took sides. Opposition to the Aaronian takeover bid included "hate-mail", "death threats", and "bleak prophecies" from white supremacists.[154] Reminiscent of the (non-Aaronian) Nazi theme in Weimar Germany's 1932 presidential election, "Old man, you must step aside",[155] support for the challenger featured the "Bad Henry" pop song, with its raucous message, "Move over Babe"

---

[154] Honig, pp. 286–287. Note *.286* is 2/7ths to three decimal places.

[155] See Chapter 11, "The Last Elections of Weimar".

because Henry's coming "and he's swinging and he'll break the 714".[156]

This bleak (to some) prophecy was fulfilled on April 8, 1974, before 53,755[157] fans at Atlanta, when Honig's solo homer slammed into the left field bullpen.[158]

Did Aaron then lose motivation? A winding down is evident in his annual figures: 1973, 40; 1974, 20; 1975, 12; 1976, 10. Honig says, "It was only in his last two seasons that he began to struggle", but in a 7-BR frame the picture is more of a doddle cum tiptoe through a table,[159] as follows (Aaron's cumulative totals on the right):[160]

5/7ths	= .714		(1973) 713
2/7ths$^{1/4}$	= .731) mean .733	(1974) 733
6/7ths^2	= .735)	
6/7ths^2	= .735) mean .745	(1975) 745
4/7ths$^{1/2}$	= .756)	
4/7ths$^{1/2}$	= .756	(1976) 755

p of cumulative totals < .05.

The clincher is the apparent "drawing power" of 7 also in Aaron's early career:

4/7ths^4	= .107	(1957) 110
1/7th	= .143	(1958) 140
3/7ths^2	= .184	(1959) 179
3/7ths^2	= .184) mean .222	(1960) 219
5/7ths^4	= .260)	
5/7ths^4	= .260	(1961) 253

Note: 7-BR shown on left are again inclusive within their size-orderly range. Aaron's cumulative totals (right) have $p < .05$.

We can deduce from this that Aaron's 755 was not a one-off hit (almost) on a 7-BR, but had ample precedents.

To return to "the 714", how did this once barrier itself get to that figure?

---

[156] D. Q. Voigt (1983), p. *714* = Ruth's record!? Was this coincidence intended? Compare this and Honig's "286" (above) with two similar examples in "The Last Elections of Weimar".

[157] 53,755 hardly differs from $12^{-1/4} = .53728$. Also, the "755" is Aaron's career total.

[158] Voigt, p. 234.

[159] Including all 7-BR from .714(3) to .755(9).

[160] Aaron's annual figures from Wolff (Ed., 1993).

FIG 12.3. The "House" that Ruth Built: The architect and his builders.

The Evolution of Ruth's 714

Of many memorable seasons which added lustre to the Babe Ruth legend, that of 1923, the Yankees' first in their new home, the Yankee stadium cum "house that Ruth built", was most highly rated by himself. The Yankees topped the year out with their first World Series win (against the New York Giants), to which Ruth contributed 3 HRs and a Series batting average of *.368* (e^{-1} to 3 decimals).[161]

The other season most deserving of the No. 1 spot is surely 1927, with the magic 60 HRs by Ruth and the magic .714 (110/154 = 5/7ths exactly) win ratio for the Yankees, which was a team and league record. The coincidence of Ruth's other record, the 714 we are presently concerned with, and the (point) .714 did not escape the eye of Honig.[162]

---

[161] Garraty and Carnes (Eds., 1999).

[162] p. 162.

The end of Ruth's career in baseball came in 1934 when the Babe was overtaken by age.[163] On its journey to 714 his cumulative total[164] of homers generally stops off near 7-BR. Its second half goes like this (7-BR shown on left):

3/7ths	= .429)	mean .469 (1928)	470
5/7ths^2	= .510)		
5/7ths^2	= .510	(1929)	516
2/7ths$^{1/2}$	= .535		
6/7ths^4	= .540		
4/7ths	= .571	(1930)	565
1/7th$^{1/4}$	= .615	(1931)	611
3/7ths$^{1/2}$	= .655	(1932)	652
3/7ths$^{1/2}$	= .655)	mean .684 (1933)	686
5/7ths	= .714)		
5/7ths	= .714	(1934)	708
5/7ths	= .714	(1935)	714

p of cumulative totals = .01.

While we can be confident of an association between on the one hand, the number 7 and, on the other, Ruth's 714 and its evolution, our cumulative figures for 1929–1933 can also be plotted on the 12-BR table as a diagonal straight line close to $108^{-1/7}$, $96^{-1/8}$, $84^{-1/9}$, $72^{-1/10}$, and $60^{-1/11}$. If 1934 and 1935 had continued this trend, Ruth would have finished on ($36^{-1/13}$ = .759) 759 instead of 714, and would have exceeded Aaron's 755. And so to Oh.

Sadaharu Oh: On the Way to a World Record

Australia has its "Breaker" Morant, [165] but Japan has its triple breaker Sadaharu. As the No. 1 player of the Tokyo Giants, the foremost team of the Japanese major league, in successive years, 1975, 1976, and 1977, Oh passed the three leaders in the all-time U.S. ML HRs table, as follows (Oh's cumulative totals shown in brackets):

---

[163] Voigt, p. 157.

[164] Including all years with 3-figure totals. Source: Wolff (Ed., 1993)

[165] Harry Harbord Morant, Australian anti-hero, implicated in the murder of prisoners and executed by firing squad during the South African (Boer) War at the turn of the last century but one (1899–1902). The "Breaker" had been drover, horseman, versifier and balladist (see *The Australian Encyclopaedia*, 1996).

1975	Willie Mays	660	(667)
1976	Babe Ruth	714	(716)
1977	Hank Aaron	755	(766)

Although it appears that the flow of "one-way bangers" from Oh's bat would have been reduced in U.S. ML conditions, his mixed parentage — Japanese mother, Chinese father — brought countervailing discrimination. As a piece of pure speculation, was Sada's (as his brother knew him) trademark one-legged "flamingo" stance at the batting plate a symbolic repudiation of the "taint" of racial dualism? That Oh was highly competitively motivated is clear from his autobiography, but somehow he could apparently reconcile this with a non-adversarial attitude to his opponent during play.

On the eve of his conquest of Aaron's record "Oh-mania" surged in Japan. When autograph seekers besieged his family residence, Oh took a policeman's *bullhorn* to address the throng. It is interesting to recall that *Aaron's* record-breaking home run had gone into the left field *bullpen*. Resonance seems a key concept for the explanation of numeric phenomena, so here is speculative collateral support for the "resonance" between 755 (as $4/7$ths$^{1/2}$) and 868 (as $4/7$ths$^{1/4}$).

Oh's way to 868 is littered, particularly in its later stages, with, not 7-BR, but e-BR near-clones. His last 12 years show (alphanumeric references are to our e-BR table):[166]

1969	400	E2	=	.400
1970	447	G7	=	.443
1971	486	G4	=	.482
1972	534	E6	=	.534
1973	585	F3	=	.582
1974	634	F2	=	.632
1975	667	H7	=	.666
1976	716	H5	=	.720
1977	766	G3	=	.763
1978	805	?		
1979	838	I4	=	.833
1980	868	H3	=	.873

p of cumulative totals < .01.

Note: in this correlation, H3 replaces $4/7$ths$^{1/4}$ to represent Oh's final 868.

---

[166] Oh's annual figures from Oh and Falkner (1984).

Forward to the Past

Comparing the ways different HR leaders' figures accumulated, we may be struck by similarities, though whether these are "significant" is not always easy to determine. In one example, Aaron's tally for the early 1960s seems to reflect Ruth's for the early 1920s, so that, if Ruth's figure is raised to a certain power, the result is close to Aaron's 40 years on (subject to the usual changes in decimal point placement). Take 1920, at the end of which Ruth's career total stood at 103; then .103 to the power of 2/3 is .220, versus Aaron's 219 at end of 1960. For the next three years Aaron's figure can be recovered from Ruth's, with the modified exponent of 3/4. Thus, 1921, Ruth 162; $.162^{3/4} = .255$ approximately, similar to Aaron's 255. In 1924 another change, but still a simple relation: Ruth's 284, divided by Aaron's 366, treated as .366 and raised to the power of 1/4, gives *365* ($284/.366^{1/4} = .365$ approximately).

What is striking is, the averages for both players (Ruth, 1920–1929, Aaron, 1960–1969) are related as in the last (1924) example, as follows:

Ruth   305.1
Aaron   386.3, with $305.1/.3863^{1/4} = .387 \approx 386.3$.

"Standard deviation" (*S.D.*) is a measure of the average amount by which the individual instances (data) being averaged deviate (differ) from the average (mean).

In the present example the *S.D.* are:

Ruth   135.2
Aaron   111.3

These numbers almost exactly replicate the following *e*-BR :

The square of e^{-1} (e^{-2}, E1 in the table) = .1353.

The 4th power of the larger factor *of the larger factor* of e^{-1}
(D15 in the table) = .1114.

p of *SD* < .01.

It is as if Aaron in the 1960s was replaying Ruth's "golden years" — in a different key.

"Break This Rock Where'er You Will ..."[167]

We have now looked at (1) end-of-career totals for the leaders in HRs and SOs, (2) for Oh, Aaron and Ruth, totals cumulated to years prior to retirement, (3) *averaged* cumulative totals for Ruth's twenties and Aaron's sixties. Following up (3) we now average the totals type (2) for the trio Oh, Aaron and Ruth. The results again show "coincidences".

First, the means. These are as follows (including all years at end of which the total has three digits):

Oh   509.2
Aaron   457.1
Ruth   436.7

As for coincidences, 509.2 is similar to $5/7\text{ths}^2 = .5102$. Recall that Ruth's famous 714 corresponds to 5/7ths. So here is yet another square : square root relation in terms of 7-BR, but across different measures.

Then 436.7 is an almost exact replica of the important number $12^{-1/3} = .4368$. And $436.7/509.2 = .8576$, close to *6/7ths* $= .8571$. Here we go again ...

As with Ruth and Aaron's twenties and sixties the standard deviations (*S.D.*) are extremely close to table numbers, this time 12-BR, and show unmistakable "quantisation" or "proportionality" when compared to that table:

$24^{-1/2}$ $= .2041$) mean .2071   Ruth   207.1
$108^{-1/3}$ $= .2100$)
$108^{-1/3}$ $= .2100$) mean .2142   Aaron 214.1
$96^{-1/3}$ $= .2184$)
$84^{-1/3}$ $= .2283$
$72^{-1/3}$ $= .2404$ Oh   240.7

p of *S.D.* < .01

Note: 12-BR series reflects the size-ordered table supplement.

The cohesiveness of these figures (means and *S.D.*) flies in the face of differences in time: Ruth's career 1914–1935 vs. Aaron's from 1954 to 1976 and Oh's from 1958 to 1980; space, U.S. vs. Japan; and even collection criteria, U.S., to end of regular season,

---

[167] "... the name — remains there still" — the mint rock of memory, impregnated with a place name, as a souvenir.

excluding World Series, Oh's apparently including post-season games.[168]

Although Ruth's 207.1 and Aaron's 214.1 *S.D.* figures might probably be judged not "significantly" different,[169] viewed our way the yearly fluctuations in the build-up of their career totals were categorically distinct, with Ruth beating Aaron in the consistency stakes by a short head as well as Oh by a length.

A "Bifocal" Survey of Batting and Pitching Statistics

Home runs and strike-outs are only two, albeit peaks, of the batting and pitching landscape, whose other features take the total of all-time ML leaders' tables to about two dozen (30, including those for current players).

For these other performance kinds, ranging from the essential batter's average to the pitcher's percentage of wins, we take only the leader in each case.

Fortunately, we can combine a visit to the tables completed to end of 1995 season with one to those updated to 1998.[170] This will give us a bifocal or "diachronic" view of the data.

The 7-Connection

Most of the figures in our samples are 3- or 4-digit whole numbers; the rest, mainly decimal fractions. Around one-third of the cases from each sample could be correlated with numbers in our 7-BR table ($p = .01$ and $< .05$ for 1995 and 1998 respectively).

Interestingly, the statistic or category with the No. 1 spot in the sequence of tables,[171] batting averages, is itself headed by baseball legend, Ty Cobb, with .367, which we recognise as approximately $e^{-1} = .368$. Cobb's figure has been the mark since his retirement in 1928.

---

[168] Oh and Falkner, p. 8.

[169] An '*F*' test of variances (square of *S.D.*) gives $f = 1.19$, well below (on the wrong side of) the figure for $p = .05$.

[170] Sources: *The 1996 Information Please Sports Almanac*, pp. 133–136 and *The 1999 ESPN Information Please Sports Almanac*, pp. 125–128.

[171] These tables are not in alphabetical order.

"Meaningless" Averages

Averaging numbers as disparate as: for Batting, 2245 (Runs, Ty Cobb again), 14,053 (At Bats, Pete Rose), or .690 (Slugging Average, Babe Ruth), or for Pitching, .692 (Winning Percentage, Bob Caruthers), 7356.0 (Innings Pitched, Cy Young), or 505 (HRs allowed, Robin Roberts)[172] seems pointless twice over: these statistics are for different types of performance and the numbers are incommensurate, for example, thousands and fractions < 1. Let us, however, leave no stone unturned and take the average of the first three digits (the maximum available across the board), disregarding the decimal point, if any. We then have:

To end of 1995 season:

Batting	(mean of 17)	347.8[173]	approx. $24^{-1/3}$	= .3467
Pitching	(mean of 13)	380.3	approx $48^{-1/4}$	= .3799
	Mean	364.1	nearly e^{-1}	= .3679

To end of 1998 season:

Batting	(mean of 17)	346.9	approx. $24^{-1/3}$	= .3467
Pitching	(mean of 13)	388.2	?	
	Mean	367.6	approx. e^{-1}	= .3679

Mean of both means	365.8	approx. $7/9^4$	= .3660

We may note, particularly, the near clones of $24^{-1/3}$ and $48^{-1/4}$ at 1995 and e^{-1} at 1998,[174] also of $7/9^4$ across both years.

Puzzling as these averages are, it is evident they can hardly be due entirely to chance.

As America's "national pastime" is still a huge crowd-puller, let us now sojourn for a while on the spectator side of baseball. Our first numeric stop takes in the capacities of ballparks.

---

[172] Note: these figures apply to season's end, both 1995 and 1998.

[173] A decimal point has been inserted after the third digit.

[174] Compare the following pairing of test cricket win ratios at 1992 (see, eg, table in Chapter 1, "The Numbers Show"): England .348, W. Indies .385, Mean = .366, approx. e^{-1} (or $7/9^4$!). As the Showman said, "The same numbers keep repeating."

Going to the Game: the Potential Attendance

The New York Yankees

The Almanac[175] shows the Yankees' first home venue (from 1901 to 1902) was Baltimore's Oriole Park, then (from 1903 to 1912) it was Hilltop Park, New York, but there are no figures for these grounds. Then follow:

1913–1922	Polo Grounds II	38,000	$\approx 48^{-1/4} = .37992$
1923–1973	Yankee Stadium I	67,224	$\approx 24^{-1/8} = .67216$
1974–1975	Shea Stadium	55,101	$\approx 36^{-1/6} = .55032$
1976–	Yankee Stadium II	57,545	$\approx 84^{-1/8} = .57473$

The p of the correlations of ground capacities with our 12-BR table is below .01.

To add to previous evidence of the 7-connection in baseball, we find the start-up capacity of the restored Yankee Stadium (Mark II) in 1976 was 57,145, digitally just 2 more than 4/7ths = .57143 to five decimal places. We recall Ruth's HRs total was equivalent to 5/7ths (.714). Still further evidence concerns the average capacity of the home fields of all ML teams at 1995, as follows:

Average Capacity of all Major League Home Venues in 1995[176]

Mean (of 28)	51,069	approx. $5/7^2 = .51020$
Standard deviation (S.D.)	7,354	approx. $6/7^2 = .7349$
Coefficient of variation		
(C.V. = S.D./Mean)	.1440	approx. $1/7 = .1429$

$p < .01$.

The "Babe's" 714 seems to resonate in the capacity mean, as $.714^2 = .510$ close to 51069. By 1998, with the advent of the Tampa Bay Devil Rays and the Arizona Diamondbacks to the American and National leagues (and unaffected by the formerly American Milwaukee Brewers' switch to the Nationals), the total number of ballparks had increased to 30. The average capacity fell below 50,000 and correlates were no longer based on 7:

---

[175] *The 1996 Information Please Sports Almanac*, p. 541.
[176] *The 1996 Information Please Sports Almanac*, pp. 541–542.

Average Capacity In 1998[177]

Mean (of 30 incl. Kingdome[178])	49,424	≈ G16	= .49393
S.D.	6,668	≈ H7	= .6659
C.V.	.1350	≈ E1	= .1353

$p < .01$.

Mean of separate means for AL and NL:

(Incl. Kingdome)	49,270		
(sub'g SAFECO Field)	48.786		
Mean	49,028	≈ $72^{-1/6}$	= .49028

$p = .02$.

So much for the average number of spectators who could, theoretically, attend a game. What of the actual numbers?

Going to the Game: the Actual Attendance

However popular baseball remained, long-running disputes between players and owners hurt attendance, so that the 1995 season average per game fell from the previous year's 31,611 to 25,257, remarkably near $(1-e^{-1}$ or F2$)^3$ = .25258 ($p < .005$).

As a proportion of average *capacity* in 1995, attendance shows (25,257/51,069 =) .49457 ≈ F16 = .49393. Strangely, .49457 resembles the mean *capacity* in *1998*, which was, we recall, 49.424.[179]

In 1998 average attendance was back up to 29,388, the proportion to capacity being (29,388/49,424 =) .59461 ≈ mean of F3 and G1[180] = .59425.

If the alternative figure for capacity, based on the separate ML means is substituted, the ratio is 29,388/49,028 = .59941, nudging $60^{-1/8}$ = .59942 ($p = .002$).

Where major league games have their thousands of spectators, major league teams play host each *year* to millions of their or their opponents' fans. That the numeric factor is not stretched beyond breaking point by the change of scale is next seen.

---

[177] *The 1999 ESPN Information Please Sports Almanac*, pp. 557–559.

[178] The Kingdome: the venue of the Seattle Mariners till *1999*, when came a move to SAFECO Field.

[179] Including The Kingdome.

[180] The size-ordered supplement to Table B shows these numbers are together.

Popular Ballparks of 1998 Show 12-BR Were Just the Ticket

At least the top five totals of tickets sold in each (major) league for the 1998 regular season, taken together, can be fitted to our 12-BR table with $p < .01$. The NL figures match bases from 48 to 108, always to the power of -1/4, as follows:[181]

	(1,000s)		
Colorado	3789	$\approx 48^{-1/4}$	$= .3799$
Arizona	3603	$\approx 60^{-1/4}$	$= .3593$
Atlanta	3361	$\approx (72^{-1/4})$ Av.	$= .3368$
		$(84^{-1/4})$	
St. Louis	3195	$\approx 96^{-1/4}$	$= .3195$
Los Angeles	3089	$\approx 108^{-1/4}$	$= .3102$

A question:

Let us play advocate of the conventional wisdom — Why does support for these teams plus the AL five have any recognisable "form" at all? Why is ticket take-up not just the amorphous creation of star quality, or lack of it, winningness or losingness, prosperity or recession — of whatever is likely to boost or depress the entertainment market?

Then, why does this "form", stretching from coast to coast, Atlanta to L.A., manifest convincingly in terms of 12? (Why not 7 or e?) How can coordination of the 1,000s, 10,000s and 1,000,000s of individual decisions — to go, or not, to the game or (within the limits of the present evidence) to buy, or not buy a ticket — succeed so well that in 3/10 instances the difference from the correlate amounts to ≤ 500 tickets out of near or over 3 million, as follows:

St Louis	3,195,021	near $96^{-1/4}$	$= .3194715$	Difference = 306
Cleveland (AL)	3,467,299	near $24^{-1/3}$	$= .3466806$	Difference = 493
New York (AL)	2,949,734	near $132^{-1/4}$	$= .2950234$	Difference = 500

---

[181] Source: *The 1999 ESPN Information Please Sports Almanac*, p. 78.

Tangible forms — the giraffe neck, the bird nest — have much to do with function, but what possible function can be imagined for merely *numerical* forms (i.e., quanta). Why not che sera, sera, go as you please …?

We, at least, now make our way to that part of the record where are found traces of battles long past, from which, season by season, stepped forth the divisional champions,[182] led by the team with the highest winning percentage for each year in question.

Winningmost Win Ratios: Average For All Years Since 1969

In 1969 the major leagues were split into East and West divisions.

Unlike in test cricket, games in baseball are pressed to a conclusion: there are no draws. The percentage of wins is then simply wins/games x 100. At *1995* the 27 top annual win ratios since 1969[183] showed:

Mean (of 27)	.6319	$\approx F2$	= .6321
S.D.	.0264	$\approx C2$	= .0255
C.V.	.0418	$\approx 24^{-1}$	= .0417

At *1998* the updated figures were:[184]

Mean (of 30)	.6335	$\approx F2$	= .6321 as before
S.D.	.0285	$\approx E13$	= .0279
C.V.	.0450	$\approx E11$	= .0449

The mean of both means is .6327.

Both these averages include a figure for the problem year 1994. Because of the premature cancellation of the baseball season as a result of the players' strike, the record is devoid of official divisional champions for this year. If the 1994 (unofficial) figure of .649 is taken out, we have:

1995	Mean (of 26)	.6312	
1998	Mean (of 29)	.6329	
	Mean	.6321	$\approx F2 = .6321$

---

[182] Except, that is, for 1994 — see next section.

[183] Based on wins and games in *The 1996 Information Please Sports Almanac*, pp. 115–116.

[184] Based on wins and games in *The 1999 ESPN Information Please Sports Almanac*, pp. 107–108.

In view of the evident role of $1\text{-}e^{-1}$ (F2) in "fixing" the overall upper limit of the major league baseball winning percentage, it is interesting to recall the similar role of powers of this constant in test cricket (see Table 1 in Chapter 6, "Quantisation Effects in Test Cricket").

Postscript

Homeric Feats and Homeric Feet

The outstanding individual performances of 1998 in the HR department were those of Mark McGuire of the St. Louis Cardinals and Sammy Sosa of the Chicago Cubs. Both broke the record set by Roger Maris in *1961* of *61* annual (single season) HRs,[185] McGuire with a mighty 70 and Sosa with an immoderate 66.

Given McGuire wins on quantity, how do these incoclasts compare for quality, judged by average distance travelled by their missiles. The figures are (mean land feet):[186]

> Mark McGuire 418.5
>
> Sammy Sosa   404.8

Careful inspection of our 12-BR table size-ordered supplement shows the following segment accurately reflects the present contingencies:

$$(84^{-1/5}) \quad .4122 \quad \left.\vphantom{\begin{matrix}a\\b\end{matrix}}\right\} \text{ mean .4187}$$
$$(72^{-1/5}) \quad .4251$$
$$(96^{-1/5}) \quad .4014 \quad \left.\vphantom{\begin{matrix}a\\b\end{matrix}}\right\} \text{ mean .4048}$$
$$(36^{-1/4}) \quad .4082$$

The p of chance association of our means with this mixed bunch of numbers is 1/100 (.01). It seems McGuire wins out on quality too.

---

[185] Maris's breach of Ruth's record of 60 (set in 1927) came *13* years after Ruth's death and McGuire's demolition of Maris's record came *13* years after Maris's — an eerie sidelight on *7* as a factor in the ML HRs table (see C. Wachs, J. Bennett, and K. Lipscomb, "Inside the Numbers", in *The 1999 ESPN Information Please Sports Almanac*, p. 70.)

[186] Means calculated from data in *The 1999 ESPN Information Please Sports Almanac*, pp. *76–77!*

Discussion

Voice from the Past: You're no a mathematician?

Author: No, I'm interested in numbers.[187]

Voice from the Past: You couldna do tax?

Author: *You* said I was thorough — or was it slow?

Mainstream Scientist: A nice little exercise, but, of course, the whole thing has no scientific credibility whatsoever. You must start with some particular problem and review the literature; then frame your hypotheses and work out your experimental design — including what test to use and the confidence level — collect your random sample and test it for statistical significance, and then, from the results of this test, decide whether to accept or reject the null hypothesis and your alternative hypothesis — I'm sorry, but I can't see that you have done any of this.

Author: The problem is *general* — it's about the world. At the same time, it *is* particular — one aspect of the world. It's about the world as *number*. You see, the world is not quite the place we thought it was — neither the object world, nor the event world ...

During our little excursion we have been more prospectors than tourists — fossickers, if you like.[188] Our finds have not been gold or opal, but numbers — a kaleidoscope reflecting deeds of the great Babe Ruth, who *was* baseball, of other all-time leaders, top teams, and the rest. From the abundant evidence — and some of it has a probability of less than .01 — we establish that there *is* a numeric factor in baseball —

Mainstream Scientist: ... But don't you know that, if you are allowed to take reciprocals, powers, means, and so on, you can fit *any* number to *any* base, regardless of what it is. Your "preferred" numbers are just the numbers *you* prefer!

Author: No! Our tables originated from clues in published data. They reflect numerical outcomes in diverse areas — tests on numerous samples have shown this. It is *nature* which prefers these numbers, at least to numbers in general, drawn, let's say, from a barrel or out of the air ... Can't you see that applying tables to data is like putting a prism, or, if you prefer it, a diffraction grating in the path of light from some source to

---

[187] "Numbers on their own form only a tiny part of mathematics",
   "Mathematics is [*not*] mostly a matter of numbers." (Stewart, 1995, p. 31).
[188] Fossicker: in Australia, someone who searches for gold, etc., particularly in old workings or tailings.

produce a spectrum of colours? If the different frequencies weren't there in the light already, this wouldn't happen.

Voice from the Past: What like a physicist are you?

Author: I have the usual interest. A physicist once said, knowledge is less important in science than imagination.

Mainstream Scientist: You certainly have that! Everywhere you look there are ratios, or numbers of some kind. How can it be thought that the *same* numbers apply to experimental psychology, ball games, demography and politics — I'm thinking of your South Australian and Weimar material — not to mention the solar system?[189]

Author: Psychology —

Voice from the Past: Hrmmph!

Author: … is not a bad place to start. When I became interested in the problem of vigilance — the way critical signals can be missed or unforced errors occur — I thought *time* was of the essence. Vigilance is important for practical purposes like driving, but, as you know, it's in lab experiments that you find vigilance in its stripped-down form. Vigilance experiments use light flashes, sound pulses, and so on, for "critical" signals. These generally come at irregular times and aren't very different from the "background" or non-signal events. Repetition of "events" and "critical signals" of little or no intrinsic interest, despite their names, severely tests the observer's or monitor's ability to remain watchful. The result is that signals which are easy to discriminate at the start are often mistaken or missed, as time goes on. In a somewhat similar way, the batter in baseball or cricket may fail to detect the subtle hand movement which could betray the curve ball or "wrong 'un".

Various explanations have been put forward to account for the usual steep decline or "decrement" in performance early in a period of watch and continuation at a level below, or well below the maximum. One possible factor is *rhythm*. As you said, everywhere you look, you find ratios, and you can say the same about rhythms, whether it's the planets swinging round the sun, or the beating of a heart. Our own species depends on innumerable rhythms, with periods from ultra-short to circadian[190] or longer.

---

[189] See in following.

[190] Circadian: about a day

Time-of-day effects on efficiency are well known, but there are short-term rhythms — of a few minutes for example — which might affect any activity calling for continued attention, whether it's driving, playing a ball game, or watching for signals in a laboratory.

The first small investigation[191] I carried out concerned the average time lag between missed signals in vigilance experiments. I found evidence of a "periodicity" of 4–5 minutes, both in a sample of individual data available from one experiment and in group data from more than 100 other published experiments. That is, the distributions of average lag times tended to peak at 4–5 minutes and 8–9 minutes, with indications of a continuing "rhythmicity". As for the cause or mechanism, it seemed likely that the periodicity in the average lag time was a *resonance* effect of the bodily rhythm.

Voice from the Past: You're aye sure taking your time with it. What about baseba'?

Mainstream Scientist: Yes, what about baseball? Isn't it time you came down from your hobby-horse about vigilance?

The Showman: While you've been chewing the rag about mind games, I've been playing the numbers game; some figures here should interest you — they're from baseball —

Author: Hang on. The crowd at a sporting venue, which stands up and sits down, section by section, is performing the "Mexican wave" — a kind of resonance. We have verbal resonance, instant — no *gain* without *pain* — or, when *The Great Train Robbery* repeats likewise as "The Great *Pain* Robbery",[192] delayed. A note sounded on a violin is accompanied by harmonics[193] of the same note (overtones) and causes a nearby instrument (violin or, for example, piano with the dampers raised) to produce the same tone and overtones.

In other examples, two pendulum clocks, "communicating" via the board both are fixed to, beat in unison, as Huygens

---

[191] See Richardson (1985).

[192] Note: title of classic silent film of 1903, which became the popular name for the multi-million pound hold-up of a mail train in 1963 in England, and title of article in *Nursing Times* (U.K. journal) dated June 30, 1999.

[193] The "fundamental" note is the first harmonic; doubling the frequency gives the second harmonic, trebling, the third, etc. Notice that the bases in our 12-BR table follow a similar pattern (12, 24, 36 ...).

discovered.[194] One rhythmical process locks (or "entrains") on another, if their periods are similar or can adapt so they are in simple ratio. You have resonance in the orbital periods of planet Jupiter's Galilean satellites (named for their finder, Galileo Galilei) based on small integers — mainly 2 (on doubling). The system keeps returning to the same pattern and is harmonious and stable.

My interest in vigilance shifted to the percent or ratio of detections and of misses, and the ratio between these, that is, to the ratios as *numbers* — the "numbers of vigilance". The clue which set me fairly and squarely on the track of the numeric factor came from a *psychophysical* study by Watkins (1963). Watkins investigated six female observers' ability to detect visual signals in different noise conditions.[195]

When I came to work out each subject's overall ratio of errors to correct detections from the large number of training and experimental trials, then played around a little with the figures, I found they made a regular pattern based on 12 and 24. The correlates were: $24^{-1/4}$ (2), $12^{-1/4}$, $24^{-1/8}$, $12^{-1/8}$, and $24^{-1/16}$. As you can see, these changed each time, again by a factor of 2, either in the base or the exponent. The fit was inexact but close enough to give probability of chance below .01. It was this that convinced me of a numeric factor based on 12.

Here the number 2 has no obvious use comparable to returning the Jupiter satellites to the same configuration. There's no apparent way the subject (as organism) might benefit in terms of, for example, intra-organismic interference avoidance, from an *inter*-organismic effect.

Although it was those correlations which fired my interest in "12-BR", it turned out that, to appreciate the closer "harmony" which is actually embedded in these error-detection ratios, it is necessary to set the correlations temporarily aside. Then, with our ratios in order of increasing size, we have a list resembling that of the six top HR totals, in the reverse size order.[196] Instead of threes, we take pairs and divide the mean of the smallest pair (best performers) by the largest single ratio (the sixth). Strangely, this

---

[194] Christian Huygens, Dutch mathematician and scientist of the seventeenth century.

[195] See Richardson (1990); psychophysics is the study of the quantitative relation between physical stimuli and perception.

[196] The six ratios are .442, .454, .541, .677, .736, .828. Mean .613 (F9).

gives the *third* figure exactly to three decimal places. Unexpectedly, we find the mean of the middle pair, divided as before, gives the *fifth* figure no less exactly. Then the mean of the first two means (of pairs), divided by the mean of the third pair (worst performers), gives the *fourth* figure, with .001 difference only. Clearly, these numbers constitute a well orchestrated composition.

Mainstream Scientist: Doesn't this mean that your famous 12-BR were *not* nature's choice in this case?

Author: The 12-BR framework is there alright but it's as if, superimposed on it, there're these remarkably exact relationships, triangular in form, between sub-groups and single subjects, which suggest a complex resonance. Recall the resonance between Oh and Aaron and between the trio means. A better analogy is with the triangular effects in the Weimar figures, involving Hindenburg, the German electorate, and Hitler's and the Nazis' figures.[197]

As you know, ratio or proportion in, for example, size of objects or frequency of events, is a universal factor in perception: how we recognise people or things, or duly respond or act. Here, number is often inessential. Appreciation of harmonious or melodious intervals doesn't depend on mathematical knowledge of frequencies or their — again simple — relations. It's the same when high and low voices sing one octave apart — and maintain a 2 : 1 ratio of frequencies — as they naturally tend to do. You could think of this as a kind of selective resonance.

At least etymologically, *ratio* has to do, not with *number*, but with *reason*.[198] Numbers which we call *rational* can be expressed exactly as ratios of whole numbers and such ratios are important, as in the singer and satellite examples. But, of course, "rational" numbers, or the whole number ratios, have no monopoly of *reason*. Mightn't it be reasonable, then, for an observer or monitor as *organism* to respond, or correctly, respond, to only a *ratio* of signals — especially if these lack apparent survival, etc., value — whether the ratio is "rational" or not? — But this brings us back to resonance.

Mainstream Scientist: Aren't you just playing with words? Surely, the Jovian satellites don't keep to their pattern of orbital resonances from regard for rationality?

---

[197] See Chapter 11, The Last Elections of Weimar".
[198] The word *ratio* is from the Latin *rat*, from the Latin "to think" — *O. E. D.*

Author: I don't know. Many people, particularly scientists, including yourself, believe the universe is ruled by reason,[199] but we don't have to be like the Pythagoreans and expect it to be whole numbers all the way. Most of the "proportionality" I found in solar system data was based on "irrational" numbers — e-BR and 12-BR (powers of the bases, 12, 24, 36 …).[200]

At the same time, I did find whole number ratios, when I worked out overall averages for all the groups in another two large samples of published *vigilance* experiments. (These partly overlapped each other and my 1985 sample.) Detections averaged near 5/8ths and near 2/3rds. The shares of signals going to correct detections and misses were, therefore, 5 : 3 and 2 : 1[201] It's interesting to realise that the same simple ratios of sound frequencies produce the major sixth and octave in music.

The Watkins psychophysical data, averaged a different way, also gave small integer ratios — between the four main conditions of all training and experimental trials. The measure was again errors : detections, averaged from the ratios for individual subjects and put in increasing size order. The group averages could then be sequentially related as 3 : 4, 5 : 7, and 5 : 6. The p was below .05[202] Here small integers have a central role in contrast to the six individual ratios, both patterns representing group or sub-group effects.

Clearly, the role of the signal observer partly overlaps with that of the batter and as, I believe, the Showman has some interesting batting figures for us, it's now, "Over to the Showman!"

Voice from the Past: Och, that was heavy going, anyway. I'm glad you're finally getting back to baseba'.

---

[199] "The entire scientific enterprise is built upon the assumed rationality of nature" (Davies, 1993, p. 162).

[200] As an example from my paper "On the Importance of Identifying Numbers in Astronomical and Other Scientific Data", previously on web site http//inprint.flinders.edu.au/NRichardson/Numer.html, by courtesy of Flinders University of South Australia: synodic periods can be linked to e-BR as follows: Mercury 115.9 ≈ D3 = .1147; Venus 583.9 ≈ F3 = .5820; Mars 779.9 ≈ H1 = .7788, to mention only the inner planets (Note: synodic period is, roughly, number of Earth days until return of planet to same position relative to Earth and Sun.)

[201] Richardson (1995).

[202] Richardson (1990).

The Showman: Hrmmpf. I think you'll find these interesting, though I wouldn't swap you cricket for the Yankee game. Take your top 25 all-time batting averages — half a mo, baseball hasn't been going since the year dot; it's like the "World Series" — pushes the envelope a bit. As I was saying, take the top 25 batting averages, an' average *them*. Well, it comes to .34 something — never mind. Now, average instead the total "hits" by each player and the total "outs" (these have got to be "at bats" without a hit). Hits 'n' outs are like detections and misses in the serious mind game. Then, divide each player's hits by his outs an' work out the average hit : out ratio. The figures 'til the end of the 1995 baseball season (through 1995, as the Yanks say) go like this. (By the way, *S.D.* means standard deviation and *C.V.* means coefficient of variation. Never mind what *that* means; just try an' identify the numbers an' their relations):

Hits	2701.3	Outs	5204.5	Hits/Outs	.5191[203]
S.D.	631.7	*S.D.*	1187.5	*S.D.*	.0203
C.V.	.2339	*C.V.*	.2282	*C.V.*	.0392

You can test these bewdies[204] 'til the cows come home, but you'll never prove they're not different from chance. Take the square root of hits — make hits .27013 — an' you get .51974, an' isn't .51974 nearly the spittin' image of 52045 an' 5191 something? Fact is, you've got a 2 : 1 relation between outs 'n' hits — in *exponents*, if you shift the decimal points up front. It's like Aaron an' Oh, with the square root of 4/7ths an' the fourth root of the same again, except, this time, instead of fractions, it's *e*-BR — F5 an' G5 in your table. Don't expect to find the same thing every year, though. Come 1998, it's only the average hit : out ratio that hits you in the eye. That's because it's the same as the 1995 average, .5191.

Mainstream Scientist: This is most irregular. These figures should have been brought in earlier, before the discussion stage, or, better still, left out altogether, if they were not planned for at the design stage.

Voice From the Past: It's aye late to bring them in now.

Author: Can't you see, it's like the Weimar presidential election figures, where you had F5 and F1 digit sequences representing

---

[203] Average of players' ratios of hits to outs.
[204] *Bewdy*: Australian slang for *beauty*.

whole numbers. I mean the figures that were repeated in the U.S. presidential data?[205]

Mainstream Scientist: Baseball and politics in the same basket? 27 *hundred* hits and 27 *million* votes are supposed to be connected? How do you explain the difference of *four* orders of magnitude?

Author: Suppose the table number gives the *form* of the actual number, but not the order of magnitude? To put it another way, it doesn't fix the position of the decimal point?

The Showman: If you want an example from cricket, lovely cricket, there's Lance Gibbs's 27,000 something balls. That's like 10,000e, so there's four orders of magnitude there as well, difference, I mean. An' Gibbs's figure is part of a pattern, not a one off.[206]

Author: By the way, no one is suggesting our tables are the whole story. According to Frost and Prechter (1990), the place of honour goes to the *phi*[207] proportion, the Golden Ratio or Golden Mean, which is .618 approximately. The point is 1-.618 is .382, and .382 divided by .618 is .618.[208] Frost and Prechter refer to evidence of human preference for the *phi* proportion, as incorporated, for example, in the Golden Rectangle. The authors, whose main topic is the stock market, instance diverse areas where *phi* crops up, including physics and physiology. *Phi* is related to the Fibonacci series[209] as the limit of the ratio between adjacent Fibonacci numbers and the same authors also found empirical evidence of Fibonacci numbers themselves and of the ratios between them, including the ratios between non-adjacent Fibonacci numbers.

If you keep on factoring the reciprocal of e (.368), the larger complementary, divisible factor (we spoke of this before) also converges to .618, just like the ratio between adjacent Fibonacci numbers. Any number between 0 and 1, factored in this way, leads to the same figure. Of all the possible routes to .618, at least these two, adding Fibonacci numbers and sequentially factoring e^{-1}, then, generate bases with diverse applications. Still, our own evidence has mainly to do with 7, 12, and e.

---

[205] See Chapter 11, "The Last Elections of Weimar".
[206] See Table 3 in Chapter 6, "Quantisation Effects in Test Cricket".
[207] *Phi*: Greek letter, the 21st in the Greek alphabet.
[208] *Phi* is that number, whose *complement* is equal to its *square*.
[209] See Glossary.

The Showman: If it comes down to favourites, how about Phar Lap?[210] He was a winner: 51 races, 37 wins, and placed 5 times. Prize money? He set a new record, sir, for a neddy — that's a horse to you — bred in the jolly old British Empire, as it used to be called. His record, though, was an either-or affair, either —

Mainstream Scientist: Dubious tales of the turf; what next?

Voice from the Past: Mair procrastination, if you're asking me.

The Showman: ... £69,268 or £66,738, depending on which figure is the right one. It doesn't matter much, you can take your pick.[211] The previous record, held by an English horse called Isinglas, was £57,450.[212]

Take a good look at your 12-BR table and what do you see under 84 (that's 7 x 12, by the way) staring back at you but the same numbers, almost: $84^{-1/12}$, that's .6913; $84^{-1/11}$, that's .6684; an' $84^{-1/8}$, which is .5747.[213] So, if it comes to favourite *numbers* —

Mainstream Scientist: Seven times twelve; seven times twaddle! Sheer numerology; absolute humbug! —

The Showman: Maybe it is. It doesn't matter.; You can fit the same numbers to your *e*-base; the probability is .05. It's not likely to be chance —

Mainstream Scientist: ... The evidence for the perception and production of certain ratios is not in dispute, but surely you are not suggesting that baseball stars leave the game on purpose when their career home runs, or whatever, happen to have what you call a trans-decimal relation to some decimal fraction, or a "harmonious" proportion to a rival's figure?

Author: The players' own role in these effects is certainly intriguing. They *lived* their numbers while they were active and had to live *with* them after they stepped down. It's hard to believe our trio of Oh, Aaron, and Ruth left with no regrets for the

---

[210] Phar Lap: not a play on *Far Lap*, but Singhalese for *lightning*; champion New Zealand bred, Australian racehorse; winner of 1930 Melbourne Cup; died in mysterious circumstances in Mexico after winning Agua Caliente Cup.

[211] Which figure is correct depends on whether Phar Lap's prize money for winning his last race, the Agua Caliente Cup, was £10,313, the official figure, or £12,843, as per the ruling exchange rate (see Carter, 1971, p. 166.)

[212] De Lore (1983), p. 23.

[213] Recall that the U.S. Democrats' share of the presidential vote on November 8, 1932, was .5742 (see Chapter 11, "The Last Elections of Weimar).

"irretrievables" which might still have been theirs. Take *Ruth*, who was forced out of the major leagues when age caught up with him. In a sense, his 714 was over-determined: it didn't just equate with 5/7ths (.714 approximately), but with his team, the "Twenty-seven Yankees' " record win ratio for 1927 of also .714, in fact 5/7ths exactly. But there's a paradox because it's as if, at the same time as he was trying to head off retirement, he was pacing himself, if only subconsciously, so as to "freeze" time at "high twenty-seven".

Even before he broke Ruth's record, *Aaron* "equalised" another way by hitting 44 annual HRs, which he did *four* times, and 44 was *his* uniform number.[214] What Aaron may have had in his mind as a target, then, may well have been (714 + 44) 758.

Mainstream Scientist: Well, didn't he get 755, so he almost got there? Why not leave it at that, instead of dragging in special numbers like "lucky" seven? Remember Occam's razor.[215]

Author: He got close, but as a possible goal he missed out on this again complicates the player's attitude to his final score.

Oh is quite explicit in his book that he aimed at 900 career home runs. But 900 was just a number, not a rival's record. Yet the 868 he finished on is a lot nearer 900 than it is to Aaron's 755. Strange if motivation from the 755 just happened to run out when Oh had reached a secondary, "virtual" target in the "square root" of the same number.[216] At the same time, we have his tacit rejection of a sub-900 goal.

We spoke of our pattern of HR and SO numbers as another "house that Ruth built". What stands out is the *unity* of this fabric, how cohesive it is — paradoxically, the moreso when Oh's figure is included. Take the almost exact square root : square relation in *e*-BR between the top and next-to-top HR trios. How has contingency — if that is what it is — the Yankees' 5/7ths, Aaron's 44, Oh's rivalry with Aaron, the lure of 900, and what else besides, been turned to one constructive purpose — if that is what it is?

---

[214] Hickok (1995).

[215] William of Occam, English philosopher of the fourteenth century, held that the assumptions made to explain a fact should be kept to a minimum, hence "Occam's razor".

[216] Whether evidence exists of normal persons' sensitivity to proportions between numbers *in the abstract*, such as square : square root relations, is not known.

Nowhere does this problem seem better reflected than in classical Chinese philosophy, as presented by Needham (1956) in his massive work.[217] Needham shows there are important parallels between the Chinese and Pythagorean world views,[218] for example the concept of pre-existing harmony and the key role of numbers.

Chinese thinking was "coordinative", "associative", or "correlative". Cause and effect in our sense did not rule, but "inductance"; like affected like; things which "belonged to the same classes resonated with, or energised, each other."

Mainstream Scientist: Sympathetic magic; sheer superstition. Have you been reading Frazer?[219]

Author: Needham.[220] They used the analogy of the resonance between musical instruments, and, as we'll see, Sheldrake's approach is similar.

Mainstream Scientist: Oh, Sheldrake!

Author: Inductance or resonance meant the decline of one process was the cue for the rise of another of the same class. Take as an example of a possible reverse principle, Hitler's post-Landsberg return to the political scene and the death of Weimar Germany's "saddler" president, Friedrich Ebert, which immediately followed.[221] Also, Hitler's appointment as Chancellor on January 30, 1933, signifying democracy's failure, was followed on March 4, 1933 (*33* days later) by the inauguration as U.S. President of Democrat and champion of democracy, F. D. Roosevelt.[222]

Look at some other Chinese key words. They translate as "order", "pattern", "organism". The universe was a "hierarchy of parts and wholes suffused by a harmony of wills"; in Needham's metaphor, a "country dance", spontaneously ordered; a cosmic pattern, in which the seasons and celestial bodies all took their place. Things fitted so exactly that you could not insert a hair between them.[223] As for number, "Instead of the number

---

[217] Referred to by Prigogine and Stengers (1990), p. 48.

[218] See Chapter 3, "What-Was-His-Name with the Thingamy" re the Pythagoreans.

[219] J. G. Frazer, author of *The Golden Bough: a Study of Magic and Religion*.

[220] Quotations from Needham (1956) are from Vol. 2, pp. 382ff.

[221] Note: February 27, 1925, Hitler's refoundation of the NSDAP; February 28, 1925, Ebert's death.

[222] See Chapter 11, "The Last Elections of Weimar".

[223] Reminiscent of the "designer universe" view that the knob settings" — actual values — for physical constants like particle masses and field forces are critical for the existence of, at least, human, life (see Davies, 1992,

depending on the actual (empirical) plurality of the objects perceived or pictured, it is, on the contrary, the objects whose plurality is defined by receiving its form from a mystical number decided upon (as if in a prepared framework) beforehand."[224] Our common sense rebels against this apparent inversion of reality even if, at the same time, we may uncritically accept as an objective fact that, for example, the wonders of the ancient world numbered seven exactly, with no difference + or - of so much as one. Yet, if the word "mystical" is removed and the paradox restated as, a "plurality" receives its form from numbers *as* numbers — from "workhorse" numbers — this might well apply to, say, the capacities of the baseball parks which were at different times home to the New York Yankees.[225]

Mainstream Scientist: I recall that Needham takes a strong line against numerology. Doesn't he say that numerology is an "illusory realm", where numbers are "not the empirical and quantitative handmaid of natural phenomena, but the categorical 'damsel of Nuremberg' in which they have to be made to fit?" [226]

Author: Right. Take that table of the Chinese Taoists which goes from 1 to 9 x 9, then 8 x 9, 7 x 9, and so on, a bit like our 12-BR table in reverse, but this does not put ours on all fours with numerology of the Taoist variety. The reason is that we take reciprocals and powers and compare them with empirical data, but the Taoists went in for an apparently arbitrary, and certainly idiosyncratic logic to arrive at some alleged fact. For example: "8 x 9 makes 72", continues. "Here an even number follows after an odd one. Odd numbers govern time. Time governs the moon. The moon governs the horse. Therefore the horse has a gestation period of 11 months." [227]

---

pp. 198ff.) Terrestrially, a question mark hangs over the atmosphere: for example, too much oxygen (O_2) could set the world on fire (Davies, 1989, p. 132). Does the numerical pattern of relative abundancies by volume (see Chapter 4, "The Great Globe Itself") relate to the maintenance of atmospheric stability?

[224] In Needham, p. 287; attributed to A. Bergaigne.

[225] See in this chapter, "Going to the Game: the Potential Attendance".

[226] See Needham, p. 326. The Iron Maiden was an instrument of torture and execution in old Nuremberg, with face and bosom armed with sharp spikes to pierce a condemned prisoner through and through, as he was drawn by mechanical arms gradually into her iron embrace (Headlam, 1904, pp. 168–169).

[227] Needham, p. 271.

The Showman: 'Struth, the only thing that governed Phar Lap was when they nicked his marbles.

Mainstream Scientist: In this case they did get the period right.

Author: They did get the period right.[228] Of course, the Chinese notion of harmony, as far as it applies to human affairs, invites the question, what about hostility, rivalry, and so on? At a country dance, no less than in an Aussie Rules game,[229] competitiveness and bad blood find an outlet in at least the sneer, the jibe or the elbow without necessarily impeding the flow of action or "numbers".[230] It's tough, especially at the top, and numbers near the top of any list at all generally seem to have the most order. To take another example from physics, when water is heated from below, as it nears boiling point a dynamic structure of hexagonal "convection cells" may form. Such phenomena are termed "dissipative structures' — because they need an inflow of energy to sustain them — and are found in far-from-equilibrium conditions.[231]

For a different kind of analogy, suggestive of the same principle, we needn't go further than speech — yours or mine — which tends, as you know, to become rhythmical, when emotions run strong. Here's a literary example from Ruth's great contemporary and fellow American, Ernest Hemingway's story, "The Short Happy Life of Francis Macomber". It's set in Africa. Wannabe white hunter, Macomber, has disgraced himself by running away from his first lion, when it charged him. Now his wife Margaret, her last illusion shattered, is about to run away, from the *company*, before her tears engulf her: "*I wish it hadn't happened. Oh, I wish it hadn't happened*". [232] "It" is not just Frank's loss of nerve, but her own dalliance with professional hunter, Robert Wilson, we may suppose. The unravelling of this knot comes at "buff" time when *Margaret* shoots not the charging buffalo, but her husband dead. Was it an accident, or ...? Wilson, who has seen everything, opts for "or": "Why didn't you poison him? *That's what they do in England*," and "I'm through now ... *I was a little angry*." So, strong emotion, scalding tears or

---

[228] Note: not all periods are accurate, eg, the tiger: seven months, vs. the actual three months approximately.

[229] Aussie Rules: football code.

[230] Numbers": here, dance movements.

[231] Prigogine and Stengers, p. 143.

[232] Note the repetition of this important *seven*-syllable pattern.

simmering anger, find expression in the same rhythmical pattern — reduplicated to ensure its effect.[233]

In the far-from-equilibrium Weimar Republic of November, 1932, the German people voiced its support for the political parties presenting for election to the Reichstag. The parties' shares of votes were unmistakably related to 12-BR (see Chapter 11, "The Last Elections of Weimar") — another example of self-organisation in extreme conditions.

To return to baseball, the strong emotions aroused by the game might not only bring Ruthomania to the U.S. and Oh mania to Japan, but also contribute to our numerical patterns. As for the symmetrical home run and strike-out pattern, there is a remarkable reference by Oh to *shobu*, the "desperate and decisive" combat "between one strong batter and a strong opposing pitcher", which "bears with it the potential for victory or defeat for an entire team:.[234] Again, a "crunch" context for pattern.

The Showman: Don't forget cricket. Was there ever a series like the Bodyline? It was mayhem on the field, but look at the numbers[235] — they're a beaut set, as Paul used to say.[236]

Mainstream Scientist: Aren't you claiming correlations with table numbers for your Green Quiz figures? Extreme conditions don't apply to parks and gardens, surely?

The Showman: That's a different kettle of fish.

Author: Even if a tough-at-the-top factor kicks in at the top, there's no suggestion that it's only at the top that you get self-organisation. Paul Davies (1989) refers to the existence of "*self-organising* processes in every branch of science" (p. 87). Self-organisation is an aspect of nature's creativity and manifests at all levels of complexity, both when water freezes and crystals form and in the phenomenon of life. More especially, at the atomic

---

[233] Source: Ernest Hemingway, *The Snows of Kilimanjaro and other stories* (New York, Bantam Books, 1976).

[234] Oh and Falkner (1984), p. 252.

[235] See Chapter 9, "The Bodyline Series". For one comparison with the more "grass roots" level of the game, the overall proportion of wins at district cricket in South Australia during 119 years was not identifiable from the tables. (Data from D. Johnstone, personal communication, December 22, 1994.)

[236] Paul Keating as Treasurer (1983–1991) typically described the latest economic data as "a beautiful set of numbers".

level, *quantisation* means the energy is compartmentalised, that is, restricted to certain values and not allowed to vary in a *continuous* range. In a sense, what we have found is no more than an extension of this rule to the macroworld, though now with the reins only lightly held.

Don't forget that "discreteness" on the macro-scale *can* depend on *real* factors. For example, animal species appear to "cluster around definite rungs in an increasing ladder of sizes", according to their place in the food chain (Barrow, 1995, p. 68). In South Australia, hospital treatments and services are charged according to the "payment band" in which they fall, not the actual level of treatment,[237] though surely the payment band is related to the actual cost. This is not to say numerical effects — correlations with tables, etc. — may not add what we are calling quantisation or proportionality to discreteness in the same cases.

Mainstream Scientist: I'm glad you think real factors still operate in the real world.

Author: If only I knew where the real world begins, or ends. Even an orthodox scientist like yourself, Jeff, must have had the experience of meeting someone for the first time, then, in the next days, you meet again once, twice, perhaps three times — by chance. But is it chance, or isn't it as if your separate fates run side by side on parallel tracks, until these diverge, perhaps to come together again at some future time? Did the real world change transiently? Or only your personal world? As you'll recall, Kammerer investigated this type of event, which he termed "seriality".[238] By his "law of seriality" (*Gesetz der Serie*) there is a "lawful recurrence of the same or similar thing and events — a recurrence in time or space whereby the individual members in the sequence — as far as can be ascertained by careful analysis — are not connected by the same active cause".[239] It's like the Chinese idea of inductance and resonance, of like affecting like —

Mainstream Scientist: I'm still waiting for the evidence.

Voice From the Past: Aye, we're still waiting.

---

[237] Attributed to Dr. Armitage, Government Enterprises Minister, in *The Advertiser*, Adelaide, March 9, 1998, p. 7.

[238] Paul Kammerer, Austrian biologist of the early twentieth century, is chiefly remembered for his heterodoxical claim that acquired characteristics can be inherited.

[239] Kammerer (1919), p. 36 (in Koestler, 1974) translated by Koestler.

Author: The image is of Kammerer, in a public park or a passenger on the tram, noting each series of individuals with some common feature, or similarly equipped with umbrella or book. His "a-causal agency intrudes" by unknown means "into the causal order of things both in dramatic and trivial ways". Personal observation, at any rate, suggests that "seriality" is based on fact — whether you call it a law, conjecture, or what you please.

To return to our reality problem, physicists distinguish between *locality* and *non-locality*. A "local" event depends on local factors — an apple falls from a tree. A "non-local" event involves "action-at-a-distance". In the classic example, two particles which once interacted, then went their separate ways, remain a pair, or have the same "wave function". This is known from the correlated results of measurements performed or which can be predicted. "Quantum systems are fundamentally non-local." In its strong form, the hypothesis is, "the fate of any given particle whatsoever" ... "is inseparably linked to the fate of the cosmos as a whole ... because its very reality is interwoven with that of the rest of the universe." (Davies, 1989, pp. 176–177).

As, in principle, quantum effects apply to the macroworld, including the world of everyday experience, can true "locality" be anything but an idealisation of reality? Set against quantum "non-locality", seriality seems quite a bland notion. But what is now real? Is the chance meeting, which surpasses chance, a local, real event, or a local, real event with non-local "overtones", or, exceptionally, a local, *surreal* event?[240] But why should seriality be restricted to "stage-managing" the human drama, and not extend to the familiar clustering of associated numbers?

The Showman: Like Carlton, Collingwood, and Geelong.

Mainstream Scientist: What about Carlton, Collingwood, and Geelong?

The Showman: The A. F. L.[241] clubs of course. Their latest membership figures meet up in your 12-BR table under 60 and 72.

---

[240] The incredible reappearance of M. de Fontgibu each time plum pudding, a rarity in France, came the way of the poet and librettist, Emile Deschamps, might almost rate as surreal (see Inglis, 1990, p. 1).

[241] A. F. L.: Australian Football League.

Mainstream Scientist: I suppose these are some more of your marvellous correlations we're expected to clap our hands and go "Wow!" about?

The Showman: You're talking about probabilities of .05 or less, an' that's just the straight correlations, without the clustering — Collingwood and Geelong both on near enough 24,000 — 24,070 an' 24,064, if you want to be exact: only *six* between them. An' the cube root of a seventy-second (that's $72^{-1/3}$ to you, sir), .24037, to five decimals.[242]

Mainstream Scientist: I should think the Bulls, and so on —

The Showman: The Blues, the Magpies, an' the Cats.

Mainstream Scientist: ... Right ... balance their membership lists the same way they balance their books. The only difference is, instead of profit and loss, you have new members and ceased (or deceased) members. Your bottom line is just contingent on the actual changes. I don't accept for a moment that the memberships "received their pluralities" from an abstract number table.

If I see a $20 note on the ground, the chances are I will pick it up, and remember this incident at least for a day. If it's just an ordinary piece of plastic, I hardly notice it at all. If your interest is in coincidences — or favourite numbers — you are likely to notice these and easily persuade yourself they happen more often than can be by chance. Seek, and you will find.

Author: I see. The "comedy of life" clustering of passers-by, observed by Kammerer, might dramatise Rupert Sheldrake's theory of "formative causation" by "morphic resonance". Sheldrake's concern was with the problem of "morphogenesis"; how to understand the development to its adult forms of an embryo, or, for that matter, an atom. There are difficulties to do with differentiation, coordination, and so on, which we can, in principle, compare to our own problem of how aggregated events get numerical form. Sheldrake's theory is that form develops under the influence of previous systems of similar form. There is a "resonant effect of form upon form across space and time". Learned behaviour is also influenced by morphic resonance.[243]

---

[242] Source: *The Advertiser*, Adelaide, April 19, 2000. Note: all 16 A. F. L. club membership totals at April, 2000, can be fitted either to *e*-BR or to 12-BR; $p < .05$.

[243] Sheldrake (1995), pp. 98, 199.

According to Sheldrake, morphogenesis begins with a "morphogenetic germ" and associated "morphogenetic field", which contain the "virtual form" of the final system: "This field then orders events within its range of influence in such a way that the virtual form is actualised" (p. 79). Notice the obvious similarities with Chinese theory: for *inductance* (or resonance), we have resonance; for objects, whose plurality receives its form from a "mystical number decided upon (*as if in a prepared framework*) beforehand, we have a morphogenetic *field*.

There seems no reason why Sheldrake's theory, if valid, should not apply to numerical forms in both the object and, of particular relevance here, the event world. To return to our main example of the top HR totals, then, for morphogenetic germ we have, as the natural candidate, 5/7ths (.714), but, also, to take account of the trio means, the constant e. If human consciousness, including its deep layers, is added, we can speak of $4/7^{1/4}$ as a "virtual target" for Oh, in his post-retirement rivalry with Aaron, and one element to be coordinated with the pattern it's part of. How this might come about in terms of the theory involves the concept of hierarchy. Morphogenetic fields are hierarchically organised. A higher-level morphogenetic field restricts and patterns the "intrinsic indeterminateness" of the units within" (pp. 90–91).

Mainstream Scientist: Even if all this were true, which I do not concede for a moment, what difference does it make? You said the world is not what it's generally thought to be: what has changed?

Voice from the Past: The mills in these parts still grin' sma', but aye sure they still grin' unco slowly.

The Showman: It's still a great great one — if you don't weaken.

Author: Let's start with baseball —

Voice from the Past: —

Mainstream Scientist: —

The Showman: Why not?

Author: ... and, of course, what applies to baseball applies to cricket, and much else.

It's time to realise that, as well as the multitude of "real" factors which affect outcomes — whole numbers or decimals — there is this tendency for certain numbers to turn up more often than just the general run of numbers. Whether you call it the numeric factor or something else, the effect is the same. It's as if we were playing dice — and the dice were *loaded*.

On a world scale, we have, as well as "proportionality" in the world of objects — take again the pattern of relative abundances in the atmosphere by volume of nitrogen, oxygen, argon, and neon,[244] proportionality in the world of events. It's clear that the numbers obtained by counting or measuring are not nearly so free to roam within the limits of reasonable expectation as is generally believed, but are subject to previously unrecognised constraints. It follows that the numeric factor is applicable as a *formal element* in description and analysis.

Although absolute percentages, differences, and relative percentages are, and will likely remain handy tools, why shouldn't the "natural" numeric ratios also have a role? Instead of oxygen about 27% as abundant as nitrogen in the air, and so on, there is then your sequential *e*-BR pattern as a snapshot of the principal atmospheric gases, which makes *numeric* sense.[245] You may recall in this connection a recent news report of plants which were superficially (morphologically) distinct, but had closely related D.N.A. features. This suggested that D.N.A. could be applied as an alternative to form (morphology) as the basis for classification. The criterion would not be physical form.

Resonance means a score or other total impacts on other scores or totals: Ruth's 714 or Bradman's 270 in the third Test of the 1936–37 Ashes series[246] comes to mind. Evidence of this kind implies the possibility of an interpretation of "statistics" opposite to that by Leonard Koppett; "The word *statistic* suggests the word "static", and, in the real world, events are dynamic, not static", and "statistics are a by-product, not a cause".[247]

We need to put things in a wider perspective when we seek *causes*. To trace the *quantum* of votes won by the U.S. Democrats in the presidential election of November 1932, back to the Nazi figure in the Reichstag election, which took place two days before,[248] is by no means a "bridge too far".

---

[244] See Chapter 4, "The Great Globe Itself"

[245] See "Air, Thin Air" in Chapter 4, "The Great Globe Itself".

[246] See Chapter 9, "Resonance from a Captain's Knock".

[247] Koppett, 1991, p. 231.

[248] Recall that the Democratic and Nazi ratios were related as 8th and 4th roots of the base 84^{-1}. See "The Strangely Intertwined Careers of Hitler and Roosevelt" in Chapter 11, "The Last Elections of Weimar".

We can see a wider role for *mathematics* in shaping outcomes. This is to steer *ratios*, regardless of the nature of the objects or events — it might be the ratio of oxygen to nitrogen in the atmosphere or the ratio of the average total of hits to the average total of outs in baseball — towards "attracters" like F5 and G5 in our *e*-BR table. Paradoxically, the new role of mathematics is also to nudge whole number *totals* towards the *digit sequences of decimal fractions* derived from *e*, 7, 12, *pi*, or some other constant. Steer and nudge are, of course, metaphors for processes we may one day better understand.

Was mathematics discovered, or invented? is one of the constants of mathematical debate. From the perspective of our numbers tables, at least, where it is possible, time after time, to compare and correlate empirical data with the table entries, it seems obvious that the simple mathematics embodied in these tables reflects what is really out there.

"Out there" is a universe, whose vastness reduces us to insignificant specks, or is our place special? Another controversy of long standing. Are we, if not the raison d'être, at least the favoured ones? The biologist, Stuart Kauffman is in the forefront of those who argue that man is no accident but, as portrayed in his (1995) book title, is "at home in the universe". His view is that natural (Darwinian) selection does not act alone in evolution, but in conjunction with self-organisation, and the same general principles may govern the evolution of both biological forms and that of the products of human technology. As he puts it, "Tissues and terra-cotta may indeed evolve in similar ways" (p. 206).

What, then, of our evidence for a numeric factor, which applies both to the composition of Earth's atmosphere and the synodic periods — the number of days for return to the same alignment — of Earth's sister planets, and to the data for homo ludens — man the baseballer? Does not this evidence have a supporting role for man (or woman) "at home in the universe"?

Now, throwing caution to the winds, since, as previously indicated, mathematics is not my strength. I cannot help thinking the evidence of "proportionality, quantisation", or "discreteness" in data also has implications for ... the calculus — that mighty edifice known today (in no Freudian sense) as *analysis*.

Calculus, so to call it, and relying on the statements of others, has as its very basis the principle of *continuity*. A car which travels from A to B necessarily passes through all points in between and, in the course of doing so, if it accelerates from zero to 100 kph, it unarguably traverses a continuous range of velocities, missing none. Here, calculus is on safe ground in calculating whatever "derivative" or "integral" — I use these terms unadvisedly — may be thought appropriate to solve some related problem of practical importance, such as the braking distance applicable to a particular speed.

At the same time, it's clear that, in our earlier example of ticket sales to the top baseball venues for the 1998 season, continuity is *not* the name of the game. Recall the top five from each league taken together had $p < .01$ of correlation with our 12-BR — by chance.[249] The top five "Nationals" showed a dream fit to $48^{-1/4}$ to $108^{-1/4}$, giving at least a nod to each multiple of 12.

It follows that any conventional application of calculus in the form of (say, to be rash) a differential equation, which assumed continuously varying sales, depending on such "reals" as team performance, size of "catchment" area, and the rest, would simply and, with benefit of retrospection, be a mathematical, or "meta-mathematical" solecism.

References for Chapter 12

BARROW, J. D., *Pi in the sky: counting, thinking, and being* (Oxford: Clarendon, 1992).

BROWN, G. and MORRISON, M. (Eds.), *The 1999 ESPN Information Please Sports Almanac* (New York, 1998).

CARTER, I., *Phar Lap: the story of the big horse* (Melbourne: Lansdowne, 1971)

DAVIES, P. C. W., *The mind of God: science and the search for ultimate meaning* (Harmondsworth, Middx.: Penguin, 1993).

DAVIES, P.(C. W.), *The cosmic blueprint: new discoveries in nature's creative ability to organise the world* (New York: Simon and Schuster, 1989).

FROST, A. J. and PRECHTER, R. R., *Elliott wave principle: key to stock market profits* (Gainesville, Georgia: New Classics Library, 1990).

GARRATY, J. A. and CARNES, M. C. (Eds.), *American National Biography* (New York: Oxford Uni. Press, 1999).

GUILFORD, J. P. and FRUCHTER, B., *Fundamental statistics in psychology and education* (New York: McGraw-Hill, 1973).

HEADLAM, C., *The story of Nuremberg* (London: Dent, 1904).

---

[249] See "Popular Ballparks of 1998 …" in this chapter.

HICKOK, R., *A Who's Who of Sports Champions: their stories and records* (Boston and New York: Houghton Mifflin, 1995).

HONIG, D., *Baseball America: the heroes of the game and the times of their glory* (New York: Macmillan, 1985).

INGLIS, B., *Coincidence: a matter of chance — or synchronicity* (London: Hutchinson, 1990).

JEANS, Sir J., *Science and music* (Cambridge: Cambridge Uni. Press, 1953).

KAMMERER, P., *Das Gesetz der Serie* (Stuttgart – Berlin: Deutsche Verlags-Anstalt, 1919).

KAUFFMAN, S., *At home in the universe: the search for laws of self-organisation and complexity* (Harmondsworth, Middx.: Penguin, 1996).

KOESTLER, A., *The roots of coincidence* (London: Hutchinson, 1974).

KOPPETT, L., *The new thinking fan's guide to baseball* (New York: Simon and Schuster, 1991).

LANG, K. R., *Astrophysical data: planets and stars* (New York: Springer-Verlag, 1992).

De LORE, B., *Melbourne Cup winners* (Sydney: View Productions, 1983)

MACDOUGALL, T. (Ed.), *The Australian Encyclopaedia*, (Terrey Hills, N.S.W.: Australian Geographic, 1996).

MESEROLE, M. (Ed.), *The 1996 Information Please Sports Almanac* (Boston and New York: Houghton Mifflin, 1995).

NEEDHAM, J., *Science and civilization in China* (Vol. 2; London: Cambridge Uni. Press, 1956).

PRIGOGINE, I. and STENGERS, I., *Order out of chaos: man's new dialogue with nature* (London: Collins, 1990).

RICHARDSON, N., Vigilance as a table of numbers. *Perceptual and Motor Skills*, 80, 67–84 (1995).

RICHARDSON, N., Vigilance ratios implicate biological rhythms. *Perceptual and Motor Skills*, 70, 143–154 (1990).

RICHARDSON, N., Vigilance missed signals may have preferred average lags. *Perceptual and Motor Skills*, 61, 1083–1089 (1985).

SADAHARU OH and FALKNER, D., *Sadaharu Oh: a Zen way of baseball* (New York: Times Books, 1984).

SADOUL, G., Tr., MORRIS, P., *Dictionary of films* (Berkeley: Uni. of California, 1972).

SHELDRAKE, R., *A new science of life: the hypothesis of formative causation* (London: Harper & Collins, 1995).

STEWART, I., *Nature's numbers: discovering order and pattern in the universe* (London: Weidenfeld and Nicolson, 1995).

VOIGT, D. Q., *American baseball Vol. 2: from the commissioners to continental expansion* (University Park and London: Pennsylvania State Uni. Press, 1983).

WATKINS, W. H., Effect of certain noises upon detection of visual signals. Unpublished doctoral dissertation, Uni. Of Texas, 1963. (NTIS No. AD-294 582).

WOLFF, R. (Ed.), *The Baseball Encyclopedia: the complete and definitive record of major league baseball* (New York: Macmillan, 1993).

Appendix to Chapter 12

American and National Home Runners in League with Numbers Tables Raise Questions of Significance

After an "out of whack" 1997 the 1998 U.S. ML season proved bounteous in HRs.[250]

A numeric-factor-based approach shows this bounty was not indiscriminate in nature but was shared out between the major leagues, if not necessarily according to intrinsic merit (how is this to be judged?), at least according to tables of numbers.

Take the average number of homers tallied by each team. The figures are:

American League (AL)   178.5
National League   (NL)   160.3

The difference between these figures is not large and might in the normal way (of statistical reasoning) be due merely to "random" changes in relative fluency. Accepting this possibility, we can test it by an (in our sense non-numerical) "*t*-test", *t* being a statistic, whose calculated value is compared to a "*t* table" to arrive at the *p* of chance. The value of *t* in this case is .1329. For the 28 "degrees of freedom" involved (30 teams in both leagues, minus 2) the *p* is .1, twice the .05 level conventionally treated as "probably significant".

A quick check with our *e*-BR table shows the AL's 178.5 is an almost direct hit on E14 (.1784) and the NL's 160.3 differs

---

[250] See Brown and Morrison (Eds.), 1998. Baseball editor Karl Ravech calls 1998 the most prolific season for home runs and possibly the best ever season in the history of baseball.

little from D2 (.1597). The p of these correlations is less than 1/100 (< .01) by a binomial test.

If there are only two possibilities, chance or not, as the reason for the difference between our means being just the size it is or favouring the AL, it seems we must, at least, exclude chance.

Then the average number of runs each team's contribution to its league average differed from that average is given by the standard deviation (*S.D.*) statistic, readily obtained from any calculator with statistical functions. The *S.D.* are:

AL   40.71

NL   34.34

A conventional answer to the question, are these figures (statistically) different? is given by an F test,[251] which gives $F = 1.62$. This is well below the value required for p .05, that is, for "probable" significance.

In fact, our 12-BR table shows (point) .4071 and (point) .3434 come near or very near $36^{-1/4}$ and $72^{-1/4}$, with the numeric factor's characteristic 2 : 1 ratio of, in this case, bases. As the p of these correlations with this particular table is only .01, it seems we can be fairly sure there was a real (veridical) difference in variability, with the American teams leading in this measure as well as in number of HRs.

Glossary of Baseball Terms[252]

Apple: common slang term for the ball.

Average (Batting Average): ratio hits / at bats.

Big Bang: big hit, home run, power play.

Bleachers: the seats which are cheapest and furthest from the action at a ballpark.

Bullpen: warm-up enclosure for relief pitchers.

Defense: the team "in the field".

Home Run: a hit enabling the batter to touch all four bases in turn.

Hit: a hit ball which enables the batter to reach a base safely.

---

[251] Guilford and Fruchter (1973), pp. 224–225.

[252] Based mainly on P. Dickson, *The Dickson Baseball Dictionary* (New York, Facts on File, 1989).

Homer: home run.

Homeric: adjective.

Inning: fractional part (1/9th) of a game.

Major league (ML): one of the two U.S. major leagues: the American League and the National League.

Offense: the team "at bat".

Out: when the batter fails to reach first base while at bat.

Plate: short for home plate, the pentagonal slab of white rubber which serves as the batting base.

Ruth-Aaron numbers: see General Glossary.

Slugging Average: bases / at bats

Strike-out: the "outing" of a batter after three strikes.

World Series: "best-of-*seven* games" series played each October between the ML champions to decide the "world championship".

Green Quiz Question No. 12

There's only one city has a coathanger for a bridge an' a sweetheart of a harbour. S—'s figure matches up with an e-BR "product" (like the figure in Question No. 11, only different). If you know your table you'll know the product of each pair of factors comes in the column which follows the factors, so you have your groups of three columns.[253] In S—'s case, the factors are the factors of $1/e$.

What is the location of the product of these factors in the table (Appendix B). Give the letter and column number.

How many hectares of P'n'G has S— got, give or take one?

---

[253] Exception: the product of columns 1 and 2 is in column 4, whereas column 3 shows the *quotient* of columns 1 and 2.

CHAPTER 13
A FLIGHT OF THE IMAGINATION: REPRISE

Author: Do you remember, Jeff, at the Institute, there was that business that we thought at first was a genuine close encounter of the third kind? Then it was put about it was just a student prank — the people in the A.I.[254] department were implicated — and we believed *that*. Then you went on to become a fully-fledged scientist (and, I'm afraid, closed your mind to the faintest suggestion of unorthodoxy), while I ... I dropped out. But I always had, at the back of my mind, that there might be something in — how could I ever forget that name? — *Eeyip*'s garbled prattle about numbers, and tables ...

Then one day I came to take a closer look at the figures you had scribbled down for your proposed paper — "On the Mentality of a Visitor from Planet —", I think, was the title you had in mind for it — what hopes you had of early advancement![255] — but, of course, you dropped it like a hot brick, when it came out about the "hoax" ...

To cut a long story short, what really got me hooked on what you call numerology was the Eeyip affair. I could only think the A.I. people must have been feeding stats from the Almanack[256] into their computer and somehow hit on the right algorithm. I never did have a chance to confer with you after we went separate ways. Of course, Watkins (1963) came into it as well and, publicly at least, I've stuck to Watkins and kept Eeyip under wraps for discretion's sake.

Mainstream Scientist: Do you mean to say, you still believe in a little green man, with a computer instead of a brain, who came

---

[254] A.I.: artificial intelligence.

[255] The complete title of Jeff's ambitious paper was: "On the Mentality of a Visitor from the Planet — ; Types of Solecism Current Outside the Solar System; Towards a New Taxonomy of Unreason in Our Galaxy".

[256] *Wisden's Cricketers' Almanack.*

from Planet — ? — They'll be taking *you* away in the *green cart*[257]

Author: Yes, Jeff, it's what I was meaning to tell you — Eeyip is back, with new evidence from the magnum computers of Planet — [258]

Eeyip: Ee—yip!

Voice from the Past: He's aye sure taken his time about it.

Mainstream Scientist: The little — ![259]

The Showman: Odsbodikins!

Glossary[260]

Analysis of Variance: a method of investigating data by comparing variability between groups or sets with variability within the same groups or sets.

Base: a fixed number which can be raised to any power for some purpose.

Binomial test: a test based on the probabilities (*p*) of possible outcomes in terms of "successes" and "failures" where an event can either happen (a "success") or not (a "failure") in a number of different "trials".

Common fraction: also simple or vulgar fraction — in which both the numerator and denominator are whole numbers.

Complementary factor: here one of a pair of *divisible* factors which total 1.

Continuous: describes a variable, eg, temperature, which can take any value within its appropriate range.

Correlation: association.

Data: or "raw" data — especially a collection of numbers.

Denominator: the lower part of a fraction.

Digit: numeral.

---

[257] *Green cart*: Australian colloquialism for conveyance used to take the insane to the mental institution.

[258] Name withheld, by request.

[259] Expletive deleted.

[260] Follows mainly K. Klaebe, *Dictionary of Mathematics* (North Ryde, NSW: Harcourt Brace Jovanovich, 1986) and W. and T. A. Millington, *Dictionary of Mathematics* (London, Cassell, 1972).

Empirical: from observation or experiment.

Exponent: index, eg, the "2" in x^2.

e: a mathematical constant = 2.7183 approximately. Is an "irrational" number, ie, cannot be expressed exactly as the ratio of whole numbers. Approximated by the function $(1 + 1/x)^x$, where x is a very large number. Is the base of "natural" logarithms.

e-based ratios: derivatives of *e*; here mainly sequential factors of e^{-1}, together with roots and powers of these.

Fibonacci series: the series of whole numbers 1, 1, 2, 3, 5, 8, 13 ... , where each number is the sum of the two preceding numbers.

Integer: whole number.

Irrational number: one which cannot be expressed as the ratio of two integers.

Macroworld, macroscale: that of ordinary experience, direct or indirect.

Mark: standard.

Mean: average.

Median: the middle number in a size-ordered collection or group of numbers.

Microworld, microscale: the atomic or sub-atomic world or scale.

Number-line: an infinite line on which numbers may be represented on both sides of a zero point.

Numerator: the upper part of a fraction.

Numerics: here means understanding numbers by identifying them as particular derivatives of particular bases and sorting out the relationships between them or the patterns they form.

Numerology: study of the hidden meaning of numbers.

Perfect number: a prime number which equals the sum of its divisors (factors), including 1.

pi: the Greek letter π; expresses the relation between the diameter of any circle and its circumference.

Poisson test: used instead of a binomial test when the probability of a success $[p(x)] > .10$.

Prime number or prime: an integer which has no integer divisor except itself and 1.

Product: result of multiplying one number by another.

Proper fraction: where the numerator is smaller than ($<$) the denominator.

Proportionality: here, the tendency for empirical quantities to be related in simple ways (eg, as square root : square) or, less directly, as derivatives of the same base (12, e, ...)

Psychophysics: investigates the quantitative relation between physical stimuli and perception.

Quantisation: by analogy with an atom which can take only certain, discrete energy values, not any value in a continuous range of values, *quantisation* is used here for the tendency of empirical quantities in the macroworld to parallel discrete numbers from tables.

Quotient: result of dividing one number by another.

Rational number: one which can be expressed as the ratio of two integers.

Real number: includes whole numbers and fractions. Exception: "imaginary" numbers (used in maths).

Reciprocal: the result of dividing a number into 1. Mathematically, raising a number to the power of minus 1, eg, the reciprocal of x is x^{-1}.

Root number: here, index, eg, in "the 4th root of 1/12", the root number is 4.

Ruth-Aaron numbers: pairs of consecutive integers, like Ruth's 714 (career HRs) and Aaron's record-breaking 715 (as of April 8, 1974), where the sum of the prime factors of one number is equal to that of the other. 714 and 715 have the unique additional property that their product is equal to the product of the first *seven* primes (2, 3, 5, 7, 11, 13, 17). (See "Home Runs, Strange Numerics, and Form in the Event World" and Hoffman, 1999, pp. 179ff..)

Sequential factor (of e^{-1}): one of a pair of complementary, divisible factors of e^{-1}, or one of a pair of complementary, divisible factors *of a factor* of e^{-1}, etc.

Significant: when used in a statistical sense, not due to chance variation.

Symbols: < smaller than, > larger than, ≤ equal to or less than, ≥ equal to or more than, ≈ approximately equal to.

Synchronicity: co-occurrence of events, which are meaningfully, but not causally, related.

Synodic period: of a planet, the time between the return of the same straight-line pattern composed by the Sun, the Earth, and another planet; usually given in Earth days.

Trans-decimal correlation: a whole number matches a decimal fraction except for the decimal point.

12-based numbers: derivatives of 12; the series 12^{-1}, 24^{-1}, 36^{-1} ... together with various powers of these bases.

Variable: whatever can take different values, as in ball-games, the speed of the ball, or a player's batting average.

Variance: a measure of the average amount the individual values in a collection or set of values vary from the mean of the set.

Zen: a school of Buddhism.

Answers to Green Quiz [261]

1. Kuala Lumpur (134), E1 = .135
2. Barcelona (271), London (267), F5 = .269
3. Toronto (160), D2 = .160
4. Hamburg (81), C6 = .082.
5. Tokyo (333), E15 = .334
6. Milan (112), D15 = .111
7. Melbourne (463), D18 = .464
8. Brisbane (216), C18 = .215
9. Copenhagen (376), E9 = .375
10. Montreal (380), G19 = .380
11. Singapore (144), F19 = .144
12 Sydney (198), F7 = .197

---

[261] Source: *The Advertiser*, Adelaide, 20.10.98. Note: *p* of all 14 P'n'G figures with 3 digits (including as "successes" all those in the Green Quiz except No. 4) < .01 by binomial test.

APPENDIX A

Part 1. Table of Ratios Based on 12 and Multiples of 12
(12-Based Ratios:12-BR)

Base (b)	12	24	36	48	60	72
b^{-1}	.0833	.0417	.0278	.0208	.0167	.0139
$b^{-1/2}$	.2887	.2041	.1667	.1443	.1291	.1179
$b^{-1/3}$	.4368	.3467	.3029	.2752	.2554	.2404
$b^{-1/4}$	.5373	.4518	.4082	.3799	.3593	.3433
$b^{-1/5}$	.6084	.5296	.4884	.4611	.4409	.4251
$b^{-1/6}$	.6609	.5888	.5503	.5246	.5054	.4903
$b^{-1/7}$	.7012	.6351	.5993	.5752	.5572	.5428
$b^{-1/8}$	.7330	.6722	.6389	.6164	.5994	.5859
$b^{-1/9}$	.7587	.7025	.6715	.6504	.6345	.6218
$b^{-1/10}$	.7800	.7277	.6988	.6790	.6640	.6520
$b^{-1/11}$	.7978	.7491	.7220	.7033	.6892	.6779
$b^{-1/12}$	.8130	.7673	.7418	.7243	.7109	.7002
$b^{-1/13}$	.8260	.7831	.7591	.7425	.7298	.7197
$b^{-1/14}$	.8374	.7969	.7742	.7584	.7464	.7368
$b^{-1/15}$	.8473	.8091	.7875	.7725	.7611	.7519
$b^{-1/16}$	.8562	.8199	.7993	.7851	.7742	.7654
$b^{-1/17}$	.8640	.8295	.8099	.7963	.7860	.7776
$b^{-1/18}$	.8711	.8381	.8195	.8065	.7966	.7885
$b^{-1/19}$	.8774	.8460	.8281	.8157	.8061	.7984
$b^{-1/20}$	.8832	.8531	.8360	.8240	.8149	.8075
$b^{-1/21}$	.8884	.8596	.8431	.8317	.8229	.8157
$b^{-1/22}$	.8932	.8655	.8497	.8386	.8302	.8233
$b^{-1/23}$	.8976	.8709	.8557	.8451	.8369	.8303
$b^{-1/24}$	.9016	.8760	.8613	.8510	.8432	.8368
$b^{-1/25}$	.9054	.8806	.8665	.8565	.8489	.8428
$b^{-1/26}$	.9089	.8849	.8712	.8617	.8543	.8483
$b^{-1/27}$	.9121	.8890	.8757	.8664	.8593	.8535
$b^{-1/28}$	.9151	.8927	.8799	.8709	.8640	.8584
$b^{-1/29}$	.9179	.8962	.8838	.8750	.8683	.8629
$b^{-1/30}$	.9205	.8995	.8874	.8789	.8724	.8671
$b^{-1/31}$	.9230	.9026	.8908	.8826	.8763	.8711
$b^{-1/32}$	.9253	.9055	.8941	.8861	.8799	.8749
$b^{-1/48}$	.9495	.9395	.9281	.9225	.9182	.9148
$b^{-1/64}$	.9619	.9516	.9455	.9413	.9380	.9354
$b^{-1/96}$	.9744	.9674	.9634	.9605	.9582	.9564

-1/128 ·9808. ·9755 9724 ·9702
-1/192 ·9871· ·9836· -9815·
-1/256 ·9903· ·9877· ·9861·
-1/384 ·9935· 9918· ·9907·

APPENDIX A

Part 2 *Continued*

.6137	$(132^{-1/10})$	.6976	$(108^{-1/13})$	.7464	$(60^{-1/14})$
.6164	$(48^{-1/8})$	.6988	$(36^{-1/10})$	.7465	$(144^{-1/17})$
.6196	$(120^{-1/10})$	.7002	$(72^{-1/12})$	.7491	$(24^{-1/11})$
.6218	$(72^{-1/9})$	.7012	$(12^{-1/7})$	.7503	$(132^{-1/17})$
.6261	$(108^{-1/10})$	.7012	$(144^{-1/14})$	.7518	$(96^{-1/16})$
.6335	$(96^{-1/10})$	.7025	$(24^{-1/9})$	.7519	$(72^{-1/15})$
.6345	$(60^{-1/9})$	.7033	$(48^{-1/11})$	.7546	$(120^{-1/17})$
.6351	$(24^{-1/7})$	.7039	$(96^{-1/13})$	.7581	$(84^{-1/16})$
.6365	$(144^{-1/11})$	.7056	$(132^{-1/14})$	.7584	$(48^{-1/14})$
.6389	$(36^{-1/8})$	.7104	$(120^{-1/14})$	.7587	$(12^{-1/9})$
.6415	$(132^{-1/11})$	.7109	$(60^{-1/12})$	.7587	$(144^{-1/18})$
.6421	$(84^{-1/10})$	.7112	$(84^{-1/13})$	.7591	$(36^{-1/13})$
.6471	$(120^{-1/11})$	.7157	$(108^{-1/14})$	.7593	$(108^{-1/17})$
.6504	$(48^{-1/9})$	.7180	$(144^{-1/15})$	.7611	$(60^{-1/15})$
.6520	$(72^{-1/10})$	.7197	$(72^{-1/13})$	.7624	$(132^{-1/18})$
.6533	$(108^{-1/11})$	.7218	$(96^{-1/14})$	.7645	$(96^{-1/17})$
.6604	$(96^{-1/11})$	.7220	$(36^{-1/11})$	.7654	$(72^{-1/16})$
.6609	$(12^{-1/6})$	.7222	$(132^{-1/15})$	.7665	$(120^{-1/18})$
.6609	$(144^{-1/12})$	.7243	$(48^{-1/12})$	.7673	$(24^{-1/12})$
.6640	$(60^{-1/10})$	.7268	$(120^{-1/15})$	.7698	$(144^{-1/19})$
.6657	$(132^{-1/12})$	.7277	$(24^{-1/10})$	.7706	$(84^{-1/17})$
.6684	$(84^{-1/11})$	.7287	$(84^{-1/14})$	.7710	$(108^{-1/18})$
.6710	$(120^{-1/12})$	.7298	$(60^{-1/13})$	.7725	$(48^{-1/15})$
.6715	$(36^{-1/9})$	.7319	$(108^{-1/15})$	.7734	$(132^{-1/19})$
.6722	$(24^{-1/8})$	.7330	$(12^{-1/8})$	.7742	$(36^{-1/14})$
.6769	$(108^{-1/12})$	.7330	$(144^{-1/16})$	.7742	$(60^{-1/16})$
.6779	$(72^{-1/11})$	.7368	$(72^{-1/14})$	.7760	$(96^{-1/18})$
.6790	$(48^{-1/10})$	.7370	$(132^{-1/16})$	.7773	$(120^{-1/19})$
.6823	$(144^{-1/13})$	.7376	$(96^{-1/15})$	.7776	$(72^{-1/17})$
.6836	$(96^{-1/12})$	.7414	$(120^{-1/16})$	.7800	$(12^{-1/10})$
.6869	$(132^{-1/13})$	.7418	$(36^{-1/12})$	.7800	$(144^{-1/20})$
.6892	$(60^{-1/11})$	.7425	$(48^{-1/13})$	.7816	$(108^{-1/19})$
.6913	$(84^{-1/12})$	.7442	$(84^{-1/15})$	.7818	$(84^{-1/18})$
.6919	$(120^{-1/13})$	.7463	$(108^{-1/16})$	.7831	$(24^{-1/13})$

APPENDIX A

Part 2 *Continued*

.7834	$(132^{-1/20})$	.8091	$(24^{-1/15})$	.8295	$(24^{-1/17})$
.7851	$(48^{-1/16})$	.8098	$(84^{-1/21})$	.8302	$(60^{-1/22})$
.7860	$(60^{-1/17})$	.8099	$(36^{-1/17})$	.8303	$(72^{-1/23})$
.7864	$(96^{-1/19})$	.8121	$(120^{-1/23})$	.8314	$(84^{-1/24})$
.7871	$(120^{-1/20})$	.8126	$(96^{-1/22})$	.8317	$(48^{-1/21})$
.7875	$(36^{-1/15})$	.8130	$(12^{-1/12})$	.8318	$(120^{-1/26})$
.7885	$(72^{-1/18})$	.8130	$(144^{-1/24})$	.8319	$(144^{-1/27})$
.7893	$(144^{-1/21})$	.8149	$(60^{-1/20})$	.8331	$(96^{-1/25})$
.7913	$(108^{-1/20})$	.8157	$(48^{-1/19})$	.8346	$(132^{-1/27})$
.7920	$(84^{-1/19})$	.8157	$(72^{-1/21})$	.8352	$(108^{-1/26})$
.7925	$(132^{-1/21})$	.8158	$(108^{-1/23})$	.8360	$(36^{-1/20})$
.7960	$(96^{-1/20})$	.8159	$(132^{-1/24})$	.8368	$(72^{-1/24})$
.7961	$(120^{-1/21})$	.8176	$(84^{-1/22})$	.8369	$(60^{-1/23})$
.7963	$(48^{-1/17})$	.8192	$(120^{-1/24})$	.8374	$(12^{-1/14})$
.7966	$(60^{-1/18})$	.8195	$(36^{-1/18})$	.8374	$(144^{-1/28})$
.7969	$(24^{-1/14})$	.8197	$(144^{-1/25})$	.8375	$(120^{-1/27})$
.7978	$(12^{-1/11})$	.8199	$(24^{-1/16})$	.8376	$(84^{-1/25})$
.7978	$(144^{-1/22})$	.8200	$(96^{-1/23})$	.8381	$(24^{-1/18})$
.7984	$(72^{-1/19})$	.8226	$(132^{-1/25})$	.8386	$(48^{-1/22})$
.7993	$(36^{-1/16})$	.8228	$(108^{-1/24})$	.8390	$(96^{-1/26})$
.8001	$(108^{-1/21})$	.8229	$(60^{-1/21})$	.8400	$(132^{-1/28})$
.8010	$(132^{-1/22})$	.8233	$(72^{-1/22})$	.8408	$(108^{-1/27})$
.8013	$(84^{-1/20})$	.8240	$(48^{-1/20})$	.8425	$(144^{-1/29})$
.8044	$(120^{-1/22})$	.8248	$(84^{-1/23})$	.8428	$(72^{-1/25})$
.8046	$(96^{-1/21})$	.8257	$(120^{-1/25})$	.8428	$(120^{-1/28})$
.8057	$(144^{-1/23})$	.8260	$(12^{-1/13})$	.8431	$(36^{-1/21})$
.8061	$(60^{-1/19})$	.8260	$(144^{-1/26})$	.8432	$(60^{-1/24})$
.8065	$(48^{-1/18})$	.8268	$(96^{-1/24})$	.8433	$(84^{-1/26})$
.8075	$(72^{-1/20})$	.8281	$(36^{-1/19})$	.8445	$(96^{-1/27})$
.8083	$(108^{-1/22})$	.8288	$(132^{-1/26})$	.8450	$(132^{-1/29})$
.8087	$(132^{-1/23})$	.8292	$(108^{-1/25})$	.8451	$(48^{-1/23})$

APPENDIX A

Part 2 *Continued*

.8460	$(24^{-1/19})$	.8593	$(60^{-1/27})$	.8774	$(12^{-1/19})$
.8460	$(108^{-1/28})$	.8596	$(24^{-1/21})$	.8789	$(48^{-1/30})$
.8473	$(12^{-1/15})$	.8598	$(108^{-1/31})$	.8799	$(36^{-1/28})$
.8473	$(144^{-1/30})$	.8610	$(120^{-1/32})$	.8799	$(60^{-1/32})$
.8478	$(120^{-1/29})$	.8613	$(36^{-1/24})$	.8806	$(24^{-1/25})$
.8483	$(72^{-1/26})$	.8617	$(48^{-1/26})$	.8826	$(48^{-1/31})$
.8487	$(84^{-1/27})$	.8627	$(84^{-1/30})$	.8832	$(12^{-1/20})$
.8489	$(60^{-1/25})$	.8629	$(72^{-1/29})$	.8838	$(36^{-1/29})$
.8496	$(96^{-1/28})$	.8631	$(96^{-1/31})$	.8849	$(24^{-1/26})$
.8497	$(36^{-1/22})$	.8639	$(108^{-1/32})$	.8861	$(48^{-1/32})$
.8498	$(132^{-1/30})$	.8640	$(12^{-1/17})$	.8874	$(36^{-1/30})$
.8509	$(108^{-1/29})$	.8640	$(60^{-1/28})$	.8884	$(12^{-1/21})$
.8510	$(48^{-1/24})$	.8655	$(24^{-1/22})$	.8890	$(24^{-1/27})$
.8519	$(144^{-1/31})$	.8664	$(48^{-1/27})$	.8908	$(36^{-1/31})$
.8525	$(120^{-1/30})$	.8665	$(36^{-1/25})$	.8927	$(24^{-1/28})$
.8531	$(24^{-1/20})$	.8668	$(84^{-1/31})$	.8932	$(12^{-1/22})$
.8535	$(72^{-1/27})$	.8671	$(72^{-1/30})$	.8941	$(36^{-1/32})$
.8536	$(84^{-1/28})$	.8671	$(96^{-1/32})$	.8962	$(24^{-1/29})$
.8543	$(60^{-1/26})$	.8683	$(60^{-1/29})$	.8976	$(12^{-1/23})$
.8543	$(132^{-1/31})$	.8707	$(84^{-1/32})$	.8995	$(24^{-1/30})$
.8544	$(96^{-1/29})$	.8709	$(24^{-1/23})$	.9016	$(12^{-1/24})$
.8555	$(108^{-1/30})$	.8709	$(48^{-1/28})$	.9026	$(24^{-1/31})$
.8557	$(36^{-1/23})$	.8711	$(12^{-1/18})$	.9054	$(12^{-1/25})$
.8562	$(12^{-1/16})$	.8711	$(72^{-1/31})$	.9055	$(24^{-1/32})$
.8562	$(144^{-1/32})$	.8712	$(36^{-1/26})$	.9089	$(12^{-1/26})$
.8565	$(48^{-1/25})$	.8724	$(60^{-1/30})$	.9121	$(12^{-1/27})$
.8569	$(120^{-1/31})$	.8749	$(72^{-1/32})$	.9151	$(12^{-1/28})$
.8583	$(84^{-1/29})$	.8750	$(48^{-1/29})$	.9179	$(12^{-1/29})$
.8584	$(72^{-1/28})$	.8757	$(36^{-1/27})$	.9205	$(12^{-1/30})$
.8585	$(132^{-1/32})$	.8760	$(24^{-1/24})$	.9230	$(12^{-1/31})$
.8589	$(96^{-1/30})$	.8763	$(60^{-1/31})$	.9253	$(12^{-1/32})$

APPENDIX B

Part 1. Ratios Based on e^{-1} and its Sequential Factors and $1-e^{-1}$ and its Factors[1] (e-Based Ratios: $e\text{-BR}$)[2]

	1	2	3	4	5	6	7	8	9	10	
b^{32}						.00666					A
b^{16}		.000650	.000173			.08159			.000394		B
b^{8}	.000335	.0255	.01316	.00292	.00523	.2856	.00149	.000506	.0199		C
b^{4}	.01832	.1597	.1147	.0541	.0723	.5344	.0387	.0225	.1409	.00317	D
b^{2}	.1353	.3996	.3387	.2325	.2689	.7311	.1966	.1500	.3754	.0563	E
base (b)	.3679	.6321	.5820	.4822	.5186	.8550	.4434	.3873	.6127	.2373	F
$b^{1/2}$	.6065	.7951	.7629	.6944	.7201	.9247	.6659	.6223	.7828	.4871	G
$b^{1/4}$	.7788	.8917	.8734	.8333	.8486	.9616	.8160	.7889	.8847	.6979	H
$b^{1/8}$	.8825	.9443	.9346	.9129	.9212	.9806	.9033	.8882	.9406	.8354	I
$b^{1/16}$	.9394	.9717	.9667	.9554	.9598	.9903	.9504	.9424	.9698	.9140	J
$b^{1/32}$	.9692	.9858	.9832	.9775	.9797	.9951	.9749	.9708	.9848	.9560	K
$b^{1/64}$	.9845	.9929	.9916	.9887	.9898		.9874	.9853	.9924	.9778	L
$b^{1/128}$	.9922			.9943	.9949		.9937	.9926		.9888	M
$b^{1/256}$										.9944	N

factors of col. 1   factors of col. 2

base (b)	11	12	13	14	15	16	17	18	19	20	21	22	
b^{32}		.000490						.00213					A
b^{16}		.0221			.000154			.0462					B
b^{8}		.1488	.000778	.00101	.01240			.2149		.00142	.00957		C
b^{4}	.00202	.3857	.0279	.0318	.1114	.00354	.000935	.4635	.000433	.0377	.09783	.00369	D
b^{2}	.0449	.6210	.1670	.1784	.3337	.0595	.0306	.6808	.0208	.1942	.3128	.0608	E
base (b)	.2119	.7881	.4087	.4223	.5777	.2440	.1749	.8251	.1443	.4407	.5593	.2465	F
$b^{1/2}$	.4604	.8877	.6393	.6499	.7601	.4939	.4182	.9084	.3799	.6639	.7478	.4965	G
$b^{1/4}$	.6785	.9422	.7995	.8061	.8718	.7028	.6467	.9531	.6163	.8148	.8648	.7046	H
$b^{1/8}$	.8237	.9707	.8942	.8979	.9337	.8383	.8042	.9763	.7851	.9027	.9299	.8394	I
$b^{1/16}$	.9076	.9852	.9456	.9476	.9663	.9156	.8967	.9881	.8860	.9501	.9643	.9162	J
$b^{1/32}$	-9527	.9926	.9724	.9734	.9830	.9569	.9470	.9940	.9413	.9747	.9820	.9572	K
$b^{1/64}$	.9761		.9861	.9866	.9915	.9782	.9731		.9702	.9873	.9910	.9784	L
$b^{1/128}$	.9880		.9930	.9933		.9890	.9865		.9850	.9936	.9955	.9891	M
$b^{1/256}$	.9940					.9945	.9932		.9925			.9945	N

factors of col 5   factors of col 6   factors of col 11   factors of col 12

[1] Factors are divisible, complementary factors. For example, col. 5 base, .2689, divided by col 6. base, .7311, gives col 1 base, .3679. Each horizontal pair gives corresponding col. 1 figure. The column following each pair of factors gives their product. Note: products of the horizontal pairs in cols. 1 and 2, whose bases are e^{-1} and $1-e^{-1}$, are shown in col. 4, whereas col. 3 contains their quotients.

[2] This table first appeared in *Perceptual and Motor Skills*, 1995, 80, 67-84.

APPENDIX B

Part 2. *e*-Based Ratios (*e*-BR) in Order of Size With Row and Column References to Part 1

.000154	(B15)	.08159	(C6)	.4965	(G22)
.000173	(B3)	.09783	(D21)	.5186	(G5)
.000335	(C1)	.1114	(D15)	.5344	(E6)
.000394	(B9)	.1147	(D3)	.5593	(F21)
.000433	(D19)	.1353	(E1)	.5777	(F15)
.000490	(A12)	.1409	(D9)	.5820	(F3)
.000506	(C8)	.1443	(F19)	.6065	(G1)
.000650	(B2)	.1488	(C12)	.6127	(F9)
.000778	(D13)	.1500	(E8)	.6163	(H19)
.000935	(D17)	.1597	(D2)	.6210	(E12)
.00101	(C14)	.1670	(F13)	.6223	(G8)
.00142	(C20)	.1749	(F17)	.6321	(F2)
.00149	(D7)	.1784	(E14)	.6393	(H13)
.00202	(D11)	.1942	(E20)	.6467	(H17)
.00213	(A18)	.1966	(F7)	.6499	(G14)
.00292	(D4)	.2119	(F11)	.6639	(G20)
.00317	(D10)	.2149	(C18)	.6659	(H7)
.00354	(D16)	.2325	(F4)	.6785	(H11)
.00369	(D22)	.2373	(F10)	.6808	(E18)
.00523	(D5)	.2440	(F16)	.6944	(H4)
.00666	(B6)	.2465	(F22)	.6979	(H10)
.00957	(C21)	.2689	(F5)	.7028	(H16)
.01240	(C15)	.2856	(D6)	.7046	(H22)
.01316	(C3)	.3128	(E21)	.7201	(H5)
.01832	(D1)	.3337	(E15)	.7311	(F6)
.0199	(C9)	.3387	(E3)	.7478	(G21)
.0208	(E19)	.3679	(F1)	.7601	(G15)
.0221	(B12)	.3754	(E9)	.7629	(G3)
.0225	(D8)	.3799	(G19)	.7788	(H1)
.0255	(C2)	.3857	(D12)	.7828	(G9)
.0279	(E13)	.3873	(F8)	.7851	(I19)
.0306	(E17)	.3996	(E2)	.7881	(F12)
.0318	(D14)	.4087	(G13)	.7889	(H8)
.0377	(D20)	.4182	(G17)	.7951	(G2)
.0387	(E7)	.4223	(F14)	.7995	(I13)
.0449	(E11)	.4407	(F20)	.8042	(I17)
.0462	(B18)	.4434	(G7)	.8061	(H14)
.0541	(E4)	.4604	(G11)	.8148	(H20)
.0563	(E10)	.4635	(D18)	.8160	(I7)
.0595	(E16)	.4822	(G4)	.8237	(I11)
.0608	(E22)	.4871	(G10)	.8251	(F18)
.0723	(E5)	.4939	(G16)	.8333	(I4)

APPENDIX B

Part 2 *Continued*

.8354	(I10)	.9501	(J20)	.9853	(L8)
.8383	(I16)	.9504	(K7)	.9858	(K2)
.8394	(I22)	.9527	(K11)	.9861	(M13)
.8486	(I5)	.9531	(H18)	.9865	(M17)
.8550	(G6)	.9554	(K4)	.9866	(L14)
.8648	(H21)	.9560	(K10)	.9873	(L20)
.8718	(H15)	.9569	(K16)	.9874	(M7)
.8734	(H3)	.9572	(K22)	.9880	(M11)
.8825	(I1)	.9598	(K5)	.9881	(J18)
.8847	(H9)	.9616	(I6)	.9887	(M4)
.8860	(J19)	.9643	(J21)	.9888	(M10)
.8877	(G12)	.9663	(J15)	.9890	(M16)
.8882	(I8)	.9667	(J3)	.9891	(M22)
.8917	(H2)	.9692	(K1)	.9898	(M5)
.8942	(J13)	.9698	(J9)	.9903	(K6)
.8967	(J17)	.9702	(L19)	.9910	(L21)
.8979	(I14)	.9707	(I12)	.9915	(L15)
.9027	(I20)	.9708	(K8)	.9916	(L3)
.9033	(J7)	.9717	(J2)	.9922	(M1)
.9076	(J11)	.9724	(L13)	.9924	(L9)
.9084	(G18)	.9731	(L17)	.9925	(N19)
.9129	(J4)	.9734	(K14)	.9926	(M8)
.9140	(J10)	.9747	(K20)	.9926	(K12)
.9156	(J16)	.9749	(L7)	.9929	(L2)
.9162	(J22)	.9761	(L11)	.9930	(N13)
.9212	(J5)	.9763	(I18)	.9932	(N17)
.9247	(H6)	.9775	(L4)	.9933	(M14)
.9299	(I21)	.9778	(L10)	.9936	(M20)
.9337	(I15)	.9782	(L16)	.9937	(N7)
.9346	(I3)	.9784	(L22)	.9940	(N11)
.9394	(J1)	.9797	(L5)	.9940	(K18)
.9406	(I9)	.9806	(J6)	.9943	(N4)
.9413	(K19)	.9820	(K21)	.9944	(N10)
.9422	(H12)	.9830	(K15)	.9945	(N16)
.9424	(J8)	.9832	(K3)	.9945	(N22)
.9443	(I2)	.9845	(L1)	.9949	(N5)
.9456	(K13)	.9848	(K9)	.9951	(L6)
.9470	(K17)	.9850	(M19)	.9955	(M21)
.9476	(J14)	.9852	(J12)		

APPENDIX C

Part 1. Ratios Based on Fractions

Base (b)	1/10	1/9	1/8	1/7	1/6	1/5	2/9	1/4	2/7	3/10	
	1	2	3	4	5	6	7	8	9	10	
b^{64}											
b^{32}											
b^{16}											
b^{8}											
b^{4}	.000100	.000152	.000244	.000416	.000772	.00160	.00244	.00391	.00666	.008100	D
b^{2}	.0100	.0123	.0156	.0204	.0278	.0400	.0494	.0625	.0816	.0900	E
base	.1000	.1111	.1250	.1429	.1667	.2000	.2222	.2500	.2857	.3000	F
$b^{1/2}$	.3162	.3333	.3536	.3780	.4082	.4472	.4714	.5000	.5345	.5477	G
$b^{1/4}$	.5623	.5774	.5946	.6148	.6389	.6687	.6866	.7071	.7311	.7401	H
$b^{1/8}$	.7499	.7598	.7711	.7841	.7993	.8178	.8286	.8409	.8550	.8603	I
$b^{1/16}$	.8660	.8717	.8781	.8855	.8941	.9043	.9103	.9170	.9247	.9275	J
$b^{1/32}$	.9306	.9336	.9371	.9410	.9455	.9509	.9541	.9576	.9616	.9631	K
$b^{1/64}$	.9647	.9663	.9680	.9701	.9724	.9752	.9768	.9786	.9806	.9814	L
$b^{1/128}$	.9822	.9830	.9839	.9849	.9861	.9875	.9883	.9892	.9903	.9906	M
$b^{1/256}$	.9910	.9915	.9919	.9924	.9930	.9937	.9941	.9946	.9951	.9953	N

APPENDIX C

Part 1 *Continued*

Base (b)	1/3	3/8	2/5	3/7	4/9	1/2	5/9	4/7	3/5	5/8	
	11	12	13	14	15	16	17	18	19	20	
b^{64}											
b^{32}											
b^{16}								.000129	.000282	.000542	B
b^{8}	.000152	.000391	.000655	.00114	.00152	.00391	.00907	.0114	.0168	.0233	C
b^{4}	.0123	.0198	.0256	.0337	.0390	.0625	.0953	.1066	.1296	.1526	D
b^{2}	.1111	.1406	.1600	.1837	.1975	.2500	.3086	.3265	.3600	.3906	E
base	.3333	.3750	.4000	.4286	.4444	.5000	.5555	.5714	.6000	.6250	F
$b^{1/2}$	.5774	.6124	.6325	.6547	.6667	.7071	.7454	.7559	.7746	.7906	G
$b^{1/4}$	.7598	.7825	.7953	.8091	.8165	.8409	.8633	.8694	.8801	.8891	H
$b^{1/8}$	.8717	.8846	.8918	.8995	.9036	.9170	.9292	.9324	.9381	.9429	I
$b^{1/16}$	.9336	.9405	.9443	.9484	.9506	.9576	.9639	.9656	.9686	.9711	J
$b^{1/32}$	.9663	.9698	.9718	.9739	.9750	.9786	.9818	.9827	.9842	.9854	K
$b^{1/64}$	.9830	.9848	.9858	.9868	.9874	.9892	.9909	.9913	.9921	.9927	L
$b^{1/128}$	.9915	.9924	.9929	.9934	.9937	.9946	.9954	.9956	.9960	.9963	M
$b^{1/256}$	.9957	.9962	.9964	.9967	.9968						N

APPENDIX C

Part 1 Continued

Base (b)	2/3	7/10	5/7	3/4	7/9	4/5	5/6	6/7	7/8	8/9	9/10	
	21	22	23	24	25	26	27	28	29	30	31	
b^{64}									.000194	.000532	.0012	Z
b^{32}				.000100	.000322	.000792	.00293	.00721	.0139	.0231	.0343	A
b^{16}	.00152	.00332	.00459	.0100	.0179	.0281	.0541	.0849	.1181	.1519	.1853	B
b^{8}	.0390	.0576	.0678	.1001	.1339	.1678	.2326	.2914	.3436	.3897	.4305	C
b^{4}	.1975	.2401	.2603	.3164	.3660	.4096	.4823	.5398	.5862	.6243	.6561	D
b^{2}	.4444	.4900	.5102	.5625	.6049	.6400	.6944	.7347	.7656	.7901	.8100	E
base	.6667	.7000	.7143	.7500	.7777	.8000	.8333	.8571	.8750	.8888	.9000	F
$b^{1/2}$	.8165	.8367	.8452	.8660	.8819	.8944	.9129	.9258	.9354	.9428	.9487	G
$b^{1/4}$	.9036	.9147	.9193	.9306	.9391	.9457	.9554	.9622	.9672	.9710	.9740	H
$b^{1/8}$	.9506	.9564	.9588	.9647	.9691	.9725	.9775	.9809	.9834	.9854	.9869	I
$b^{1/16}$	.9750	.9780	.9792	.9822	.9844	.9862	.9887	.9904	.9917	.9927	.9934	J
$b^{1/32}$	.9874	.9889	.9895	.9911	.9922	.9931	.9943	.9952	.9958	.9963	.9967	K
$b^{1/64}$	.9937	.9944	.9948									L
$b^{1/128}$	.9968	.9972	.9974									M

APPENDIX C

Part 2. Ratios based on Fractions in Order of Size with Row and Column References to Part 1

.000100	(D1)	.0179	(B25)	.1837	(E14)
.000100	(A24)	.0198	(D12)	.1853	(B31)
.000129	(B18)	.0204	(E4)	.1975	(E15)
.000152	(D2)	.0231	(A30)	.1975	(D21)
.000152	(C11)	.0233	(C20)	.2000	(F6)
.000194	(Z29)	.0256	(D13)	.2222	(F7)
.000244	(D3)	.0278	(E5)	.2326	(C27)
.000282	(B19)	.0281	(B26)	.2401	(D22)
.000322	(A25)	.0337	(D14)	.2500	(F8)
.000391	(C12)	.0343	(A31)	.2500	(E16)
.000416	(D4)	.0390	(D15)	.2603	(D23)
.000532	(Z30)	.0390	(C21)	.2857	(F9)
.000542	(B20)	.0400	(E6)	.2914	(C28)
.000655	(C13)	.0494	(E7)	.3000	(F10)
.000772	(D5)	.0541	(B27)	.3086	(E17)
.000792	(A26)	.0576	(C22)	.3162	(G1)
.00114	(C14)	.0625	(E8)	.3164	(D24)
.0012	(Z31)	.0625	(D16)	.3265	(E18)
.00152	(C15)	.0678	(C23)	.3333	(G2)
.00152	(B21)	.0816	(E9)	.3333	(F11)
.00160	(D6)	.0849	(B28)	.3436	(C29)
.00244	(D7)	.0900	(E10)	.3536	(G3)
.00293	(A27)	.0953	(D17)	.3600	(E19)
.00332	(B22)	.1000	(F1)	.3660	(D25)
.00391	(D8)	.1001	(C24)	.3750	(F12)
.00391	(C16)	.1066	(D18)	.3780	(G4)
.00459	(B23)	.1111	(F2)	.3897	(C30)
.00666	(D9)	.1111	(E11)	.3906	(E20)
.00721	(A28)	.1181	(B29)	.4000	(F13)
.00810	(D10)	.1250	(F3)	.4082	(G5)
.00907	(C17)	.1296	(D19)	.4096	(D26)
.0100	(E1)	.1339	(C25)	.4286	(F14)
.0100	(B24)	.1406	(E12)	.4305	(C31)
.0114	(C18)	.1429	(F4)	.4444	(F15)
.0123	(E2)	.1519	(B30)	.4444	(E21)
.0123	(D11)	.1526	(D20)	.4472	(G6)
.0139	(A29)	.1600	(E13)	.4714	(G7)
.0156	(E3)	.1667	(F5)	.4823	(D27)
.0168	(C19)	.1678	(C26)	.4900	(E22)

APPENDIX C

Part 2 *Continued*

.5000	(G8)	.7559	(G18)	.8888	(F30)
.5000	(F16)	.7598	(I2)	.8891	(H20)
.5102	(E23)	.7598	(H11)	.8918	(I13)
.5345	(G9)	.7656	(E29)	.8941	(J5)
.5398	(D28)	.7711	(I3)	.8944	(G26)
.5477	(G10)	.7746	(G19)	.8995	(I14)
.5555	(F17)	.7777	(F25)	.9000	(F31)
.5623	(H1)	.7825	(H12)	.9036	(I15)
.5625	(E24)	.7841	(I4)	.9036	(H21)
.5714	(F18)	.7901	(E30)	.9043	(J6)
.5774	(H2)	.7906	(G20)	.9103	(J7)
.5774	(G11)	.7953	(H13)	.9129	(G27)
.5862	(D29)	.7993	(I5)	.9147	(H22)
.5946	(H3)	.8000	(F26)	.9170	(J8)
.6000	(F19)	.8091	(H14)	.9170	(I16)
.6049	(E25)	.8100	(E31)	.9193	(H23)
.6124	(G12)	.8165	(H15)	.9247	(J9)
.6148	(H4)	.8165	(G21)	.9258	(G28)
.6243	(D30)	.8178	(I6)	.9275	(J10)
.6250	(F20)	.8286	(I7)	.9292	(I17)
.6325	(G13)	.8333	(F27)	.9306	(K1)
.6389	(H5)	.8367	(G22)	.9306	(H24)
.6400	(E26)	.8409	(I8)	.9324	(I18)
.6547	(G14)	.8409	(H16)	.9336	(K2)
.6561	(D31)	.8452	(G23)	.9336	(J11)
.6667	(G15)	.8550	(I9)	.9354	(G29)
.6667	(F21)	.8571	(F28)	.9371	(K3)
.6687	(H6)	.8603	(I10)	.9381	(I19)
.6866	(H7)	.8633	(H17)	.9391	(H25)
.6944	(E27)	.8660	(J1)	.9405	(J12)
.7000	(F22)	.8660	(G24)	.9410	(K4)
.7071	(H8)	.8694	(H18)	.9428	(G30)
.7071	(G16)	.8717	(J2)	.9429	(I20)
.7143	(F23)	.8717	(I11)	.9443	(J13)
.7311	(H9)	.8750	(F29)	.9455	(K5)
.7347	(E28)	.8781	(J3)	.9457	(H26)
.7401	(H10)	.8801	(H19)	.9484	(J14)
.7454	(G17)	.8819	(G25)	.9487	(G31)
.7499	(I1)	.8846	(I12)	.9506	(J15)
.7500	(F24)	.8855	(J4)	.9506	(I21)

APPENDIX C

Part 2 *Continued*

.9509	(K6)	.9814	(L10)	.9921	(L19)
.9541	(K7)	.9818	(K17)	.9922	(K25)
.9554	(H27)	.9822	(M1)	.9924	(N4)
.9564	(I22)	.9822	(J24)	.9924	(M12)
.9576	(K8)	.9827	(K18)	.9927	(L20)
.9576	(J16)	.9830	(M2)	.9927	(J30)
.9588	(I23)	.9830	(L11)	.9929	(M13)
.9616	(K9)	.9834	(I29)	.9930	(N5)
.9622	(H28)	.9839	(M3)	.9931	(K26)
.9631	(K10)	.9842	(K19)	.9934	(M14)
.9639	(J17)	.9844	(J25)	.9934	(J31)
.9647	(L1)	.9848	(L12)	.9937	(N6)
.9647	(I24)	.9849	(M4)	.9937	(M15)
.9656	(J18)	.9854	(K20)	.9937	(L21)
.9663	(L2)	.9854	(I30)	.9941	(N7)
.9663	(K11)	.9858	(L13)	.9943	(K27)
.9672	(H29)	.9861	(M5)	.9944	(L22)
.9680	(L3)	.9862	(J26)	.9946	(N8)
.9686	(J19)	.9868	(L14)	.9946	(M16)
.9691	(I25)	.9869	(I31)	.9948	(L23)
.9698	(K12)	.9874	(L15)	.9951	(N9)
.9701	(L4)	.9874	(K21)	.9952	(K28)
.9710	(H30)	.9875	(M6)	.9953	(N10)
.9711	(J20)	.9883	(M7)	.9954	(M17)
.9718	(K13)	.9887	(J27)	.9956	(M18)
.9724	(L5)	.9889	(K22)	.9957	(N11)
.9725	(I26)	.9892	(M8)	.9958	(K29)
.9739	(K14)	.9892	(L16)	.9960	(M19)
.9740	(H31)	.9895	(K23)	.9962	(N12)
.9750	(K15)	.9903	(M9)	.9963	(M20)
.9750	(J21)	.9904	(J28)	.9963	(K30)
.9752	(L6)	.9906	(M10)	.9964	(N13)
.9768	(L7)	.9909	(L17)	.9967	(N14)
.9775	(I27)	.9910	(N1)	.9967	(K31)
.9780	(J22)	.9911	(K24)	.9968	(N15)
.9786	(L8)	.9913	(L18)	.9968	(M21)
.9786	(K16)	.9915	(N2)	.9972	(M22)
.9792	(J23)	.9915	(M11)	.9974	(M23)
.9806	(L9)	.9917	(J29)		
.9809	(I28)	.9919	(N3)		